READERS' GUIDES TO ESSENTIAL CRITICISM

CONSULTANT EDITOR: NICOLAS TREDELL

Published

Readers' Guides to Essential Criticism
Series Standing Order
ISBN 978–1–4039–0108–8
(*outside North America only*)

You can receive future titles in this series as they are published by placing a standing order. Please contact your bookseller or, in the case of difficulty, write to us at the address below with your name and address, the title of the series and the ISBN quoted above.

Customer Services Department, Macmillan Distribution Ltd,
Houndmills, Basingstoke, Hampshire, RG21 6XS, UK

The Fiction of Pat Barker

MERRITT MOSELEY

Consultant editor: Nicolas Tredell

palgrave
macmillan

First published 2014 by
PALGRAVE MACMILLAN

Palgrave Macmillan in the UK is an imprint of Macmillan Publishers Limited, registered in England, company number 785998, of Houndmills, Basingstoke, Hampshire RG21 6XS.

Palgrave Macmillan in the US is a division of St Martin's Press LLC, 175 Fifth Avenue, New York, NY 10010.

Palgrave Macmillan is the global academic imprint of the above companies and has companies and representatives throughout the world.

Palgrave® and Macmillan® are registered trademarks in the United States, the United Kingdom, Europe and other countries

ISBN: 978–0–230–29330–4 hardback
ISBN: 978–0–230–29331–1 paperback

This book is printed on paper suitable for recycling and made from fully managed and sustained forest sources. Logging, pulping and manufacturing processes are expected to conform to the environmental regulations of the country of origin.

A catalogue record for this book is available from the British Library.

A catalog record for this book is available from the Library of Congress.

Printed in China

To my beloved grandchildren

Contents

A Note on Texts

All page references to novels by Pat Barker in this Guide, including those within critical extracts, are to the editions listed below.

Union Street (London: Virago, 1982)

Blow Your House Down (London: Virago, 1984)

Liza's England (originally published as *The Century's Daughter*) (New York: Picador, 1986). Pagination is the same as for the UK Virago paperback.

The Man Who Wasn't There (New York: Picador, 1988). Pagination is the same as for the UK Virago paperback.

Regeneration (New York: Plume, 1991). Pagination is the same as for the UK Penguin paperback.

The Eye in the Door (New York: Plume, 1993). Pagination is the same as for the UK Penguin paperback.

The Ghost Road (New York: Plume, 1995). Pagination is the same as for the UK Penguin paperback.

Another World (New York: Farrar, Straus & Giroux, 1998). Pagination is the same as for the UK Penguin paperback.

Border Crossing (New York: Farrar, Straus & Giroux, 2001)

Double Vision (New York: Picador, 2003)

Life Class (New York: Anchor, 2007)

Toby's Room (London: Hamish Hamilton, 2012)

Acknowledgements

I wish to thank Pat Barker, for helpful conversation; Nicolas Tredell, series editor, for commissioning this book and for his careful reading of the typescript; the professionals at Palgrave Macmillan, with whom it is a pleasure to work; the staff of Ramsey Library at the University of North Carolina at Asheville, for all their help obtaining books and articles; my departmental colleagues, for many years of friendship and critically stimulating conversation; and, as always, my wife Madeline, for all that she is and does.

Introduction

Pat Barker (born in 1943), the author of twelve novels, has been since 1982 one of Britain's most critically esteemed novelists. Beginning with *Union Street*, published in that year, she developed a reputation for politically engaged fiction dealing with the post-industrial culture of north-eastern England, particularly the lives of its working-class women. In 1983 she was named in the initial *Granta* list of the twenty 'Best of the Young British Novelists', alongside a group of other authors who were then (mostly) younger than she and in many cases much better known: for example, Rose Tremain (English, 1943–), Salman Rushdie (Indian British, 1947–), and Martin Amis (English, 1949–). Her first few books were published by the feminist publisher Virago, whose founder and director, Carmen Callil, was her first sponsor. In 1991 she moved to Viking Penguin; at the same time she turned to historical fiction about the Great War, with *Regeneration*. This move caused comment among some observers about a move away from focusing on women (though her 1988 novel *The Man Who Wasn't There*, published by Virago, had already featured a young male protagonist). She explained in a 1991 interview with Flora Alexander that publication by Virago, a feminist publisher, meant that her novels would be ignored, and reviewed only by women.[1] *Regeneration* also marked a move toward writing about a broader range of demographic types, as her novels since the onset of what came to be called the '*Regeneration* Trilogy' (which finally included, in addition to *Regeneration, The Eye in the Door* [1993] and *The Ghost Road* [1995]) include more middle-class characters, particularly writers, artists, and social workers.

Though Barker was by no means ignored by literary commentary during the first period of her career, serious criticism of her work accelerated following the publication of the *Regeneration* trilogy and perhaps especially after *The Ghost Road* won the Booker Prize in 1995. To date there have been nine books devoted entirely to her work. Sharon Monteith's *Pat Barker* (part of the Writers and Their Work series from the British Council, 2001) was the first general monograph, followed by John Brannigan's *Pat Barker* (2005), David Waterman's *Pat Barker and the Mediation of Social Reality* (2009) and Mark Rawlinson's

Pat Barker (2010). There have been two collections of critical essays: the first was *Critical Perspectives on Pat Barker*, edited by Sharon Monteith, Margaretta Jolly, Hahem Yousaf and Ronald Paul (2005); it was followed by Pat Wheeler (ed.), *Re-reading Pat Barker* (2011). The centrality of the *Regeneration* trilogy to Barker's work is attested by Karen Patrick Knutsen's *Reciprocal Haunting: Pat Barker's Regeneration Trilogy* (2010); and the fact that within the trilogy the first novel is seen as paramount (perhaps because of its use as a set text in British A-level examinations) explains Karin Westman's short volume *Pat Barker's Regeneration: A Reader's Guide* (2001) and Sarah Gamble's student handbook, *Regeneration* (York Notes, 2009). There has been a relative outpouring of periodical criticism of Barker's work, though somewhat maldistributed: like the monographs, critical essays have focused primarily on the *Regeneration* trilogy.

The aim of this book is to provide a comprehensive introduction and a guide to the essential criticism of Barker's fiction, for the use of students—and any readers—interested in learning more of what critics have written on her novels. Every attempt has been made to ensure that the accounts in the chapters that follow are accurate and useful in identifying the particular areas of interest and the critical approaches of the critics mentioned. Overviews and quotations serve as a starting point. Interested readers are invited to use the Bibliography in order to turn to the full-length works of criticism. Like Barker criticism itself—and for that reason—this book attends especially to the *Regeneration* trilogy: both to the trilogy as a literary unit, which has developed its own critical heritage, and to the individual books comprised in it.

The organization of this volume is first chronological, then thematic. The chapters are arranged by the dates of publication of the novels they discuss; within them, their contents are sorted by themes. Pat Barker's first four novels are covered in Chapters One and Two. The *Regeneration* trilogy receives the next four; Chapters Seven and Eight are devoted to the five novels that followed the trilogy. Within each chapter the essential criticism of the novels has been treated under thematic headings such as 'Class', or 'Therapy', or 'Trauma'. Readers will understand that such categorization, designed as an aid to navigation, need not imply that any of the scholars and critics—especially authors of full-length critical studies of the author's oeuvre (Sharon Monteith, John Brannigan, Mark Rawlinson and David Waterman)—are limited to any one topic.

Attempting to offer general truths about the entire oeuvre of a prolific and resourceful novelist is difficult, as is generalizing about the critical discourse on her work; doing so successfully may be impossible. But there are some themes that may be identified as central to Pat Barker's fiction.

One of these is *gender*. Barker has almost always been accepted as a feminist novelist, though, after her first three novels, a broadening approach and (in the trilogy) a focus primarily on men's experience have led to more complex explanations of her feminism. John Brannigan, for instance, writes in *Pat Barker* (2005) that 'Gender identity and formation has been a concern throughout her work, and her novels have always borne out the lesson that male and female identifies are only understood in relation to each other.'[2] Many critics have seen the *Regeneration* trilogy (and, by extension, other novels with major male characters) as dramatizing a crisis in masculinity (e.g. Greg Harris's 'Compulsory Masculinity, Britain, and the Great War' [1998][3]). Margaretta Jolly, in 'Towards a Masculine Maternal' (2005), writes of a figure she calls 'the masculine maternal' and assigns to it the capacity of 'dissolution of gender as it is expressed through the binaries of sadism and masochism, violence and nurture'.[4] In 'Pathologized Masculinity in Pat Barker's *Double Vision*' (2011), Marie-Luise Kohlke discusses what she calls Barker's 'pathologisation of masculinity', stipulating that 'Since the publication of her first novel, the figure of the male attacker and/ or sexual predator has persistently haunted Pat Barker's fiction.'[5] Sarah C. E. Ross, in 'Regeneration, Redemption, Resurrection' (2005), links early and late novels by identifying the 'fundamental strand' which ties together the early novels, the *Regeneration* trilogy, and the books after that as 'her preoccupation with the nature of evil itself'.[6] Beyond questions of gender in binary male–female terms, her novels since at least *Regeneration* have also explored male homosexuality with depth and understanding.

Kohlke's reference to attack and predation identifies a second theme critics find generally in Barker's fiction: *trauma*. From the beginning her fiction has given stark representations of victimization. Brannigan quotes the phrase 'figures of utter ruin' from *Double Vision* and insists that 'Every one of Barker's novels contains some such figures—the skull visible through the skin, the tortured, screaming mouth, or the staring, petrified eyes.'[7] In conjunction with the experience of trauma, the novelist is at least equally concerned with the human response to it, and the later consequences of that victimization are always at issue, whether immediate or in long-term aftermath through memory. Margaretta Jolly notices, as 'the most unpleasant aspect of Barker's unflinching depiction of working-class life ... her characters' own submission to and even complicity in their degradation. Oppression is physicality internalized.'[8] By contrast, Sharon Monteith asserts in 'Warring Fictions' (1997) that it is 'this stoical endurance on the part of men and women that characterizes each of her novels, at their most gritty and at their most lyrical [...]'.[9]

Another key topic and theme is *class*. Her early novels were seen as part of a tradition of working-class fiction and written from a radical position. In 'Crime and Rehabilitation' (2001), Mark Greif, who links her to George Orwell (pen name of the English author Eric Blair, 1903–50), claims that she 'may be the most important progressive novelist to reach full artistic maturity in the past 10 years'.[10] Brannigan further incorporates her work into the tradition, naming predecessors like D. H. Lawrence (English, 1885–1930) and Robert Tressell (pen name of the Irish writer Robert Croker, 1870–1911)—best known for *The Ragged Trousered Philanthropists*, a radical social critique published in 1914—and Sid Chaplin (1916–86), and more recent authors of working-class fiction like Alan Sillitoe (from Nottingham, 1928–2010), Stan Barstow (Wakefield, Yorkshire, 1928–2011) and John Braine (Bradford, Yorkshire, 1922–86). These three figures of the 1950s and 1960s are best known (respectively) for *Saturday Night and Sunday Morning* (1958), *A Kind of Loving* (1960), and *Room at the Top* (1957). Brannigan goes on to argue for the important difference between her work and theirs, defined largely by her attention to rounded female characters, lacking in their mostly male-centred fictions.[11]

Another recurrent feature, perhaps more insistently noticed after *Liza's England* and then the World War I novels, is *history and memory*. John Brannigan links *Another World* with Barker's other novels through its central concern with 'the ethics of historical memory in the present'.[12] One other oddly specific generalization comes from Mary Trabucco, who writes in 'Fire and Water in *Border Crossing*' (2011), 'In each of her novels there is a familiar interpenetration between history, memory, and medicine that suffuses and complicates her work.'[13] Others point out the oddly recurrent feature (odd at least in fiction that is mostly realistic) of ghosts and other forms of spectral presence.[14] She never writes outright ghost stories that require or expect the reader to accept the reality of ghosts, but there are spectral appearances in a majority of her novels; spiritualism figures largely—and is sometimes comic, sometimes poignant but never just fraudulent—and waking dreams, nightmares, and visitations by the deceased form a significant part of her fictional world.

As for the technical aspects of Barker's fiction, Sharon Monteith, in *Pat Barker* (2002), identifies one of the 'key features' of her work as the way in which, while she focuses straightforwardly on the subject of her fiction, she is also acutely aware of (and interested in exploring) ambiguities.[15] Monteith also (somewhat unusually) insists on the author's humour, 'at the edge of tragedy', a feature which, perhaps unjustly, figures very little in most critical discussions of Barker.[16]

The most contested issue in the project of placing Barker's work is its relationship to realism and, if it is not judged to be realism, the question of to what extent it is postmodern. Pat Barker, in many interviews and authorial commentaries (for instance in the acknowledgements of her historical novels), has seemed clearly dedicated to a realistic account of what can be known about the past, verisimilitude, and an awareness of the key difference between what is fiction and what is nonfiction. John Brannigan's book rather oddly, but conveniently, demonstrates serially most of the possible positions on the question of realism. For instance, in a comment on her use of memory, he calls her work 'social realist fiction', and this placement makes sense in light of his partial assimilation of her work to that of earlier writers like Tressell and Braine.[17] Further along, he complicates this identification by suggesting that her 'early reputation' as a realist needs to be qualified by the recognition that she is something of a symbolist: he links her to early modernist writers in the symbolist tradition like Joseph Conrad (Polish-English, 1857–1924) and American Kate Chopin (1850–1904).[18] A bit *further* along, while acknowledging that realism is probably the best term to use as a general summing up of her fictional approach, he then adds a list of features which militate against the accuracy of that description, before making a somewhat unconvincing attempt to define her work as postmodernist.[19] Sarah Ross declares that 'realist' has replaced 'feminist' as the common categorization of Barker's work; she studies the interaction of feminism and realism, and calls attention to Barker's 'unflinching interrogation of the nature of evil in several social, political and historical forms'; she concludes that Barker's work aligns 'socialist feminism and conscientious realism [...]'.[20] The main argument developed by critics who wish to distinguish Barker's fiction from realism is that she is a postmodernist, though this requires some subtle definitions of postmodernism and careful argumentation. In 'Matrix, Metramorphosis, and the Readymade' (2011), Maria Holmgren Troy writes that in 'problematizing the boundaries between individual characters' subjectivity and between her novels as well as other authors' works, Barker goes beyond conventions of realism, a narrative tradition with which her novels have often been associated'.[21] She goes on to distinguish Barker's fiction from realism, though the way she defines realism, for the purposes of this distinction, is narrow and somewhat tendentious. And Catherine Bernard, in 'Pat Barker's Critical Work of Mourning' (2007), links Barker's work with historiographical metafiction, the term introduced into critical theory by Linda Hutcheon, through her 'concern with the repressed voices of History, with those long deprived with [*sic*] discursive agency [...]'; she also refers to Barker's 'paradoxical take on realism', though without ever quite identifying what constitutes the paradox.[22]

One feature often associated with the postmodern novel, though not exclusively so, of course, is *intertextuality* (a term current since the 1970s to refer to the complex relationship between a text and other texts, called intertexts, and sometimes considered to be the basic condition of literary textuality). And many critics have commented on Barker's artful use of a variety of intertexts, some of them fictional (e.g. other World War I novels; *The Strange Case of Dr Jekyll and Mr Hyde* [1886] by Scottish author Robert Louis Stevenson [1850–94]) and some of them visual (for instance, the paintings of the Spanish romantic painter Francisco Goya) or scientific (e.g., medical texts related to the treatment of Great War officers). There are many examples, most of them for obvious reasons specific to particular texts and intertexts; but Troy, in distinguishing Barker's work from realism, does cite her 'ways of referring to other literary works in her novels and her "recycling" of similar events or scenes in different contexts in her own oeuvre' as a feature that illustrates postmodernism.[23]

BIOGRAPHY

Pat Barker was born on 8 May 1943, in Thornaby-on-Tees, in the north of England. She declines to identify her mother; and there has been some confusion about her father. She grew up thinking that he was an Air Force officer killed in the war; the biographical note in the *Granta* Best of Young British Novelists issue says 'Her father was killed in action during World War Two, and she was brought up mainly by her grandmother.'[24] She gradually learned more about her parentage, first being told that her father had been an officer who didn't marry her mother and disappeared into the war, and even later learning that her mother did not know who her father was. The shame involved may have been one reason that her mother left her, when she did marry. It is true that the daughter grew up mostly with her grandmother and grandfather, after her mother married when she was seven. Her grandmother worked in a fish and chip shop, while her grandfather was a labourer. He was also a veteran of the Great War and traces of that influence, and even of the specific injury he received (a bayonet wound in the abdomen, which she was permitted, as a treat, to insert her hand into) appear often in her fiction. Her grandmother's first husband had been a spiritualist minister, and the child's reading in some of his books, left in a house with limited reading material, also bears fruit in the concern some of her early fiction shows with spiritualism, particularly as an important feature of the period after World War I.

     She was educated at a grammar school and then went to London where she studied at the London School of Economics and Political Science, receiving a BSc in 1965. From that year until 1970 she worked as a teacher. In 1978 she married David Barker, a professor of zoology, and they had two children, John and Annabel. David Barker died in 2009, after a lengthy illness. He had been a professor of zoology at

Durham University and the Barkers lived in Durham. Their daughter is now also a novelist, Anna Ralph.

Pat Barker's writing career began with what has been described as 'a series of middle-class novels of manners and social refinement', all unpublished.[25] She took a short creative writing course with the English novelist Angela Carter (1940–92), who encouraged her to write out of her own background, so she began to write about the subject matter her life had made available to her: the stories of poor women working to bring up their families and to make a living under difficult conditions. Carter showed her work to Carmen Callil, the founding publisher of Virago, the groundbreaking feminist press, who accepted *Union Street* and published it in 1982.

It would be wrong to put too schematic an emphasis on divisions in the Barker oeuvre, but it is possible to see her career as loosely divided into three acts.

The first comprises her four early novels: *Union Street* (1982), *Blow Your House Down* (1984), *Liza's England* (originally published in 1986 as *The Century's Daughter*), and *The Man Who Wasn't There* (1989). These are set among members of the working class in north-eastern England—though many of these working-class characters are not actually *in* work, demonstrating the devastation wrought by Britain's loss of industrial employment. The women are more likely to have jobs than the men, though their jobs are poorly paid, degrading work in cake factories or chicken processing plants, as cleaners of pubs or richer women's homes or as prostitutes. Life is grim and fairly hopeless. Moments of transcendence, where they exist, are symbolic or spiritual rather than material. It is to these early novels that John Brannigan's summary comment applies most stringently: 'The most obvious and persistent theme is one of dereliction—physical, economic, social, emotional and psychological.'[26] And Margaretta Jolly concurs, especially on that psychological devastation: 'the most unpleasant aspect of Barker's unflinching depiction of working-class life is her characters' own submission to and even complicity in their degradation. Oppression is physicality internalized.'[27]

The first three novels, in particular, illustrate Barker's feminism. They focus on women's lives, while men are relatively peripheral, though when they do appear they figure as predators, as bad husbands or as neglectful sex partners. The first, longest, and most gripping chapter of *Union Street* features a child's rape; *Blow Your House Down* is about the threat posed to prostitutes by a Yorkshire-Ripper-like murderer who also rapes and tortures his victims; Liza, widowed after marriage to a weak and unsatisfactory husband, is assaulted in her old age by malevolent local lads. *Union Street* won the Fawcett Society Book Prize, a US award. *The Man Who Wasn't There* turned to a male protagonist, though it remained focused on north-eastern working-class life. All four of these novels, though they ramify over a long history, particularly in *Liza's England* (whose original title, *The Century's Daughter*, makes clear her representation of a very long historical movement), are set in nearly contemporary times.

With *Regeneration* she shifted dramatically and opened the second act of her novelistic career. It was the first of a trilogy of novels set in 1917–18. It moved away from the industrial north-east, being set mostly at Craiglockhart Hospital in Scotland, where British officers were treated for war trauma, with scenes also in London, on the Western Front, and (the industrial setting) in Salford, in Lancashire. It was a man's world, though the novel includes female munitions workers. In class terms, too, *Regeneration* marked a shift. One of its main historical figures is Siegfried Sassoon (1886–1967), a member of the landed gentry, interested in golf and fox hunting, and another is Dr W. H. R. Rivers (1864–1922), an upper middle-class physician and anthropologist. Since Craiglockhart is an officers' hospital, most of its patients are upper and middle class. One exception is Billy Prior, an invented figure who, by being from the working class, helps Barker to keep an anchor there, as well as to provoke interclass commentary and conflict, particularly with Rivers. Prior is also bisexual, and fairly open about it (while Sassoon and Wilfred Owen, both homosexual, are guarded about their natures).

When *Regeneration* was followed by *The Eye in the Door*, it became clear that Barker was working on a series. Its action follows closely on that of *Regeneration*, and the characters and themes are largely the same, though Billy Prior is more central in this volume. *The Eye in the Door* received the *Guardian* Fiction Prize. She closed the series with *The Ghost Road*, which resolves the arc of plot, or partially does so, by showing the deaths of Prior and Owen.

The trilogy distinguished itself in Barker's work, then, by a new focus on men, on war, on mostly middle-class characters, on sexual and gender fluidity, and on therapy; and by being a historical novel—traditionally a form that accepts the facticity of 'history' and combines imagined characters with real personages whose actions conform to what is actually known about them. Her 'Author's Note' in *Regeneration* declares that 'Fact and fiction are so interwoven in this book that it may help the reader to know what is historical and what is not' (251). She follows this statement with acknowledgement of her sources in eight different academic libraries, an article and book by Dr Rivers, and even a book called *Hysterical Disorders of Warfare*. *The Regeneration Trilogy* (published in one volume under that name in 1996), and the Booker Prize for *The Ghost Road* gave Barker a level of visibility and prestige previously unknown. A theatrical film based on *Regeneration* was released in the same year, and a volume combining *Union Street* and *Blow Your House Down* also appeared that year, responding to interest arising from the trilogy. The author was named 'Author of the Year' by the Booksellers' Association, also in 1996. In 2008, to celebrate the 40th anniversary of the Booker Prize, there was a new competition, called 'The Best of the Booker', and *The Ghost Road* was one of the six shortlisted books.

Pat Barker was made a Commander of the Order of the British Empire, 'for services to literature', in the New Year's Honours list of January 2000.

The third act of Barker's career is ongoing. In it she turned, following the War books, to novels which, while they may include similar themes, are freestanding, in the sense that there are no carried-over characters (with the exception noted below). Some of them return to the post-industrial north-east, for instance *Another World* and *Border Crossing*. Though there are working-class characters (and a Great War veteran, also working-class), the central figures are bourgeois: photographers, social workers, sculptors, lecturers. The interest in trauma remains and continues, and these novels include child murderers, atrocities in Sarajevo, and vividly recalled battlefield killings. There is a fierce engagement with the horrors of the contemporary world, often overtly or covertly dependent on the news about events like the murder of Jamie Bulger by two ten-year-old boys, the wars in Afghanistan and Bosnia, and the destruction of millions of British cattle during the foot-and-mouth epidemic.

In 2007 Pat Barker published *Life Class*. Its milieu is that of artists studying at the Slade School of Art in London, but, in a reversion away from the contemporaneous localization of her books since *The Ghost Road*, its time is just before and during the Great War. While its persons do not serve as infantrymen, as in the trilogy, the war impinges power-fully on the characters' lives. This return to the historical period that inspired her most admired fiction also signals a return to series fiction. *Toby's Room*, published in 2012, was a sort of prequel *cum* sequel to *Life Class*, showing something of the characters before the onset of the action depicted in the first book, then following them after it, though still contained within the war years and the multiple traumas of the war. Profiles of the author published since *Toby's Room* suggest that she indeed plans a second trilogy, but may leave the Great War behind and show the afterlives of her characters in the 1930s.

But *Union Street*—the novel by that title, and, symbolically at least, the milieu it concerns, the kind of social and political and geographical matrix that liberated Pat Barker to write about what she knew, is where her career begins.

CHAPTER ONE

Beginnings

Pat Barker's first novel, *Union Street* (1982), was a remarkably assured and artful beginning to her career. Michael Gorra's review in the *Hudson Review* praised the novel as 'an almost hellish cycle of seven stories about the working-class women who live along the Union Street of the title'.[1] He went on: '*The New Statesman* called *Union Street* on its publication in England "the long-overdue working class masterpiece," but such pigeonholing, however well-intentioned, is inadequate to Barker's work, and limits its audience—as does the equally likely description of it as a feminist novel'.[2] An ensemble piece about women living in a decaying north-eastern industrial city, it focuses on seven women loosely connected by similarities of theme, by geography (they live in Union Street, while quite a few of them have backgrounds in a much worse neighbourhood of abandoned homes, still standing and inhabited, and serving as a reminder or reproach—Wharfe Street). They are treated from youngest to oldest.

The first chapter, 'Kelly Brown'—even the first page—announces the novel's themes of fragility and deprivation; the opening sentence reads, 'There was a square of cardboard in the window where the glass had been smashed' (1) and within two pages the narrator has provided the information that Kelly and her older sister share one bed; that the bedroom is cold; that they are uneasy about 'him', an otherwise unidentified man linked to her mother, whose bedroom is beyond their wall; and that they live in an industrial city: 'Outside, a man's boots slurred over the cobbles: the first shift of the day' (1). More troubling is an argument between the girls over the disposal of sanitary napkins, which shows Kelly, in thought, rejecting adult sexuality.

This striking beginning hints at some of the themes that Barker will develop in *Union Street*. Men are usually tangential or irrelevant, except when present and threatening. Women's sexuality is problematic, hardly a gift to be welcomed. Life is hard, and women, even sisters or mothers and daughters, compete with each other for resources and scarce satisfactions.

Kelly's father is absent, and she longs, probably unrealistically, for his return. Yearning for an adult male leads to the key event in her story, rape by a stranger. The aftermath of the rape separates Kelly from the other children her age, and makes her a problem for her family and neighbours, and she 'acts out' by attacking and defiling a rich family's home and her school. At the end of her chapter, having found a dead and abandoned baby, she meets an old woman in the park and they share a moment of closeness together.

The following chapters provide an array of women's lives, moving chronologically through woman's life. Joanne Wilson (chapter 2) is a young woman working in the cake bakery and struggling with an unwanted pregnancy; as she complains to Joss (a midget and one of the few sympathetic men in *Union Street*, perhaps because he is not acknowledged as a man), 'I'm trapped! Worse than he'll ever be' (104). All the women could say the same. Lisa Goddard (chapter 3) is a burdened young mother, pregnant again, first seen slapping her child in the supermarket, who gives birth to a daughter, rejected by her mother because she is a girl.

Muriel Scaife, in the next chapter, is another wife and mother, a bit older, whose husband is disabled, though her mother diagnoses laziness. In the course of the chapter he suffers a haemorrhage, described with appalling vividness: 'It was like nothing she had ever seen before: so black, so foul-smelling, it didn't seem like blood at all,' (163) and dies leaving a son uncertain how to be a man.

Chapter 5, 'Iris King', introduces one of the central and in some ways most powerful women in the novel. Iris works, has her own money and dominates her husband Ted, who is cowed and marginal and desexed. She enjoys cleaning and helping the other women in Union Street. The narrator explains: 'All this was meat and drink to her. She loved life. She loved to feel life bubbling and quickening all around her, and took it for granted that life included old age, suffering and death' (196). This affirmation is undercut by Iris's violent reaction against her daughter Brenda, unmarried and pregnant; she pressures Brenda to get a late abortion, and when the baby is born alive she kills it and buries it in rubble and bricks, where Kelly will find it, or has already found it, in chapter 1.

'Blonde Dinah', of chapter 6, is an aged prostitute from Wharfe Street. Despite the title, the chapter is equally focused on George Harrison, a retired steelworker, whose wife hates having him around; in an earlier chapter she casually wishes he would die. Finding Blonde Dinah on his walks, George has sex with her, reflecting that he has never seen his wife Gladys naked, and seems to receive new life, comparing himself to the younger and dead John Scaife.

The final chapter closes the circle by linking with the first. Focused on the old and helpless Alice Bell, it shows what the life of deprivation and struggle and childbearing leads to. Crippled, resisting social workers and neighbourly help, she has a stroke. Refusing to go into a home, she makes her way to the park, clearly determined to die under her own terms. Her encounter with Kelly Brown is retold from her point of view; in addition there is something that can only be thought of as a vision: she looks towards a tree that stands out against the red sky.

■ At first it seemed to be bare like all the others, though with a jagged-ness of outline that suggested not winter but death. By now the murmur had become a shout, a fierce, ecstatic trilling; and when she looked more closely she saw that the tree was full of birds, clustering along its branches, as thick and bright as leaves. And all singing. But then, as she came closer still, as her white hair and skin took on the colours of blood and fire, she saw more clearly, and in a moment of vision cried. It isn't the birds, it's the tree. The tree is singing. (264) □

(Kelly had seen the same tree and within it 'the murmur had become a fierce, ecstatic trilling' [65].) In the end—as both women have 'gone'—Kelly home, Alice to death—'there were only the birds, soaring, swooping, gliding, moving in a never-ending spiral about the withered and unwithering tree' (265).

Though, as a first novel, *Union Street* was not so widely reviewed as her later works would be, it garnered respectable and in many cases very laudatory reviews. In the *Washington Post*, Elizabeth Ward praised the novel's maturity, its construction, its daring, and its willingness to use so many linked aspects of human life as its subject. She compared it very favourably with what one expects from a first novel.[3] Ivan Gold, in the *New York Times*, also praised the breadth and thoroughness of the novel, writing that it explored every possible dimension of living, family, grieving, loving and hating.[4]

The issues addressed by literary criticisms of *Union Street* include those, noted by reviewers and others, that can be nicely accessed through the multiple meanings of the title. As John Brannigan points out in 'The Small World of Kelly Brown' (2005), '"Union" establishes an association with working-class labor, a history of struggle against exploitation, as well as the more suggestive resonances of unity, togetherness, family, and sexual union.'[5]

The first of these associations carries the greater irony. 'Union' declares an affiliation with the long tradition of organized labour in Britain. But unions play no role in the novel. Barker has pointed out that the people in the society from which she came were unemployed and disabled men and single mothers in inadequate employment—'none of these people even belonged to a union; they were the people that even the labor movement was blind to'.[6] In 'Writing from the Margins' (1995), George Wotton (206) locates the novel in a 'critical moment' in the deindustrialization of the traditional working class—'a winter of particular discontent' (presumably the strikes during the Heath administration of the 1970s, signalled by shortages of coal).[7] What are the problems in working-class life, to which the novel and its title point? Brannigan identifies the 'traumatic impact of the decimation of particular economic and social structures'; David Waterman, in *Pat Barker and the Mediation of Social Reality* (2009), identifies the dereliction in post-industrial areas as a challenge to 'romantic stereotypes of working-class life'; in *Pat Barker* (2010), Mark Rawlinson cites Thatcherism as a 'cause of the further social immiseration of economically marginal urban communities' (though Thatcherism may be an anachronistic diagnosis, her election as Prime Minister having occurred only in 1979).[8] Commentators such as Monica Malm, in '*Union Street*: Thoughts on Mothering' (1998), and Ian Haywood, in *Working-Class Fictions* (1997), point to the substitution of women's drudgery—working in cake factories or, in the next Barker novel, the chicken processing plant—for the old-time, heavy-industrial work like steelmaking and shipbuilding as part of the movement away from the ideas summed up by the word 'union'.[9] Sharon Monteith memorably calls men 'denuded by the collapse of heavy industries in the north ... disempowered patriarchs'.[10] In dissent from the consensus that working-class life has been disempowered, fragmented, and immiserated by the loss of heavy industry, with destructive effects on unity and community, Penny Smith, in 'Remembered Poverty' (1995), insists that in *Union Street* 'we remain within a working-class community which is seen to be an organic entity'.[11]

Class

Barker's relationship with working-class life and fiction has been subject to some dispute. For some critics her novels demonstrate continuity with the tradition of English working-class fiction; among these seems to be John Brannigan, who writes that *Union Street* connects with 'earlier intrepid cartographers of working-class community, with George Orwell, Richard Hoggart [English critic, 1918–], Raymond Williams [Welsh novelist and critic, 1921–88], and the social realism in literature, drama, film and television of the late 1950s and early 1960s'.[12] Ian

Haywood spots a 'strong reliance' on D. H. Lawrence (English novelist, 1885–1930), though he goes on to stipulate she 'adapts Lawrence to her own feminist agenda' (145), and Blake Morrison, in *The New Yorker*, detects 'an air of *Sons and Lovers* [Lawrence's 1913 novel] about *Union Street*'.[13] Barker herself, in a 2006 interview with Fiona Tolan, denied belonging to a particular literary tradition, because the tradition of working-class fiction made little room for good books about women.[14] It is in that feminism, that insistence on the importance of women's lives, that rejection of what John Kirk in 'Recovered Perspectives' (1999) calls the 'reductive and gender blind' views on working-class life of Orwell, and Paulina Palmer, in *Contemporary Women's Fiction* (1989), calls the 'masculine ethos that distinguishes much of this fiction', that most critics base their discrimination of Pat Barker's work from the received working-class genre.[15] Hitchcock is another who emphasizes the feminine focus as an important departure from the tradition.

John Brannigan raises the issue of representation and exploitation when he writes that working-class fiction runs the 'risk of appropriating working-class experience for middle-class forms of representation, and the risk of marginalising working-class subject matter by attempting to invent distinctive working-class forms of expression'.[16] One of the uncommon negative critiques of *Union Street* comes from Kathryn and Philip Dodd, in 'From the East End to *Eastenders*' (1992), who contrast it unfavourably with the success of the *Eastenders* television serial, of all things, which has been broadcast by the British Broadcasting Corporation since 1985. The Dodds declare that the book 'is very much about the working class, not of it' though it is unclear how that distinction functions; and that it is implicated in 'extreme versions of nineteenth-century naturalism...the same detached stance of the zoologist-observer...the concomitant obsessions with animal analogies'.[17]

Sex and Gender

What about the other suggestion of the title—'unity, togetherness, family, and sexual union'? Perhaps the easiest to dispose of is sexual union. There is no shortage of sex in the novel, almost all of it ranging from the unbelievable to the repulsive: rape, at the most extreme, or piston-like, loveless knee-tremblers in the railway underpass; grudging thrice-yearly allowances; the kind of act that impregnated eighteen-year-old Joanne Wilson, who says, 'I'll tell you summat else: it was no bloody pleasure. A sparrow couldn't've farted quicker' (99). As for family, there are few intact families and no 'happy ones'. As for unity and togetherness, critics mostly agree, the connotations of 'union' are ambiguous at best. Paulina Palmer puts the judgement strongly that the women in Union Street are neither rebellious nor 'part of [Richard] Hoggart's community of hearth-loving, plump-armed matrons always ready with the tea'.[18] Other commentators agree: in 'Working-Class Women, Labor, and the Problem of Community' (2005), Sarah Brophy comments on Barker's 'ironic qualifications of any tendency to idealize female solidarity in the working-class communities'; both Malm and Waterman observe the competitiveness among women, Waterman insisting that if there were solidarity among the workers at the cake factory they would sabotage the management, not one another, while Brophy calls the competing women 'anonymous and infantilized'.[19] Falcus writes that Barker rejects 'easy assumptions of supporting working-class female communities'.[20] She sums up the position of those who problematize feminist or feminine solidarity, sisterhood, and women's supportive relations: 'Despite some critics reading in these three novels [she is also discussing *Blow Your House Down* and *Liza's England*] "an acknowledgement of the power of female solidarity" (Rennison, 2005, p. 27), it is clear that bonds between women are fraught with difficulties and are often more adequately described in the light of Irigaray's argument as relationships based on rivalry and competition.'[21] She refers here to a diagnosis by Luce Irigaray (1930–), in *An Ethics of Sexual Difference* (1993), who argued that because masculine ethical criteria lead to the repression of mother–daughter love, relations between women are more likely to be characterized by competition than by collaboration and sisterly support. There is no shortage of maternal violence (in the Lisa Goddard chapter, for instance), which along with domestic violence of the usual sort, between husbands and wives, Falcus traces to its causes in 'poverty, unemployment and exhaustion'.[22] Some critics, indeed, disagree, at least in part, with Margaretta Jolly calling the 'union' in Barker's title 'the recognition of some measure of mutual support within the women's community' and Rawlinson diagnosing the misogyny of men as 'lodged in the interactions of the women of Union Street [...]'.[23] Ian Haywood approaches the question of community through the novel's structure, maintaining that the seven chapters with seven different focal characters permit a 'pioneer psychological and emotional representation' of working-class women, but also emphasize their separation from each other.[24]

The diagnosis of misogyny is a key part of the feminist analysis of the novel, or the analysis of the novel's feminism. John Brannigan declares that 'Barker is thoroughly feminist not just in pursuing these anguished cries of oppressed women, but also in showing such oppression as the product of bankrupt social economy.' Kirk also insists on the inseparability of feminist and class analysis.[25] Beyond the failure of women to form supportive networks, on the street or in the factory, other commentators (e.g. Palmer and Falcus) have highlighted the difficulties of the mother–daughter relationship, with Falcus declaring mother–daughter relationships (along with other female connections) 'bonds based on "a complex mixture of fascination and distaste"'.[26]

As for men, critical judgements of them range from Rawlinson's diagnosis that they are 'both pathetic and terrible, superfluous and indispensable, materially absent and ideologically omnipotent' to Sharon Monteith's comment, accepting that men are victims of an industrial collapse, that 'they are not uniformly demonized'.[27] An intermediate position may be Ian Haywood's statement that they are 'written off' in the sense that the 'only sympathetic men in the novel are sexually unthreatening or inert'—for instance, the relatively sympathetic Joss, a midget treated as comic, and John Scaife, first an invalid and next a corpse.[28] Haywood's summary, along with the rape of Kelly Brown in the first chapter, help to explain why no critic detects anything positive in the 'sexual union' portion of Brannigan's summary (above). Brophy provides an elegant summary of the feminist project by saying that *Union Street* (and *Liza's England*) 'render a multifaceted account of the complex structures of feeling inhabited by working-class women, highlighting the gaps that persist between their dreams of fulfillment and their everyday struggles for survival'.[29] Barker's own commentary about feminism in her early novels is interesting: interviewer Fiona Tolan points out that in her first three novels, 'you worked to give a very powerful voice to a number of disenfranchised characters, particularly working class women', and asks if she considers herself a feminist; Barker replies, 'Only in the sense that I would never describe myself as an unfeminist writer. [...] But with the proviso that anything you do to change the condition of one gender will inevitably involve changes for the other.'[30]

Approach and Technique

Much commentary on *Union Street* focuses on its ideas: its politics, its position regarding the working class, post-industrial conditions in north-eastern England, its feminism. James Procter, in 'The Return of the Native' (2011), places it among novels of empire, noting the connections with British military activity in Northern Ireland, and links Kelly's 'becoming-feral'—when she defiles her school with her own excrement—to the 'dirty protest'—a hunger strike, accompanied by the defiling of cells, mounted by some imprisoned IRA members in Ulster in 2001.[31] But it deserves, and has received, considerable criticism of its method. Some of this has to do with the question of realism: Flora Alexander, in *Contemporary Women Novelists* (1989), calls Pat Barker 'basically a realist writer', adding, however, that she 'modifies her realism by excluding aspects of working-class life that might appear wholesome and attractive, and concentrating on an examination of poverty and the squalor and degradation that it engenders'.[32] Alexander goes on to argue that the author's 'unsentimental, unflinching' rendering of the degrading facts of the life she represents creates 'what is effectively a political statement about the lives of women who have for all practical purposes been silenced'.[33] John Brannigan distinguishes her work from social realism, in part by writing that she uses 'omnipresent' rather than omniscient narration; his understanding of this is that the narrative moves between focal characters while remaining fixed in their own consciousness and perceptions, rather than permitting the narrator to know more than the characters themselves, though the implicit claim that realism necessarily relies on full-bore omniscience is questionable, as a consideration of some classic realist texts will indicate.[34]

The type of narration, and the nature of the narrator, have attracted considerable critical attention. In *Dialogics of the Oppressed* (1993), Peter Hitchcock, in an essentially Bakhtinian analysis, that is, responding to Russian literary theorist Mikhail Bakhtin (1895–1975), diagnoses the omniscient narrator of *Union Street* as a 'practitioner of one of Bakhtin's favorite arts, double-voiced discourse, an ability that allows the narrator to move in and out of the language of the sign community that is the focus of the story'.[35] This multiple voicing, he explains, 'organizes what Bakhtin calls a social purview or worldview of a sort'.[36] In 'Towards a Masculine Maternal', Margaretta Jolly calls Barker's practice 'a "maternal" form of narrative as her most minimal political hope'; this is in the context of an essay on the 'masculine maternal', and thus used in a specialized application, a sense in which maternity may be expanded to encompass male as well as female nurturing.[37] John Brannigan is not referring to the narrator, but to the narrated, that is the consciousnesses of the various characters, though of course this material reaches the reader mediated through the discourse of the omniscient or omnipresent narrator, when he describes an imaginary community being constructed through the 'intersubjective consciousness of the narrative'. Rawlinson's explanation of the narrative technique comes in a discussion of the difficulty readers have in deciding how old Kelly Brown is; he observes that the narrative evokes the reader's prejudices (about whether Kelly's persona is age-appropriate, for example) 'in order to confront them'. In other words, Barker's writing about the working class relies on a 'scenic technique which plays down the authority of the third-person narrator' and uses the 'figurative rather than denotative dimensions of style'.[38]

The narrator is, whether maternal or not, omniscient though not imperiously so; that is, the narrator's voice gives repeated inside views into the consciousness of main characters. The novel is divided into seven chapters, each of them named for one of the women on Union Street, and this organization, along with its thematic implications, has quite properly attracted plenty of critical commentary. In 'Warring Fictions', Sharon Monteith writes that 'there is no single protagonist for the reader to identify as representative; promoting empathy with a single idiosyncratic character might also serve to alienate their experiences from those around them. Instead, Barker charts a historical trajectory, or a working class continuum, through the lives and memories of seven women [...].'[39] Brophy comments on the ambiguity produced by some implications in the novel that the seven women are all one woman, or are all women—the 'seven stages of woman' idea—and offers a suggested consequence: 'The phrasing hesitates between the specific and the generic—is "that girl" Lisa herself, or Joanne, or any girl?—suggesting the one life that is lived by the women of Union Street, as well as the profound disconnections experienced by each woman as she moves from one stage and type of labor to the next.'[40] Here, Kirk writes—in a way he diagnoses as characteristic of Barker's work in general—'there is a persistent effort to create a collective experience and consciousness, rather than the individualistic one associated with the novel of middle-class life [...]'.[41] Falcus, using the concept of 'women's time' attributed to the Bulgarian-French philosopher Julia Kristeva (1941–), sees the structure as revealing the cyclical quality of women's lives; she continues (citing Jolly) that the seven stages represent a repetitious rather than linear order to women's lives, adding that 'this cyclical time takes on both negative and positive aspects, as it leads to restrictions on women's lives and yet also offers the hope of more loving and supporting relationships between women'.[42] John Brannigan seems to be making a similar point in his comments about the 'intersubjective consciousness of the narrative'—that is, the leakage of information and knowledge from one of the women's consciousnesses into another, in a way he calls ghostly; this feature, he argues, constructs an imaginary community.[43]

Kelly and Alice

Of the seven sections of *Union Street*, a disproportionate amount of criticism has been focused on the first, 'Kelly Brown', and the last, 'Alice Bell'. There are several reasons why this should be so. Kelly's section is longer, and more sensational and poignant, as she experiences a rape connected with her longing for an absent father, and the effects of that rape distance her from friends and family; and Alice's section ends with her death. Kelly and Alice also show the continuities of the women in Union Street. Kelly observes older girls and women and sees her own future self in them. Alice thinks back and 'remembers' experiences and sensations that belong to other women in the book; and she thinks of herself as having been so many women. So the two of them foreground the idea of representative, even interchangeable, women's lives, and that of the intersubjectivity of women's minds. Flora Alexander argues strongly for an interdependence that culminates in that last moment. Shared experiences—life on the same street; work in the cake factory; shared experiences in present and past; Kelly's discovery of Iris's aborted grandchild: 'At some points the characters' consciousnesses blend so that one woman is able to remember the experience of another as if it were her own. Thus Alice Bell in her last hours shares fragments of the consciousness of some of the younger women, and a sense of collective identity is established.'[44]

Finally, they are linked through an event that both ends the novel—the approach to Alice's death—and ends Kelly's section, in which the two of them, young and old, share a moment of union and possibly transcendence. In 'Matrix, Metramorphosis, and the Readymade', Maria Troy has written powerfully about this moment, which she calls 'a moment of acute matrixial awareness': 'Indeed, *Union Street* is an excellent example of how Barker's narrative technique allows for a focus on subjectivity-as-encounter and transubjectivity, an enlarged and partial subjectivity that involves more than one character—that is, matrixial subjectivity.'[45] Her analysis of the last pages enables a somewhat optimistic reading of the ending of the novel, as she points out that, on her way home from her meeting with Alice, Kelly shows a 'non-traumatic interest in sexuality' and that 'it seems like Kelly, with the help of her matrixial encounter with Alice Bell, has started to move beyond her trauma'.[46] That ending includes not only a sympathetic meeting between the old and the young—both victims of trauma—and some sort of transcendent recognition of each other; it also includes a moment of symbolic transcendence, represented by the vision of a tree full of singing birds.

Other critics have suggested different ways to read that ending. Brannigan compares it to the posthumous poem 'Lady Lazarus' by the American poet Sylvia Plath (1932–63) and explains: 'Barker presents Alice here as the chimerical embodiment of a mythic symbol of renewal [...] at the same time as she serves to bring the disparate, troubled women of Union Street into an imaginary unity.'[47] Brophy is much less impressed by the ending as a 'happy' or unifying or redeeming moment. 'But to read the encounter between Alice and Kelly in the park as evidence of their "mutual recognition" of each other's opposition relationship to the "Establishment," and "a strong statement on the sisterhood of class"'—here she refers to Peter Hitchcock's *Dialogics of the Oppressed*—'is, I think, to overstate the case.'[48] She suggests that the symbolism of transcendence—that is, the singing tree—is not so clearly applicable to Kelly and Alice. Ian Haywood dismisses the moment of transcendence as 'both sentimentally feminist and mystical'.[49]

Though the applicability of the moment of transcendence may be in question, the tree of singing birds is clearly symbolic, and Barker's use of symbolism is of great critical interest. Peter Hitchcock calls attention to the many examples of 'thin domestic boundaries'—he instances thin walls, broken windows and fireplaces—which 'become symbolic of class as well as gender porousness, permitting a punishing regime of neighbourly surveillance'.[50] John Brannigan has several times pointed to the multiple examples of broken shells. In his analysis, these symbols, which include windows, eggshells, and conkers, indicate the fragility of protective systems.[51] Alexander comments on the role of repeated motifs, especially unwanted pregnancy and the association between pregnancy and death, in producing the interdependence of the lives and experiences in Union Street.[52]

Style

Finally, a number of critics have been struck by the freedom, or vitality, of the language in *Union Street*. Reviewing the novel on its first American appearance, Elizabeth Ward wrote in approval of the brutality of the language because it corresponded to the brutality of the vision of life in the novel, and to moderate it would be a falsification.[53] George Wotton writes incisively about Barker's use of 'bad language': it is 'not simply a reflexive technique for producing an illusion of verisimilitude, a device used by the author to show, through the frequent use of "swear words", how "real" or "authentic" are her working-class characters or situations'. He points out that dialect and malapropisms are traditional ways of portraying working-class characters. Barker is successful in creating 'a genuine working-class voice without recourse to what Common called "the traditional outbreaks of funny spelling"'.[54]

One of the authorial challenges Barker faced in this novel was aligning her language with that of her characters, rather than giving the narrator a linguistic register that patronized the language of the inhabitants of Union Street. Kirk writes that the sense of community (which, of course, is itself problematic to many critics) 'is sharpened by Barker's use of dialogue and dialect' in which, he maintains, the narrator's voice merges with those of the characters.[55] This practice, on a textual level, is homologous to the structural practice, identified by John Brannigan, of an omnipresent rather than omniscient narrator.

Film

The relationship between author, narrator, reader, and characters is equally complex in Barker's next novel, *Blow Your House Down*. But before turning to that book it is necessary to say something about the film made from *Union Street*. The first thing to say is that almost no reader of *Union Street* would recognize it as the source material for *Stanley and Iris*, directed by Martin Ritt and released in 1990. The film-makers extracted the character of Iris King from the fifth section of the novel; moved her and the whole story to the United States; made her a widow with a heart of gold, still deeply in love with her dead husband, and a cake-froster by profession (perhaps an acknowledgement of the role of the cake factory in *Union Street*, though Iris is not among its employees); and chose an American actress, Jane Fonda (1937–), for the role. The character played by Robert De Niro (1943–) is wholly new: an illiterate cook whom Iris teaches to read, after which he becomes in inventor in Detroit (the film is set in New England).

Barker has often expressed bemusement over the process by which her novel turned into a vehicle for Fonda and De Niro. In a 1991 interview with Donna Perry, before the film's release, she seemed to expect a more political result, saying 'There is a definition of literature which excludes making political points of any kind. This is a reason for making *Union Street* an American film. It is easier to circumvent social criticism by set-ting it in America. Here such criticism would not be accepted; it would be very difficult to raise the money. They would say it is politically unaccept-able; they would say it is too depressing a portrait of life in Britain.'[56]

The reviewers of *Stanley and Iris* were mostly unimpressed. True, Vincent Canby, in the *New York Times*, gave the film credit for the originality of its focus, the unusual world that it revealed to an audi-ence for whom a modern New England factory town would be exotic, and its honesty.[57] By contrast, Peter Travers in *Rolling Stone* called the film a 'hollow and unconvincing fairy tale', a 'celebration of get-rich-quick aspirations, which shoehorns a serious issue into a formulaic Hollywood love story'.[58] And the reviewer for the *Time Out Film Guide*, belying Barker's expectations that an American transplantation would permit a more honest treatment of the politics, concludes that 'the end-ing, despite good intentions, is American cinema at its tackiest and most hollow'.[59] In her interview with Donna Perry, Barker spoke wryly about the aftermath of the film, which saw her become briefly famous. She said the reporters unable to distinguish fact from fiction came to her neighbourhood; 'they wanted to look up Iris King and ask her how she felt about being played by Jane Fonda'.[60]

BLOW YOUR HOUSE DOWN (1984)

Union Street was published in 1982; *Blow Your House Down* followed it in 1984. This novel was immediately perceived as having much in common with *Union Street*: it follows several women, living in a shattered north-eastern city, and embodies a feminist critique of their plight. At the same time it differs from *Union Street* in that the device for cohesiveness among these disparate narratives is not geography, all the women living nearby, nor is it that they show a 'seven ages of women' scheme; instead, these women are united in being (or in one case mistaken for being) prostitutes.

It begins in a way that reminds the reader of *Union Street*: two sisters, sharing a room, bickering in a petty way, their mother leaving them on their own, a shadowy male figure ('Uncle Norman') in an unclear but apparently residential and sexual relationship. One difference stands out: this scene takes place at night. Brenda goes out, accompanies a friend Audrey to the pub. Gradually it appears they are prostitutes. And they are living in a crisis; there is a murderer on the loose, killing prostitutes. Reference to the Royal Wedding between Prince Charles and Lady Diana Spencer, which took place on 29 July 1981, places the action in that year, when Peter Sutcliffe, the 'Yorkshire Ripper' eventually convicted of killing thirteen women and attempting to kill seven others, was still on the loose.

The conversation among the women includes frank canvassing of the threat they face, and what one ought to do to avoid becoming a victim: for instance,

■ 'Stick to your regulars,' said Audrey. 'That's your best bet.'
'That's what I told her. She said he was somebody's regular.' (11) □

But they also discuss their lives outside of their sex work, men in general (of whom they have, unsurprisingly, no very high opinion), and their children. Clearly one of Barker's aims is to render these women in their ordinariness. They are like other women, just with a different job. The narrow range of possible employment for them helps to explain their decision. The major alternative seems to be work in the chicken factory, a disgusting and deadening kind of work of which several of them have experience. But, as Brenda thinks, rising from a degrading servicing of her regular George and brushing the gravel from her knees, '*Christ,* what a way to earn a living' (27).

The most forthright and confident of the prostitutes may be Jean, something of a loner, a lesbian whose lover is missing (and is found dead before the novel ends). Unlike most chapters of the novel, rendered in omniscient third-person narration, Jean's is narrated by her. She explains why she is a prostitute.

■ I like this life. I'm not in it because I'm a poor, deprived, inadequate, half-witted woman, whatever some people might like to think. I'm in it because it suits me. I like the company. I like the excitement. I like the feeling of stepping out onto the street, not knowing what's going to happen or who I'm going to meet. I like the freedom. □

Jean is one of the most important characters in this ensemble, in part because she demonstrates the most agency and in demonstrating it, explains the significance of the novel's epigraph, from the German philosopher Friedrich Nietzsche (1844–1900) in *Beyond Good and Evil* (1886): 'Whoever fights monsters should see to it that in the process he does not become a monster. And when you look long into an abyss the abyss also looks into you.'

The opposite of Jean is Kath Robson, a veteran prostitute now on the downward path. Brenda, who had been mentored by Kath, now thinks, 'It was like sitting by the bedside of a very old woman, so old that memory and mental facilities have all decayed...And yet Kath wasn't old. What would she be? Thirty-three? Thirty-four?' (16). Kath becomes the next victim of the ripper, in a really hideous act of violence, vividly rendered by Barker, made more sickening by her decision to write it from the perspective of the killer himself.

Finally there is the story of Maggie, a worker in the chicken factory who is attacked as she walks home from work, thinking of her husband. It is unclear if she is another victim of the Ripper, though there is no sexual part to her attack; she is smashed in the head rather than knifed; she is rescued by a passing prostitute, Brenda, the woman from chapter 1. Whether or not her attacker took her for a prostitute, she later reveals that the police had thought she was a prostitute. Her recovery, the difficulty of life knowing that her husband is suspected by the police of having assaulted her, and her realization that she can no longer work in the chicken factory, constitute the last part of *Blow Your House Down*. It ends with a scene of aviary transcendence similar to that in *Union Street*: 'The sky flames. Then, gradually, as the birds continue to descend, the red gentles through purple and gold to rose, until at last every bird is lodged, and the singing dies away' (170). This is somewhat less obviously redeeming than its counterpart with Kelly and Alice, since none of the human characters in the novel—not even the living prostitutes and of course not the victims—seems to witness this moment of illumination.

As with *Union Street*, reviews were mostly positive. Nicci Gerrard in *The Guardian* reviewed *Blow Your House Down* with other feminist novels and commented on its toughness, its unsentimentality, and its resolute avoidance of propaganda, features that, she said, it shared with *Union Street*.[61] Katha Pollitt in the *New York Times* linked its strengths to those of its predecessor and identified the powerful feminism in the book's message about sexual violence as a threat to all women and the tendency of the justice system to treat its victims as criminals them-selves.[62] She had reservations, though, about the story of Maggie, which implied that women need male protection. But Pollitt celebrated Barker for giving readers, in full, the inner lives of women whom literature has traditionally ignored or treated as objects, and thus humanizing and individualizing them, a project that Pollitt considers clearly feminist.[63] In the *Washington Post*, Elizabeth Ward also faulted the ending of the novel, and thought the chicken factory symbolism a little unsubtle, but strongly endorsed the depiction of Kath's murder. She commented on its language, accepting that it is obscene but insisting that to call it obscene is not enough: the obscenity is deliberate and designed to implicate the reader in the evil from which obscenity arises and to which it testifies.[64] In a 2004 interview with Rob Nixon, Barker said that the novel was better received in the United States than in Britain.[65]

Later reviews—that is, omnibus essay-reviews including *Blow Your House Down* with other Barker novels—included Kennedy Fraser's long essay in *The New Yorker*, which praises the novel for compassion and psychological insight, 'elements of the murder mystery or the psycho-logical thriller', and the ability to be 'by turns bawdy, lyrical, and cin-ematic', and calls the novel a 'Dostoyevskian *roman noir*', referring to the Russian novelist Fyodor Dostoevsky (1821–81), who often depicts downtrodden people in blighted urban settings, and evil targeted at prostitutes.[66] In the *New Labor Forum* (2004), Paul Simpson, writing about both *Union Street* and *Blow Your House Down*, calls this one 'short-shrifted', by which he means to deplore its lack of one strong, unitary plot, and expresses some disappointment about the novel's failure to follow 'the conventions of suspense novels'. He goes on to acknowledge that the author 'does not flinch from these moments of great pain, loss, self-negation or humiliation'.[67]

Later literary criticism has focused most closely on those topics that appeared in the book's reviews: the treatment of prostitution; language and 'obscenity'; the use of point of view; feminism; symbolism; the nature and effectiveness of the ending; and, something that could not appear in the reviews, the experience of teaching *Blow Your House Down*.

Prostitution

One fairly important point is that prostitutes are unusual subjects for contemporary fiction, at least when treated unsensationally. Flora Alexander writes that in *Blow Your House Down*, 'Barker continues the task of subjecting to thorough examination kinds of experience that are usually given little consideration,' and while she means work as prostitutes, it is likely that most readers know equally little about work in a chicken factory.[68] However, it is prostitution that is foregrounded; the chicken factory is the background. As Katerina Andriotis wrote in 'Pat Barker, *Blow Your House Down*, and the Prostitution Debate' (2009), the novel seems aimed to 'dispel pop-culture myths regarding prostitution'—as in Jean's statement, quoted above, dismissing most explanations of prostitutes as helpless victims.[69] (Jean is unusually free in her own choices, however.) Sharon Monteith says that, rejecting the extreme view of prostitution, Barker gives the reader its 'sheer ordinariness'.[70] In 'Pat Barker and the Languages of Region and Class' (2004), Maroula Joannou sees an effort to distinguish Barker's prostitute from the 'tart with a heart' stereotype; she also attributes to this novel the belief that marriage and prostitution are no different, perhaps putting it too strongly when, she writes, Barker 'insists' that prostitution is a job like any other.[71] Ann Ardis argues along similar lines in 'Political Attentiveness vs. Political Correctness' (1991). About Brenda (who lost her job in the chicken factory and turned to prostitution to support her family), Ardis says 'the women she worked with on the factory line are equally alienated from the products of their labor [as prostitutes]; they too switch off to get through the day. Moreover, while Edith, Brenda's mother-in-law, certainly claims both the respectability and the class status she refuses to grant Brenda, she is as alienated from her sexuality as are the prostitutes.'[72] In 'The Other "F" Word' (1990), Dale Bauer also works to minimize distinctions between the prostitutes and others, pointing out that Maggie, the victim of an unprovoked attack, is, like the prostitutes, 'cut'—'interrogated about the events of the attack and then shunned by her neighbors'.[73]

Language

Barker said in a 1989 interview with Michelle Hanson that her husband had accused her of being a pornographer hidden inside a respected novelist—a diagnosis with which she agreed.[74] Etymologically, 'pornography' means 'writing about prostitutes'. But the larger critical issue has to do with the novelist's employment of the *language* of pornography. Mark Rawlinson has discussed this at length. He explains that her pornography is 'an extended counter-statement ... and a scrupulous revision of a dismissive or exploitative misrepresentation of prostitutes'.[75] He links her 'rather stylish taboo-breaking' to the photography of British photojournalist Don McCullin (1935–) as part of an aesthetics of confrontation.[76] Ann Ardis flatly declares that the murder of Kath *is pornographic*—'in the sense that Barker shows the murderer's association of sex and violence without reassuring us that we are being offered a critique of this behavior'—a point obviously related to her decision to write this murder from the point of view of the murderer.[77] Rawlinson claims, somewhat oddly, that he notes the question of pornographic writing in Barker 'in anticipation of the claims that Barker's fiction is too derivative of influential academic scholarship' (31)—a claim that has not, in the event, been made, particularly about these early novels, which show little sign—or at least have not been accused—of being derivative of academic work.[78] Both Joannou and Brannigan comment on bodily fluids and bodily secretions, which, while not pornographic, are part of her unblinking candour about the body, what Mark Rawlinson calls her 'citation and creation of obscenity'.[79] Citation and creation—mention and use—are different, and presumably differently motivated. Barker commented that Kath's murder was 'much more explicit than anything in [her later novel] Border Crossing. And it is done from the killer's point of view. And it does involve sadistic sex. So I think that was much harder to get right.'[80] Sharon Monteith calls that passage 'almost too distressing to contemplate' and presumably that 'almost' recognizes the novelist's intention and judgement.[81]

The reader's experience of the arguably 'obscene' in Blow Your House Down is most acute, as Monteith suggests, in the scene where Kath is murdered. And it is distressing not only because of the language—for instance, 'He gathered handfuls of feathers together and started shoving them inside her cunt' (65)—but because of the narrative strategy that focalizes this chapter through the mind and sensations of the killer himself. Margaretta Jolly puts it well when she writes that 'we are made to see through the eyes of the "Ripper" as he rapes and murders a prostitute'; her diagnosis is that 'what seemed an anomalous switch in sexual focalization is clearly a deliberate challenge to any simple polarization of oppressed and oppressor'.[82] Sharon Monteith analyses the effect of this change in focalization: there is a risk of the reader identifying with the victimizer (though this risk seems slight, the novelist having taken care to make the victimizer so repellent), but points out that identifying with the victim is just as disturbing since the reader is positioned to experience the violence while helpless to act.[83] Ann Ardis generalizes about the voyeurism of any reading experience, which she takes to be greater when class boundaries are crossed; that is, when middle-class readers read about the working class.[84] John Brannigan comments more broadly on the use of varying narrative perspective, which he says shows Barker's effort to narrow the gap between the narrator's voice and that of the characters; this is particularly strong in the case of Jean's first-person narrative (which also serves the strategic purpose of putting the reader squarely at one with Jean in suspicion, as she looks into the abyss) but applies as well to the murderer's chapter, rendered in third-person narration but focalized through him. Ian Haywood seems to offer a different explanation for this alignment when he writes that 'Barker tries to deglamorize the folk-devil mystique that has accrued to the psychopathic serial killer in popular culture,' but finds that the result is to give a 'sensationalist charge to the narrative'.[85] Mark Rawlinson acknowledges the discomfort readers experience, assumes that it is purposeful, and writes that 'Readers made uncomfortable by the alignment with the aggressor are pushed to assess whether this unease is visceral or theoretical.'[86] Rather unusually, he includes not only the murder of Kath, in which we are 'made' to see through the eyes of a murderer, as Jolly puts it, but also the chapter in which Jean knifes to death one of her customers, who, it seems almost certain, was not the Ripper but a harmless punter, a strategic positioning about which most critics say little.

Gender and Sexuality

The feminism of *Blow Your House Down* may seem too obvious to need much elaboration, as it features women victimized because they are women and women raped and murdered because they are women; further, crimes against them are minimized, because they are women. Barker herself stipulated that while her book was opposed to all violence it was particularly focused on male violence against women.[87] Paulina Palmer writes that this book belongs to a new kind of novel: 'Treating violence against women as the distinguishing feature of a male supremacist society, it seeks ambitiously to investigate the interrelationship between a variety of different forms and manifestations.'[88] She goes on to distinguish two feminisms, radical feminism and socialist feminism; when she depicts the prostitutes as victims of male violence, Palmer explains, she writes in the spirit of radical feminism, but her economic analysis is socialist feminist.[89] In 'Pat Barker: In the Shadow of Monstrosities' (2005), Peter Childs defines the attitude toward prostitution as 'largely concerned with the causal factors of economic necessity and poor social welfare', which would seem to align with Palmer's socialist feminism—'it is a logical conclusion of working class gender relations in a time of mass unemployment'.[90] The grim economics behind the practice of prostitution, particularly the contrast with the only other viable employment option shown, the chicken factory, are noticed by many critics, including Joannou who sums up the chicken factory as a microcosm of patriarchy and a 'microcosm of class relations'.[91] Ardis, likewise, writes that the novel asks students—she is among those who write from the point of view of one teaching the text—'to reflect on how cultural categories such as class and gender reciprocally constitute each other [...] But Barker's work also points up the radical instability of such categories. Hence it does not exemplify class-based paradigms of analysis. Nor does it fit neatly into feminist arguments about male violence against women.'[92] The other approach through the classroom, Bauer's essay on *Blow Your House Down* as an example of feminist teaching, seems less sure about the class analysis, as it identifies Maggie (a worker in the chicken factory) as a member of the middle class—presumably because she is married, her husband has a job, and she is not a prostitute—as well as 'a model to explore in class discussions of ethics'.[93]

Symbolism

The bird symbolism has been mentioned already. Peter Childs adds an analysis of Christian symbolism and allusions, identifying Kath as a sacrificial victim, like Jesus, and identifying Maggie's section of the book as where 'Barker's chicken imagery is fully aligned with Christian symbolism'.[94] He also has some symbolic discussion of the title, in which the first two sections show pigs eaten by the wolf while the third shows the pigs fighting back. Palmer comments on the 'striking, if somewhat heavy, use of symbolism', particularly the chicken factory.[95]

Perhaps the most significant symbolic presence in the novel, if that is what it is, comes at the end. Maggie, slowly recovering from her attack, climbs a hill and looks down on the city. She sees rays of golden light falling on it; unknowingly she decides not to return to the factory; she goes home and holds hands with her husband. There follows a description from the omniscient narrator of 'a moment in every evening' when the starlings come, the sky flames then changes through other colours, and 'Above the hurrying people, above the lighted windows, above the sodium orange of the street lamps, they [the birds retiring to their rest] hump, black and silent, unnoticed, unless some stranger to the city should happen to look up, and be amazed.' What is the meaning of this ending? There is an evident connection to the ending of *Union Street*, with Maggie and Bill holding hands in place of Kelly and Alice, a change in the light, singing birds, and a moment of transcendence. John Brannigan believes that the ending is a problem because, though it is beautiful, there is no reason to think that the women in the book see it; its availability is limited to the narrator and, of course, the reader.[96] (Admittedly it would be available to a visitor to the city who happened to look up, but this still denies it to the women who live there.) Peter Childs discusses the end of Maggie's story, with her husband cradling her feet, which he reads positively (and it is true that cradling the feet of a spouse is often a marker of tenderness in Barker's fiction): 'Ending on this scene underscores the novel's emphasis on the ineffability of violence but also the silent acts of love that heal. Barker tenders no solutions other than to offer love, not violence in opposition to a barbarous world [...].'[97] Katha Pollitt's objection to the resolution of Maggie's story as prescribing male protection as an antidote to male oppression may help to explain the uneasiness some other critics express over the ending and the tendency for much criticism to ignore it.

Barker's first two novels, with their divided focus, their ensemble structure, and their multiple representations of woman over a range of ages and fates, would be followed by one focused on one woman. *Union Street* and *Blow Your House Down* had a broad range of characters over a short time; *Liza's England* would have a narrower range of characters, with one clearly central, and range over nearly a century.

CHAPTER TWO

History, Gender, and Class

Pat Barker's third novel appeared in 1986 under the title *The Century's Daughter*, before being renamed *Liza's England* ten years later. Published by Virago, like *Union Street* and *Blow Your House Down,* it makes a claim to represent more than just itself, under either title. Liza Garrett was the first child born in her town in the twentieth century and is as old as the century—that is, in her eighties—in the novel. Her experiences of maternity, of two world wars, of depression and deprivation, may make her experience a synecdoche of her century; while Sarah Brophy says that she represents both 'a generation and the twentieth century', Margaretta Jolly enlarges the claim and calls her 'the unelected representative of English history [...]'.[1] When Barker retitled the book *Liza's England*, changing the focus from time to place, she made more obvious the apparent claim that this is a Condition-of-England novel. This is no novelty; a number of critics of her first two novels had given them that name. 'Condition of England'—a term launched by Thomas Carlyle (1795–1881) in *Chartism* (1840)—usually refers to the condition of the workers or the poor in a country sharply divided between the classes. Some of the books that might be included would be *Shirley* (1849) by Charlotte Brontë (1816–55); *Sybil* (1845) by Benjamin Disraeli (1804–81); *North and South* (1855) by Elizabeth Gaskell (1810–65); *The Way We Live Now* (1875) by Anthony Trollope (1815–82); and possibly *Little Dorrit* (1857) by Charles Dickens (1812–70). Modern condition-of-England novels include *The Ice Age* (1977) by Margaret Drabble (1939–); Martin Amis's *Money* (1984); and *The Child in Time* (1987) by Ian McEwan (1948–).

And some critics have also called Barker's first two books Condition-of-England novels. Still, the narrowness of focus, temporally and geographically, especially of *Blow Your House Down* with most of the characters being prostitutes, makes them less successful capturings of the condition of England than *Liza's England*. Both John Kirk and Lyn Pykett call it that, with Pykett adding that it is also a 'study of provincial life', a phrase seemingly designed to link it with Flaubert's *Madame Bovary* (1856, subtitled 'Mœurs de province') or George Eliot's *Middlemarch* (1871–2, subtitled 'A Study of Provincial Life').[2]

Liza's England is different from its predecessors in Barker's work in having a single main protagonist, Liza Jarrett Wright, whose story it largely is. There is a second important character, Stephen, a gay social worker in his twenties, and as the novel begins it is focalized through Stephen:

> ■ 'No point being eighty, is there?' said Liza. 'If you can't be a bit outrageous'.
> And certainly she looked it, Stephen thought, with her scarlet headsquare tilted crazily over one eye, giving her the look of a senile pirate. (1) □

Liza lives in a street whose houses are scheduled to be demolished. Like Alice Bell in *Union Street*, she is attached to her house (she has lived there since 1922); like her, she fears going into what she continues to think of as the workhouse.

In fact *Liza's England* looks backward and forward in several respects. Stephen's father, dying of cancer, experiences a horrifying haemorrhage, like John Scaife in *Union Street* (and like one that Pat Barker says, in her interview with Donna Perry, she also witnessed):[3] Stephen's life represents Barker's first serious attention to male homosexuality, which will appear in a stronger flavour with some of the officers, particularly Billy Prior, in the *Regeneration* trilogy. World War I is also treated for the first time at any length, including women's work manufacturing armaments, as is spiritualism, which was practised as a religion in the author's family.[4]

Liza has a treasure box, kept under her bed, and this is the key to her rich retrospection, her exploration of 'the long country of the past']. The box triggers a flashback to her early childhood, washing day, and her difficult relations with her mother. Liza adores her father; but her mother resents her because she is a girl and finds ways to frustrate any effort she may make to read a book. Liza knows that (beyond the working-class hostility to girl children that Barker depicts in several of her novels) her mother resents her because she is herself illiterate. The family also experiences class hostility; Liza remembers accompanying her mother, who is a domestic cleaner, to her job at the Wynyards' middle-class home, where she learns sharp lessons in social humiliation.

The novel depicts working-class life in two ways, as the social setting for Liza's whole life, and as the setting from which education has permitted Stephen to remove himself—though not his father. Liza remembers a real proletarian city, despite her family's poverty. Stephen lives in a different world, one in which 'working class'—but jobless— young men have no hope of work and instead become delinquents and thus his sullen clients. Stephen's ill father still seeks re-employment, hopelessly, as a man must try to work. Barker vividly characterizes the industrial decline of the area, with its 'steelyards that no longer made steel, up railway lines axed so long ago that rose bay willow herb thronged the track' (35).

Through the book Barker weaves the past—Liza's brother's death in France, her marriage to Frank, wounded in France and a spiritualist; her deliveries and the rearing of her children—with the present, in which she inexorably declines, getting on with her dying, thinking (the narrator relates) dying was *so much like work. Like labour*' (76). And she weaves the story of Liza with the story of Stephen, which is both a counterpoint to Liza's—male and female, middle class and working class—and a continuation of it in several ways, some of them ironic. His father worked for the Wynyards, the industrialist family to whose house Liza went as a child with her mother; Liza worked alongside a Wynyard daughter in the munitions plant; and Stephen's flat is in a former Wynyards home (the same one Liza visited with her mother), now rundown and divided up for multiple occupancy. Stephen has trouble throughout the novel with some scary youths on a nearby estate; in the end they murder Liza while trying to rob her of her box, which they mistakenly think contains money.

Liza's England is politically aware and socially conscious but it is not sociology; like all Barker's novels it contains passages of great strength and great beauty. One of the finest comes when Liza gives birth to her daughter Eileen. And when Liza lies dying, she has a vision of those who have died before her, in a sort of summary of her life—her parents, other girls from the bomb factory, her brother, her husband—and she sees a tree which puts on buds again—'Against a red sky the tree blossomed and burned' (276)—and we are reminded of the visions of trees that come near the end of *Union Street* and *Blow Your House Down*.

Reviews of *Liza's England* (which were mostly really reviews of *The Century's Daughter*, its title when it appeared) were generally positive. Pauline Willis, in a short review that formed part of a roundup of women's fiction in *The Guardian*, recommended it to readers who had liked *Union Street*; Norman Shrapnel's longer review, also in *The Guardian*, balanced its praise, acknowledging that some readers might detect, and dislike, working-class romanticism, but suggesting that Barker had avoided that by the toughness and liveliness of her writing.[5] *The Sunday Times*, less sympathetic perhaps to a socialist critique of Conservative government, compared it to the Cockney soap opera

Eastenders, but then acknowledged it as unromantic, sympathetic, and realistic.[6]

The balancing of possible strengths and weaknesses continues in a longer review by Paul Driver in the *London Review of Books*. Driver declares that it is one novel that (unlike the others under review: *The Death of the Body* by C. K. Stead, *Kramer's Goats* by Rudolf Nassauer, or *Mefisto* by John Banville) has the 'air of reality' endorsed by Henry James (American novelist, 1843–1916); 'Unfortunately that one [...] is also a consciously "working-class" fiction whose claim to reality-status might be found off-puttingly vehement [...] risking a limiting categorization and, inescapably, a caricaturing treatment of its subject'; on the other hand, he continues, it is the only one of these novels that, 'making a serious attempt on reality, takes the reader completely seriously'. Beyond its reality-claims, Driver continues to recognize it as 'fully charged with moral passion, which is kept suitably in check by disciplined, unsparing observation and the author's manifest good humour', while finally calling for some 'leavening' that would have avoided the risk of 'dourness'.[7]

Like Barker's earlier books, *The Century's Daughter* may have appealed more to American reviewers. Jonathan Yardley, in the *Washington Post*, ends by calling it nothing stronger than satisfying, but sums it up by agreeing with Driver on its tough and sympathetic approach which finds value in the lives of people usually overlooked as losers.[8] Yardley calls attention to one important motif—that Liza has been repeatedly damaged by the premature deaths of the men in her life, father, brother, husband, son. In the *New York Times*, Eden Ross Lipson perhaps overstated the political specificity of the novel when she identified it as an attack on the policies of Margaret Thatcher. Having said that the novel is about two kinds of death—physical death (of which there is a great deal) and the death of long-term unemployment—she seems to suggest that Thatcherism is the cause of the latter (though in this novel, as elsewhere, Barker eschews simple or personal explanations for the loss of industrial capacity and the immiseration of the working-class). Lipson thinks less of Stephen than of Liza, as a fictional character, but comments approvingly that the novel focuses on the reality of ordinary lives rather than glamorous people.[9]

Gender

Literary criticism of *Liza's England* can be grouped around several themes or nodes. One of them is feminism and gender; though Barker's approach is clearly feminist, and recognized as such, there is an increased attention to the problems of men, including the men in Liza's life and particularly Stephen and his father. Sarah Brophy, who (like other readers) links

Liza's story to that of Alice Bell in *Union Street*, also relates Liza's account of her daughter's childbirth, by contrast, to that of Iris King and her daughter's abortion in the earlier novel. She seems to see a progression, or a deepening, here: 'the emphasis on the women's entrapment (and complicity) in a cycle of violence and degradation in *Union Street* is modified, to some degree, by the investigation in *Liza's England* of how this cycle may be interrupted, as well as by Liza's turn to historical and economic explanations for her experiences'.[10] Sharon Monteith notes the gendered division of labour shown particularly in Liza's war work as a munitions girl.[11] Several commentators point to the feminization of the working-class novel; Kirk explains well what this means: the representation of women's actions in the 1930s fills a gap 'beside the "canonical" Orwellian images of men in this period—"heroic" miners, the decent breadwinner, or the down-at-heel unemployed man'.[12]

There has been considerable discussion of maternity and matrilineality in *Liza*. Pykett points to the box as a 'matrilineal inheritance'; Margaretta Jolly's emphasis is very much on maternity; she thinks of *Liza*, alongside *Union Street* and *Blow Your House Down*, as 'Barker's other most explicitly "maternal" plot', such that, indeed, 'a maternal perspective may be the key to any regeneration of working-class culture and politics post-Thatcher'.[13] Other observers suspect sentimentalization here, and point out, as Sharon Monteith does, that any view of the novel as a 'utopian expression of matrilineage' must cope with Liza's mother's extreme cruelty to her daughter.[14] Both Brophy and Sarah Falcus question the assumption that this novel (or its predecessors) dramatize successful networks of female solidarity and support. Falcus replaces that model with one of women's continuity through reproductive capacities and gives as examples Liza's reveries about her own labour and her observation of her daughter's.[15]

In another article focused on aging, Sarah Falcus insists on the invisibility of the aged and especially of women, which 'is symbolized in colorful terms in *Liza's England* [...] as young girls pass old—in both senses—friends Liza and Mrs Dobbin on the street [...]'. She goes on to cite other critics (Julia Twigg, Germaine Greer, and Kathleen Woodward) who 'argue that there is a gendered nature to the invisibility of the old, since, for women, value rests in sexual attractiveness, which is linked to youth, and this is clearly the case here'.[16] Margaretta Jolly also comments on Liza's 'invisibility', while relating it to Frank's unacknowledged life, and Peter Hitchcock, in 'They Must Be Represented' (2000), recognizes the impulse towards invisibility as well as the paradox that 'you must be seen in order to confirm that class is there and negotiable in stable and unthreatening ways'.[17]

Pat Barker, it is often recognized, has broadened her vision of men in *Liza*. Rawlinson notes that broadening in the treatment of male–female relations; Alexander writes that where, in the first two novels, men were represented mainly as 'callous or inadequate', some of them are perceived more positively here; not freed from their role as oppressors, but seen as transmitters rather than originators of that oppression.[18] Hitchcock, while criticizing the faultiness of Stephen's and Walter's characterizations, recognizes their function as helping to examine the role of masculinity, particularly in Stephen's family; that is, masculine gender roles are seen as frustrating, too. And he defends Stephen as more than the young male foil to the old female Liza: 'it is the reversal, not the complementarity, in his narrative that throws Liza's recollections into relief'.[19]

Class

Naturally, given the subject of a working-class woman partially juxtaposed with a middle-class social worker himself risen from the working class, and the social setting of Barker's earlier books, critics have pointed to the proletarian theme in *Liza*. Sometimes it is interwoven, in their explanations, with gender, as when *Liza* is seen as representing an alternative or a challenge to the masculinist working-class texts of Orwell or Lawrence. Somewhat surprisingly, there is a suspicion of nostalgia and sentimentality—recognized or denied.

Kirk, for instance, sees Barker as 'moving dangerously close to reproducing some of the older mythographies of working-class identity she endeavors to contest', and detects a 'danger of sentimentality, or idealization' which he links to 'reactionary nostalgia', before qualifying the diagnosis by saying that this is a tendency she mostly avoids.[20] In 'Souls and Arseholes: The Double Vision of *Liza's England*' (2005), Jenny Newman registers concern that some readers may find Stephen's views sentimental, in their placing of Liza.[21] Lyn Pykett praises Barker for avoiding 'the easy nostalgia for a vanished working-class golden age of corporate spirit in back-to-back dwellings'—a nostalgia not avoided, she says, in writing about the working class by the writer and broadcaster Jeremy Seabrook (1939–)—while, surprisingly, Linda Anderson regards Pykett's argument as *itself* being covered in nostalgia—not, she explains, a nostalgia for the past but for older means of representation, particularly the nineteenth-century novel.[22]

Realism

Nostalgia, or idealization, is presumably a deficiency in realism and, as is often the case with Barker, criticism of this novel addresses itself to the question of realism. Lyn Pykett calls the novel a 'particular blending of social realism, dream and symbol'; in 'The Reimagining of History in Contemporary Women's Fiction' (1990), Linda Anderson terms it a realist novel and adds that Barker does not challenge the genre.[23] Perhaps the most detailed discussions of Barker, *Liza*, and realism come from Jenny Newman and Mark Rawlinson. Newman declares that this novel from the first has been attacked for failing to challenge 'three of the main tenets of realism: that fictitious characters should be consistent and knowable both to their readers and themselves; that they appear capable of choice; and that their story has a point, a privileged relation to the truth'.[24] This seems Linda Anderson's belief as well. Mark Rawlinson mounts a defence of Barker against what he sees as criticism (by, among others, the Dodds) of her work's 'affinity with nineteenth-century naturalism [...] that is for the way the observing narrator fixes the character in terms of "physical and manual" detail, from the point of view of an objectifying observer [...]'.[25] Rawlinson argues that Barker's method involves readers as experiencing subjects rather than as spectators.

Jenny Newman's defence is different, distinguishing Barker's work from realism by assimilating it to postmodernism, or at least putting it into a postmodern tradition. Specifically, she cites Barker's 'use of dialogue, parody, and pun, and her commitment to the communal, the choric' which 'constantly remind us that her books are textual inventions', and the refusal of her plots to complete a neat pattern or to impute a 'unifying purpose' to the characters' lives.[26] Without insisting on Barker's postmodernism, other critics point to features homologous with Newman's list; David Waterman names 'the permeability between individual and collective memory'—a feature reminiscent of Alice's consciousness in *Union Street*—and Catherine Bernard writes about the fragmentation and challenges to the coherence of the narrative embodied in the novel's reduction of Liza to 'a mere collection of signs'.[27] Newman links Liza with the women of the preceding books but singles out Frank as the link to the ones which follow.[28] This link will be most obvious in the novels about World War I, but in his woundedness, his lostness, and even his spiritualism, Frank provides a connection with Barker's next novel, *The Man Who Wasn't There*.

THE MAN WHO WASN'T THERE (1989)

This novel, Barker's fourth, published in 1989, is anomalous in several ways. It has not been overlooked, exactly; still, as Sharon Monteith, one of Barker's best and most careful critics, comments, it is 'almost uniformly sidestepped by critics of her work'.[29] 'One reason', she suggests, is that its surreal elements 'push the novel further outside the predominantly realistic framework of the earlier fiction'; moreover, the child as protagonist (unprecedented, except for the Kelly Brown chapter in *Union Street*, to which this novel is often compared), for some readers, Monteith writes in *Pat Barker* (2002), 'relegates the fiction to a space outside Barker's best work'.[30]

Though it would not be until *Regeneration* that Barker turned decisively to male characters at the heart of her fiction, there is a move away from adult women protagonists. Beyond the central figure of a young boy; beyond the non-realistic or anti-realistic method, which involves frequent shifts between Colin's life experiences and his fantasies, presented as a filmscript of a World War II movie; at 158 pages, it is Barker's shortest novel. It occurs over three days, in 'real time', Thursday through Saturday.

As the novelist said in her interview with Rob Nixon (2004), 'it's a pity it's so short, in a way. It is a transitional book. It's still set entirely in the northern working-class area, but it's transitional in its method of treating the characters, I think.'[31] The novel takes up several important themes familiar from her earlier novels and carried forward into her later ones. There is the failure of fatherhood, or masculinity. There is the troubled relationship between mothers and their children, complicated by the mother's sexuality. There is even—a frequent note in Barker's fiction—the idea that for women, war can be enjoyable. This was seen in *Liza's England*, and will recur in the World War I trilogy. Here, Colin's mother and her friend Pauline reminisce about the war (the Second World War, this time):

> ■ 'Eeh, it's a terrible thing to say, isn't it, but I wouldn't've missed it for the world.'
> 'No, nor me. In fact, I think the first two years of the war were the happiest years of my life.' (102) □

The novel opens with economical exposition: both psychological— 'Colin Harper, one eye open for snipers, turned the corner into his own road. You were supposed to walk down the middle, but the last time he'd done that Blenkinsop's dad had honked his horn and shouted, "Get off the road, you stupid little bugger!"' (9)—and historical, with socioeconomic notes:

> ■ The houses were tall and narrow, set back from the road behind low walls whose railings, pulled up in the last war to make Spitfires, had never been replaced. Before the war, his nan said, entire houses had been lived in by just one family, but now they were divided into flats, or turned into boarding houses. (9) □

We are, then, in the immediately post-World War II era, its austerity and economic decline evidenced by inadequate housing. And the first passage places Colin—first, as a warrior, then incongruously as a person just coming home; a boy, we learn, since another dad feels entitled to abuse him. We will also learn, soon, that his dadlessness sets him apart from Blenkinsop and many of his other mates.

After another paragraph of Colin plodding homeward, the novel shifts dramatically, to this: 'Gaston jerks himself awake. A sniper is crawling across Blenkinsop's roof, but Gaston has seen him. He spins round, levels the gun, and *fires*' (10). Here begins the novel's alternation of Colin's fantasy life, based on war films, with his real life of family unhappiness and maladjustment at school. Though they are never wholly detached from Colin's real life, the war scenes, presented in the present tense and sometimes in filmscript form, give an alternative Colin, a decisive, mature, courageous and dangerous operative behind enemy lines.

Scenes, deftly rendered, fill in Colin's real-life situation. His mother is indolent (she will not sign his school report). She works as a sort of waitress, wearing a sexualized fawn costume, and worries that she is getting too old. She brings her manager home to sleep with her, noisily. She and Pauline, who works at the same place, care about Colin in a sentimental way without understanding him. He is a grammar school boy, that is, a student who has earned a place in an academically ambitious school, leaving behind the other boys from his own neighbourhood. As his mother notes, reading from the report she will not sign, 'I just wish I could see the point of a lot of it. Latin: *Very fair.* English: *I enjoy reading his stories*' (13).

In addition to feeling out of place at his school and intimidated by the masters, Colin is subject to bullying by older lads around his home. And he frets about his father; though he has been told that he was 'shot down', he wants a name; later Pauline admits that Viv has no idea who his father was. His fatherlessness stands out, at his school, because for some reason the boys who have two parents have larger certificates, and he is humiliated when he realizes that everyone in the line except for one other shamefaced boy has the 'long certificate'.

This psychological crisis triggers one of the imagined flashbacks. As he is looking for his birth certificate, and telling himself it does not matter, while acknowledging that it does, the scene shifts to 'A Railway Station in France: March 1943', where Gaston, his alter ego, is travelling with false identity papers. He survives, but the man at the back of the queue—a double of the schoolmate who shares Colin's illegitimacy—panics and runs and is machine-gunned. The agent controlling the German guards in this scene is 'Von Strohm, head of the Gestapo in this region, and, in another time and place, the headmaster of an English grammar school' (18).

Colin's coming-of-age, if that is the right term for a process that covers a period from Thursday to Saturday, includes learning more about his older friend Adrian, recognizing a cross-dressing man named Bernie and incorporating him into his war routine as Bernard, and encountering a mysterious man in black, who seems to pursue him both in real life and in fantasy. There are themes that readers will recognize from early Barker texts. These include, most obviously, the absent or useless father, as well as choices about unwanted pregnancy—though played at least in part for comedy, since the father is the rear end of a pantomime horse—and even the working-class woman's preference for sons: Viv reveals that she has said to Lillian, pregnant, 'You want to pray for a lad' (87).

Finally the two parallel plots are resolved. Pauline acknowledges to Colin, recovering from an illness, that his mother cannot name his father; in the present-tense war story, an aircraft swoops down behind enemy lines and rescues two double agents (though not Gaston–Colin, shot by the guards). 'Colin, staring straight ahead, waited for the drone of the Lysander to fade. Then he gave a sharp, decisive little nod, and said, "The End"' (158).

Reviewers of *The Man Who Wasn't There* were generally approving. The novelist Shena Mackay in *The Sunday Times* particularly praised the hallucinatory scenes precipitated by Colin's fever for their mystery, and noted Barker's mastery both in Colin's development and in the social setting.[32] Norman Shrapnel, writing in *The Guardian*, reviewed it alongside a novel by the American Richard Russo (1949–) that also featured the father-and-son theme and said that Barker's book had a message worth more than those of more ambitious novels.[33] In the *New York Times* Herbert Mitgang wrote approvingly but seemed more baffled by the novel than he should have been, thinking that the title had promised a thriller and complaining that the author left too many unanswered questions for the reader.[34]

Several critics of *The Man Who Wasn't There* have suggested ways to think about its relationship to its predecessors. Some insist on discontinuity. Penny Smith, for instance, finds in this book 'a gradual turning away not only from the depiction of women, but also from the depiction of the working class', a move she links with Colin's fantasies.[35] Sharon Monteith, in her essay 'Warring Fictions', has examined the connection more deeply, and rebuts the idea that the novels change when Barker begins writing about males, declaring that the 'stoical endurance' shown by both sexes is important in each of her novels. She also points out that in this novel, as in *Liza's England*, Barker is 'attempting a distillation of historical and class memory, of the national with the personal' and further links it to *Liza* (and the trilogy) through its interest in the role of women in war; the unusual fact is that the war in this novel is the Second World War, distinguishing it in that way from Barker's focus, elsewhere, on the Great War, though the reaction of women to war's liberation is more or less the same in both cases.[36]

John Brannigan is another critic who traces continuities between *The Man Who Wasn't There* and earlier fictions, perhaps most importantly the Kelly Brown chapter of *Union Street*. Brannigan observes that both Kelly and Colin are latchkey children with unstable family lives (their mothers are similarly neglectful and have similar sexual arrangements, too). Moreover, both Kelly and Colin 'experience eerie encounters with distorted self-images and spectral fathers in scenes set in fairgrounds and parks. Both skirt around forms of misdemeanor, and seek out derelict landscapes in which to hide out.'[37] In both novels there are broken mirrors, to which Brannigan has called attention as a frequent feature of Barker's fiction. Mark Rawlinson links the novel to *Blow Your House Down* through an apparent revisiting of the same territory and its depiction of the 'struggles of the deserted mother' (hardly a trope unique to that novel, of course) but distinguishes it because of the focus through a child and the fact that *The Man Who Wasn't There* is a comedy.[38]

Gender and Class

Women *are* 'depicted' in this novel, despite Penny Smith's view, and it is equally easy to see the continuing depiction of the working class, rather than a turning away from it. The difference, perhaps, is that Colin—though firmly working class—is academically skilled and has the capacity to rise above the world of his mother, like few earlier characters in Barker's fiction, the exceptions being Richard Scaife in *Union Street* and Stephen in *Liza's England*. Like Richard, he takes learning more seriously than his family do and has more talent for it, but is uncomfortable with the possibility of rising 'above' his class by schooling. This is the awkwardness of a youth caught between two cultural worlds (sometimes represented by two parents) familiar, for instance, from Lawrence's *Sons and Lovers*. But the more aptly illuminating concept is that of 'the scholarship boy', defined by Richard Hoggart in *The Uses of Literacy* (1957). This is a boy of the working class who by academic ability, seriousness, and the opportunity of admission to a selective secondary school, 'gets on' at the cost of estrangement from his native environment and family, without necessarily becoming comfortable in the new middle-class world of academic achievement. As Alan Lovell, whose 'The Uses of Literacy: The Scholarship Boy' (1957) traces the new opportunities to the 1944 Education Act, which created grammar schools and made secondary education free for everybody—of

which Colin would be a beneficiary—comments, the scholarship boy is
defined by 'uncertainty: an uncertainty that is produced by his situation
at the friction point of two cultures'.[39]

Many critics have made this connection; for instance, while demur-
ring from Hoggart's ideas about women, Pat Wheeler identifies Colin
with the Hoggartian scholarship boy in his 'dislocation...from his
friends and his class'; Sharon Monteith makes the same identification
while stressing that Colin is not a straightforward scholarship boy, but
does reflect the discomforting features of the type—self-consciousness,
self-doubt, and anxiety.[40] John Brannigan makes an interesting alternative point, identifying the mysterious man in black who figures in both
real life and fantasy for Colin, rather than Colin himself, as a scholarship boy who has escaped his class (as Colin will do) and come back
as an outsider; the evidence for this is his 'thin, oversensitive mouth'
and his discomfort in pronouncing the word 'Mam'.[41] In 'Transgressing
Masculinities: *The Man Who Wasn't There*' (2005), Pat Wheeler perhaps
makes the same point in a different way when she attributes to Barker a
subversion of the traditional working-class representation 'by allowing
Colin an interiority and imaginative awareness'.[42] Perhaps because of
Colin's youth, *The Man Who Wasn't There* contains less visible class
antagonism than some earlier books. Waterman sees it as a transitional
work, moving from the working-class novels that preceded it to the
novels focusing on crises in masculinity that follow, in the *Regeneration*
trilogy.[43]

The challenge to masculinity in this novel comes not from war
(though war is present, imaginatively, in the war films Colin watches
and his fantasies and even his mother's memories) but from the conditions of male adolescence, exacerbated by fatherlessness. Colin's world
is devoid of significant adult men. As Sharon Monteith recognizes, his
imagination fills the absence left by his father with sensational behind-
the-scenes war narrative.[44] The man who wasn't there (the mysterious
figure in black) is, in Monteith's reading, a 'projection of his absent
father combined with his future self'.[45] Mark Rawlinson links Colin
with Kelly Brown, another fatherless child who seeks surrogates, though
in Kelly's case with far more disastrous results.[46]

The 'crisis of masculinity' or the 'cult of compulsory masculinity' is
a critical trope frequently invoked in criticism of Barker's fiction and
both Sharon Monteith and David Waterman apply it here: Monteith
says that the cult is here examined and found wanting; Waterman goes
further, declaring that 'Colin asks questions about his father, about
masculinity and sexuality, about heroes in a time of war, and ultimately
finds that it is all a sham, a cynical performance of masculinity that
reveals itself as hollow, whether in the everyday world or in the movies
or in his imagination.'[47]

In a related comment, Wheeler relates the absence of Colin's father to his feelings for his mother, which 'remain problematic throughout the novel', complicating his identification with her and his own sexual awakening.[48] And John Brannigan, reacting to Colin's traumatic discovery of his shaming birth certificate, calls his anxiety 'a linguistic or nomenclatural problem; hence Colin's desire to will the words of his father's identity into existence'.[49]

If fatherhood is, in a sense, textual, so is war. David Waterman writes that although 'the war was certainly real, Colin experiences it—and society re-experiences it—largely through the fictions of war, which nevertheless also leave their trace and continue to fascinate [...]'; John Brannigan concurs: 'the war is now less real than its narration, whether that narration is conducted through relics, testimonies, photographs, films or, indeed in the "endless war" of representation which takes place in the schoolyard'.[50] (Colin's mother, indeed, in offering a false account of Colin's father—that is, a narrative, a fiction, in the place of history—reaches to stereotypical narrative and tropes familiar from cinema when she identifies him as a flyer—i.e. one of 'the few' whose legendary flying accomplishments loom large in British memory, in part because of their frequent representation in films—shot down on a mission.)

The incorporation of the war into popular culture is of course most influential in war movies. Sharon Monteith's essay 'Screening *The Man Who Wasn't There*: The Second World War and 1950s Cinema' (2005) is the fullest treatment of this connection. She identifies the movie Colin watches, probably, as *The Man Who Never Was* (1956): 'a disturbing feature film "based on a true story" of British intelligence deceiving the Germans over the invasion of Sicily and set in 1943, like Colin's own adventure'.[51] The similar titles make her identification even more solid. But war stereotypes do not stop with serious war movies, as Monteith goes on to explain: 'the contemporary British reader in particular recognizes' the caricatures of villainous enemies 'in popular BBC television comedies like "Dad's Army" [a BBC comedy about the Home Guard during World War II that ran from 1968 to 1977] and "'Allo, 'Allo" [another BBC sitcom, 1982–92, about life in occupied France], and those echoes help to explain the comic tone of this novel'.[52] Mark Rawlinson also cites *'Allo, 'Allo* and adds another BBC drama about the resistance, *Secret Army* (1977–9, a drama of which *'Allo 'Allo* is considered a parody).[53] All these critics comment on the falsity of cinematic representation; Colin learns that films lie when they say it is easy to be brave.[54]

Film not only provides one of the chief plot elements—Colin's escape to the cinema and into cinematicity—it also provides an alternative to Colin's reality, an alternative activated both by viewing movies and by screening imaginary movies in his mind at moments of crises provoked by his problematic relationship to the father–son nexus, masculinity, and class. For instance, his headmaster Mr Sawdon, commenting on his mother's influence, tells Colin 'She can never do for a boy what a man can do. It needs a man to…to ensure that a boy's development is…healthy. *Normal.*' Cue Colin's filmscript, with

■ VON STROHM   Why do you dress as a woman? (68–9) □

Sharon Monteith notes that the structure of the novel, in its quick cuts and short scenes, derives from the cinema, and John Brannigan makes the same observation, considering the point of view or perspectivism a cinematic element.[55] Brannigan also comments on the experimental point of view, particularly 'cinematic perspectives' (79).

However Pat Barker's fiction relates to classical realism—and it is a contested relationship—undoubtedly *The Man Who Wasn't There* represents a shift away from a broadly realistic approach to representation. It also (though this is less novel) includes ghostly or psychically disturbing manifestations; and there is spiritualism here, as in *Liza's England* and later books. Sharon Monteith considers the spiritual medium a metaphor for artistry; and perhaps more telling for the trilogy which follows, with its heavy investment in psychology and psychiatry, Monteith relates mediumship to psychotherapy. Mrs Stroud, the medium, is almost a therapist herself, thus linking her to Barker's exploration of therapy in later novels.[56] Since the next three novels have a psychotherapist at the centre, and men damaged by war are the ones most in need of that therapeutic assistance, this provides an ideal introduction to *Regeneration* and the trilogy which it inaugurates.

CHAPTER THREE

The *Regeneration* Trilogy

Despite the solid record of Barker's first four novels, most of them successful enough in sales to establish her as a novelist of reliably challenging fiction; despite her recognition as one of Britain's twenty best young novelists in the *Granta* listing of 1984; despite the significant and, if not unanimous, nevertheless generally positive reviews she received for her books: nevertheless her career changed markedly in 1991 with the publication of *Regeneration*, her first historical novel, as that term is generally accepted. It was also her first novel chiefly focused on adult males (*The Man Who Wasn't There*, with a boy at the heart, had been a move in this direction). It took on one of the central subjects of British memory and cultural appreciation, the Great War—called by Anne Whitehead, in 'Open to Suggestion: Hypnosis and History in the Regeneration Trilogy' (2005), 'the "literary" war'.[1] For all these reasons and more, *Regeneration* and the two succeeding novels, which together formed the '*Regeneration* Trilogy', not only dramatically magnified Pat Barker's presence in the world of British literature, but also became, and have continued to be, the books by which she is best known. The adoption of *Regeneration* as a set text for students doing A-level English (later joined by *The Ghost Road*), and the film version of the first novel, have helped to cement the trilogy in its central position. As Richard Bradford sums it up in *The Novel Now* (2007), 'her reputation is founded principally upon her trilogy of novels [...] which explore the emotional and psychological consequences of being on active service in World War I [...]'.[2]

When *Regeneration* first appeared, it provoked considerable discussion of the change in direction some people thought it represented. Some of its reviewers, with perhaps unconscious condescension, congratulated Barker for having turned to the Great War from her earlier concerns: for instance, Paul Taylor lauded *Regeneration* for extending the author's range, and Justine Picardie, rather oddly, described her development as an emergence, first from a chrysalis, then from a ghetto, the 'ghetto' of women's fiction.[3] The quotation marks leave open Picardie's own judgement of that ghetto, but the chrysalis metaphor seems un-ironic.

Barker has often been asked about her change in subject. To Donna Perry she began by minimizing the significance of the change: 'In a sense, you can't deal with one gender in isolation from the other. I'm more interested in looking at the pressures on men, which in wartime are specific and worse than those on women are, but not, I think, essentially different.'[4] She goes on to reveal that she had always wanted to write about the war (she was, after all, brought up with a grandfather who had been wounded in that war), and began her writing career with a Great War poem, and thus 'the urge to write about it was there, but I wanted to wait until I could find a sufficiently original way of doing it because, obviously, it's been one of the most overdone topics that has ever been. And it's been done brilliantly by people who were actually there.'[5] To Candice Rodd, who asked what lay behind the change of direction, she replied that she was tired of patronization. She seemed to believe that her previous focus on working-class lives had prevented reviewers from looking beyond her sociological bona fides and recognizing that she was a literary artist.[6] To turn toward the experience of male soldiers in wartime early in the century was, given the readiness of reviewers to challenge her credentials, a very courageous move. In what seems a related observation, she told Rob Nixon that the 'voices' in her earlier novels—those of working-class north-eastern women—were not being listened to. The voices of male soldiers were listened to, but her aim was to bring out unacknowledged subtexts. She told Nixon, 'I felt I had got myself into a box where I was strongly typecast as a northern, regional, working-class feminist—label, label, label—novelist. It's not a matter so much of objecting to the labels, but you do get to a point where people are reading the labels instead of the book.'[7]

The 'label' to which her move raised the strongest challenge, perhaps, was that of a feminist novelist writing engaged fiction about women's lives and being published by the feminist press Virago; and changing the gender focus at the same time as leaving Virago complicated her case, perhaps by suggesting some opportunism. She commented to Sharon Monteith in 2004,

■ By the time I left Virago there was a backlog of things I wanted to explore about men, but then further down the line it came to be assumed that I no longer wrote about women. As you know, I have never divided men and women characters in this way and it is interesting to me that some people couldn't really conceive of foregrounding the voices of women as *not* being hostile to men—and vice versa.[8] □

Early reviews were, of course, not focused on the trilogy as such; not only was *Regeneration* obviously freestanding, it is also not at all clear when the author knew it would inaugurate a trilogy. So literary critics who comment on the trilogy do so from a perspective beyond its completion; and yet there is an impressive body of criticism dedicated to the trilogy as a system. As John Brannigan suggests, it was the success of the trilogy that ensured critical attention to Barker's work as a whole.[9] There was renewed commercial attention, too, as the re-publication of her early novels and an award from the Bookseller's Association attest.

REALITY AND VERISIMILITUDE

Questions of fidelity to reality had, of course, appeared before in criticism of Barker's fiction, but her turn to a more 'historical' novel—though even that characterization has been challenged—and particularly to the Great War, much studied, endlessly fascinating, and often treated by predecessors via both fact and fiction, opened her to much more scrutiny on her use of fiction. Not only was this the literary war; it was also, as Karen Patrick Knutsen specifies in 'Memory, War, and Trauma' (2005), a 'founding trauma', 'constitutive of the nation's identity'.[10] One must expect strict scrutiny in taking on such a central period. Several commentators expressed strong objections, most particularly Bernard Bergonzi and Martin Löschnigg.

In *War Poets and Other Subjects* (1999), Bergonzi objects to several of Barker's practices. He considers Billy Prior, for instance, a 'well-realised fictional character' but cannot accept him as a character in a historical novel about the war.[11] He considers the familiar discussion of the Austrian psychoanalyst Sigmund Freud (1856–1939) by Billy Prior in 1917 (the first translation into English of Freud's works was in 1909), the use of 'sexy' to describe combat, the emphasis on London air-raids, the propounding of a significant anti-war movement, and the use of Ireland as a refuge for pacifists—all of these, he considers anachronistic.[12] In *A War of Nerves: Soldiers and Psychiatrists in the Twentieth Century* (2001), Ben Shephard concurs: 'The novelist Pat Barker would have us believe that by 1918 officer-patients in shell-shock hospitals were discussing the finer points of Freudian doctrine with each other.'[13] There are two possible reasons for these departures from historical accuracy; one, Bergonzi argues, is the importation into a Great War story of material from World War II and Vietnam. Richard Bradford hints at the same view when he describes the author as seeming, 'somewhat presumptuously, to be visiting upon the poor victims of an early twentieth-century act of idiocy and horror the smug wisdom of their late twentieth-century counterparts'.[14] Mark Rawlinson, by contrast, considers that Barker's 'productive anachronisms (particularly the importation of late twentieth-century attitudes to self, sexuality and class)' serve to democratize the war.[15]

The other is a more literary explanation. There are two approaches to the war, Bergonzi says: 'the historical and the literary-mythic'.[16] Barker, like Sebastian Faulks (English, 1953–) in *Birdsong* (1993), takes the mythic approach, which is why her choices would not satisfy historians. He sums up:

> ■ Barker's mythic bias is why she is not very interested in getting her history right; she is more concerned in establishing a connection between the myth and certain preoccupations of the present time: gender roles (her principal male characters are partly or wholly homosexual, though Shephard says there is no reason for believing that Rivers was), feminism, psychotherapy, false memory syndrome, the sexual abuse of children [...].[17] □

John Brannigan, without sharing Bergonzi's disapproval, agrees with his premise, identifying the trilogy as not just historical fiction, but also, 'perhaps inevitably, a contemporary revisionist fiction of the war, which uses the story of the war as an index of contemporary social, cultural, sexual and political debates'.[18]

In '"...the novelist's responsibility to the past"' (1999), Martin Löschnigg mounts an equally stern challenge to Barker's use of history. He enumerates three myths that he believes Barker both accepts and furthers: one, 'the myth which I should like to call the feminist myth about the war', that is, the liberation of women by men's absence at the front and the connection with suffrage as well as the '"gendered" aspects of shellshock' derived from the work of American literary critic Elaine Showalter (1941–), especially *The Female Malady: Women, Madness, and English Culture 1830–1980* (1983).[19] The second 'myth' is that of shellshock—that is, the representation of romanticized and charismatic shellshock victims, which Löschnigg compares to the romantic figure of the nineteenth-century consumptive artist. And the third myth is 'that of the assumedly non-narratable or incommunicable nature of the war experience'.[20] Löschnigg, like Bergonzi, finds Prior unconvincing and a figure chosen to represent contemporary ideas of gender, class and sexuality.

One explanation for deviation from the strict facts (assuming the *availability* of 'true facts') about the war might be a postmodern approach, but Löschnigg, while recognizing the intertextuality involved in drawing on other accounts, primary and secondary, suggests that by declining to foreground problems of representation or suggest the fictionality of history, Barker's three novels differ from historiographic metafiction (a term coined by the Canadian literary theorist Linda Hutcheon [1947–]) and, he concludes, are 'not postmodernist novels at all. Indeed, the trilogy seems to rest upon the transparency of its discourse with regard to an objectifiable historical reality. [...] Barker tacitly adheres to an ideal of historical authenticity, even if her novels may not always live up to that ideal.'[21] It is true that her 'Author's Note' following *Regeneration* suggests a perceptible demarcation: 'Fact and fiction are so interwoven in this book that it may help the reader to know what is historical and what is not' (251).

Most of the historical accuracy-assessment (what Katherine G. Nickerson and Steven Shea, in 'W. H. R. Rivers: Portrait of a Great Physician in Pat Barker's *Regeneration* Trilogy' (1997) call her 'vertiginous blend of history and fiction'[22]) is about the war, understandably, though Anne Wyatt-Brown, in 'Headhunters and Victims of War: W. H. R. Rivers and Pat Barker' (1997), complains mildly about the difference between the Rivers of Barker's trilogy and what is known of the real Rivers—his relationship with his informants on Eddystone Island, one of the Solomon Islands in the South Pacific, or Melanesia, his knowledge or ignorance of local languages—before offering an unconvincing psychological explanation based on both Rivers's and Barker's fatherless childhoods.[23] Blake Morrison finds 'at times something very nineteen-nineties and predictable about her preoccupation with gender, emasculation, bisexuality, and role reversals' but defends the use of anachronistic idiom: 'what she loses in historical accuracy she gains in linguistic vitality, eroding the discontinuities between then and now'.[24]

Differences between the facts and Barker's fictions are less troubling to Sharon Monteith, who points out how limiting it is to revisit the historical sources and check Barker against them; to Lynda Prescott, in 'Pat Barker's Vanishing Boundaries' (2010), who celebrates a variety of 'boundary-blurring' practices including those that blend fact and fiction; and to Karen Patrick Knutsen, who oddly celebrates Barker's use of Prior and the munitionettes as an act of 'creative vandalism'.[25]

CLASS AND GENDER

More traditional questions about Barker's representations focus on class and gender. It is tempting to see her as turning away from her previous interest in the working-class and in women. After all, the characters of the trilogy are almost all men (though this is less true of the second novel, *The Eye in the Door*); and by setting her scene in a convalescent hospital for officers, given the class prejudices of the Great War armed forces, she marginalizes working-class characters (with the significant exception of Billy Prior). That is, the male 'officer class' interacts with the physicians, who are themselves male and officer-class.

There are working-class characters in the trilogy, of course, including female munitions workers, some enlisted men, and war resisters, but much of the commentary on class focuses on Billy Prior, the fictional working-class officer—or 'temporary gentleman'—invented by Barker to add to the real historical figures like the English poets Siegfried Sassoon (1886–1967) and Robert Graves (1895–1985), both ruling-class, privately educated officers. As we have seen, Löschnigg doubts the plausibility of Prior, and Bernard Bergonzi, another critic of Barker's realism, calls him 'invented and curiously dominant' but goes on to compare him to 'a visitant from the future in some work of science fiction or magic realism'.[26]

Most of the critics who have discussed class in the *Regeneration* trilogy, and the role of Billy Prior in embodying and problematizing it, write approvingly of Barker's choice. In 'Where Unknown, There Place Monsters' (2011), Pat Wheeler notes, before praising Prior as a breaker of taboos, that the literary heritage of World War I is largely middle-class: 'The predominant emotion in war poetry is arguably middle-class angst.'[27] Jay Winter, in 'Shell-Shock and the Cultural History of the Great War' (2000), acclaims Barker for having 'enlarged the dramatis personae of shell shocked soldiers in her Regeneration trilogy' by adding a working-class officer, showing that 'Trauma is democratic.'[28] The novelist told interviewer Donna Perry 'I needed Prior to bring out certain facets of Rivers's character that I couldn't bring out through Sassoon or any of the others,' and Francis Spufford quotes her as saying that he was invented to irritate Rivers.[29] Prescott calls the inclusion of Billy Prior one of her 'most impressive strokes of novelistic economy' embodying both class and gender complexities in one character.[30]

Ronald Paul's 'In Pastoral Fields' (2005) approaches the trilogy by relating Pat Barker's approach to the generally pastoral conventions of traditional Great War narratives, mostly written by or from the point of view of bourgeois officers, and argues that the role of working-class characters is part of the challenge to pastoralism. For instance, he notes the conventions of the officer/soldier relationship and specifies that 'the radical female vision of Barker's trilogy can be viewed as a conscious subversion of the pastoral conventions of such fictionalized encounters between high (officers) and low (soldiers)'.[31] The anti-pastoralism engages the other working-class characters, too:

■ by moving from the individual, pacifist protest of Siegfried Sassoon [with which *Regeneration* begins] against the mismanagement of the war to the more militant antiwar campaign of working-class socialists like Mac and Beatie [a key figure in *The Eye in the Door*], the whole thrust of

> Barker's trilogy is toward a comprehensive rejection of war as being the result of a patriarchal, class-based society, against which it is necessary to struggle.[32] □

In a vivid phrase, Paul shows that using Prior as a focalizing character gives a voice to the working-class men and 'also avoids the pastoral trope of portraying them as a mass of potentially dead animal meat'.[33]

In 'What Is Prior? Working-Class Masculinity in Pat Barker's Trilogy' (2002), Peter Hitchcock approaches Prior from another angle. He considers his function as being the decentring or destabilization of the working-class man: 'Prior destabilizes any and all attempts to narratively enclose the concept of working-class masculinity that the war requires.'[34] Hitchcock raises the question of realism, which he links to class (a linkage made differently by Bergonzi and Löschnigg).

> ■ More recently, the Regeneration trilogy has garnered class animus from the opposite direction; that is, certainly you have used real historical figures to explore the pastness of the past in World War One, but you have been too imaginative and stretched the bounds of historical fact. Bluntly when you write of women workers you are too realistic; when you write of a key moment in the history of masculinities you are not realistic enough.[35] □

John Brannigan—like Hitchcock and many commentators on Prior and class—shows class and gender as inextricably connected; he denies that women's factory work or men's shared experience in the trenches ruptures existing social structures, so that working-class identity remains, in his striking phrase, a 'cyborgian subjectivity' as a result of working conditions that render workers more machines that human beings.[36]

What *about* gender in the *Regeneration* trilogy? Barker has many times defended her apparent change in subject matter against the allegation that it constitutes a retreat from feminism. She told Donna Perry that, despite criticism she had received for supposedly abandoning the cause of feminism, she felt that, having explored what society does to women, it was necessary to examine what society does to men, since they cannot be considered in isolation.[37] Mark Greif strikingly declares that 'A feminist analysis required the analyzing of men. This goes somewhat toward explaining why what may be the most important feminist novels of the 1990s, the Regeneration trilogy, are almost entirely about men.'[38]

Though this is further than most critics are willing to go in recognizing the trilogy as feminist analysis, nevertheless there is a widespread acknowledgement that the novels centre on gender conditions, limitations, and performativity. This fact is not always welcomed—as when Blake Morrison finds the preoccupation with gender 'very nineteen-nineties and predictable', and Löschnigg, intent on what he considers Barker's promulgation of myths congratulatory of the contemporary, finds her 'particularly indebted to Showalter's gender-oriented studies of shellshock, and not, it seems, to her advantage'.[39] The debt to Elaine Showalter's *The Female Malady* (but not any resulting disadvantage) is acknowledged in her Afterword; the assimilation of the traditional masculine disorder of shellshock to the traditionally 'female malady' of hysteria suggests some of the gender complications of her fiction as well, perhaps, as some of the reasons for uneasiness expressed by military historians.

Pat Wheeler anatomizes the gendered diagnosis, in this case focusing on Siegfried Sassoon, whose 'internal conflict between feelings of anger at the government and the need to protest against the prolonging of the war, juxtaposed with his desire to return to the front to be with his men, is the template out of which Barker explores the constraints and expectations placed on men in wartime'.[40] Sassoon is one of the officers at Craiglockhart War Hospital who actually has no serious symptoms; instead, he has been sent to the hospital as an alternative to prosecuting him for his anti-war statements (and as a result of his important connections and influence, which permit him to play golf in Scotland instead of, say, going to prison). More important, particularly in light of the diagnosis of war trauma in connection with hysterical symptoms and perceived threats to masculinity, are those officers suffering from real disabilities like mutism, inability to swallow, or paralysis of the limbs. As Catherine Bernard states, in the trilogy Barker represents masculine identity as 'fractured'—as she had feminine identity in earlier novels; one result is the paralysis and aphasia, induced by trauma, which ironically imposes on men the same immobility that is traditionally feminine.[41] Mutism—hysterical inability to speak as a result of war trauma—is connected with the voicelessness of earlier characters, imposed on them by virtue of their class or, especially, female gender.

As Anne Whitehead's 'Pat Barker's *Regeneration* Trilogy' (2005) explains, in the trilogy Barker counterbalanced the traditional masculine reading of the War. 'In a situation in which all signs of physical fear were interpreted as cowardice and all alternatives to combat, such as pacifism, conscientious objection, desertion, or suicide were considered unmanly, men were forced, like women, to express their conflicts through the body.'[42] In 'Improper Heroes' (2003), David Waterman posits that in World War I, 'non-masculine, non-heroic behavior is treated as a contagious disease which must be isolated and cured, in institutions like psychiatric hospitals and prisons, institutions which function in support of the dominant ideology'.[43] In his book on Barker, he diagnoses the very diagnosis of hysteria as being linked to gender performativity.[44] And Dennis Brown, in 'The *Regeneration* Trilogy'

(2005), mentioning the 'hysteria about homosexuality'—most crucial in *The Eye in the Door*—identifies the issue he considers at the heart of Barker's work: 'a crisis in ideas about masculinity'.[45]

One surprising and sometimes controversial aspect of Barker's treatment of the war (and not just in this trilogy, but in *Liza's England* and, regarding the second war, in *The Man Who Wasn't There*) is the idea that women enjoyed it. In 'After Feminism: Pat Barker, Penelope Lively and the Contemporary Novel' (2000), Margaretta Jolly extends the idea to both sexes, when she writes that 'what makes the Regeneration Trilogy so powerful is precisely her measure of how important and even attractive the war was and still is to both sexes, in different ways'. She continues, 'her celebrated "social-realist" style balances critique of social relations as they are with a sympathy for both oppressor and oppressed'.[46]

ANTI-WAR?

The question of women's—and men's—'attraction' to war raises the question of whether it makes sense to call the trilogy 'anti-war', and there has been considerable critical discussion of this. In her interview with Rob Nixon, Barker has commented very sensibly on this issue:

> ■ It's not an antiwar book in the very simple sense that I was afraid it might seem at the beginning. Not that it isn't an antiwar book: it is. But you can't set up things like the Somme and Passchendaele and use them as an Aunt Sally, because nobody thinks the Somme and Passchendaele were a good idea. So in a sense what we appear to be arguing about is never ever going to be what they [the characters] are actually arguing about, which is a much deeper question of honor, I think.[47] □

This seems to suggest that Barker is anti-war in a more subtle way than in disapproving—as any decent observer must do—of the slaughter and mutilation of millions of men. She is raising for scrutiny some idea of what the war stands for, or does (beyond physical damage), or means. Mark Greif discounts the 'antiwar' characterization as too safe: 'an antiwar book is a book that anyone can love'. [10] But

> ■ When Barker wrote about men disciplining other men, men falling in love, dissenters escaping social strictures or informing on one another, she wasn't just writing about history. To say *Regeneration* is antiwar was like saying that [American novelist, born 1931] Toni Morrison's *Beloved* [1987] is antislavery. Barker's trilogy anatomizes regimes of gender and discipline that underpin the way we live now; it is a consummately political book [...].[48] □

A strongly dissenting view comes from Robert Boyers in *The Dictator's Dictation: The Politics of Novels and Novelists* (2005). Boyers is generally disappointed by Barker's political engagement and what he considers her insufficiently venturesome political imagination. As for the claim that Barker writes anti-war fiction, he begins by denying that she is a writer of cautionary tales (a suggestion no one has made) or 'a novelist primarily interested in ideas or positions'; he goes on to declare that the trilogy 'would seem to accept that there can be no coherent moral system by means of which to judge the behavior of people in wartime. [...] The war trilogy is decidedly not antiwar fiction, and in fact uses "history" to avoid a lively engagement with the very issues it raises.'[49]

Barker's decisions about representation of the war help to refocus the reader's attention on its consequences, its deeper meanings, rather than on its military side. Only in the later pages of *The Ghost Road* are there any scenes set at the front (though there are traumatic memories from the actual fighting earlier in the trilogy). As Patricia Johnson's 'Embodying Losses in Pat Barker's *Regeneration* Trilogy' (2005) notes, in place of battle scenes, 'the trilogy presents fragmented memories of battle through their effects on traumatized soldiers. It repeatedly employs synecdoche to bring the mangled bodies produced by war into imaginative and psychological reality.'[50] The concentration on the home front and on a limited *dramatis personae* rather than, say, the thirteen British divisions engaged on the Somme has been judged variously by critics. Bergonzi—who, we remember, is primarily a critic of the author's 'mythic bias'—criticizes the untypical representatives she foregrounds.

■ Their antiwar stance [i.e. Sassoon's and Owen's] was courageous but shared by very few, even among the poets who had been in action, and, as they knew, it was undermined by their own willing return to the Front; they were poets of immense talent and, in Owen's case, elements of greatness, but as homosexuals who did not much like women, both marginal figures in their respective cultures—Sassoon a rich, idle Cambridge dropout and Owen a failed clergyman—they were at some remove from the main currents of English life.[51] □

Bergonzi fails to acknowledge that Pat Barker's anti-war stance is different from that of Owen and Sassoon (or that Sassoon and Owen are more examples of synecdoche, that is, fictional individuals representing a class, in this case, of young officers, not homosexuals). Barker understands the opposition to war as being based on its destruction of human bodies, its lack of clear war aims, its strategic shortcomings, the bloodymindedness of the civilian population and politicians, the stubbornness of the General Staff—all these issues are beside her point, which is about the effects of the war.

What, then, are those results? In 'Pat Barker's *Regeneration* Trilogy' (2006), Nick Hubble regards it as 'not some sort of irruption into modernity but actually an intensification of the ongoing twentieth-century transition from an industrial past to a post-industrial future'— that is, 'an underlying process that has lasted for more than a hundred years'.[52] John Brannigan identifies the war as a process in which masculine and feminine exchanged places in a debilitating way.[53] Waterman depicts the war as a screen on which social contradictions are projected, a condition in which Britain risked an unimaginable loss—though this is not really shown in the novels, which begin in 1917, at a time when, though defeat of Britain did not seem very likely, war-weariness was increasing because of the enormous and apparently pointless death and destruction—because of the threat levelled against its heroism by 'hysterics, homosexuals, and pacifists' on whom blame and opprobrium could thus be placed.[54] In opposition to these 'enemies' were the traditional institutions of Britain's establishment, all of which promoted war to children ardent for some desperate glory. Sharon Monteith, always one of the most penetrating critics of Barker, addresses the question of memory, and memorialization, pointing out, in opposition to some claims that Barker's trilogy constitutes a memorial to the war, that she is actually more concerned with the effects of memorialization; and further that she is interested in human bodies as a more real and moving form of memorial.[55]

CHARACTERS

Critical discussion of the characters in the *Regeneration* trilogy focuses, more than on any others, on two men. One is the historical doctor W. H. R. Rivers, a physician, an anthropologist, a therapist for men damaged by war. He left a considerable record both in his own writing and in memoirs (for instance, his role was discussed in Siegfried Sassoon's autobiographical writings). The other is the entirely fictional Billy Prior, a working-class man made an officer for the purposes of the war (i.e., a 'temporary gentleman') who features (like Rivers) in all three of the novels, though most crucially in the third.

One useful approach to Rivers as literary character is through Rivers as historic figure, a good resource for which is Katherine G. Nickerson and Steven Shea's 'W. H. R. Rivers: Portrait of a Great Physician in Pat Barker's *Regeneration* Trilogy'. The authors comment on the known facts of Rivers's life, which support, for instance, Barker's presentation of 'the admiration Rivers engendered in his patients, students, and colleagues' and his 'capacity for reflection and self-criticism'.[56] Waterman has already been cited on details in which Barker's Rivers diverges from his real-life model.

Critics have offered a variety of summations of what Rivers stands for in the trilogy. As Blake Morrison writes, each book 'discloses new layers of his life and psyche', so it is not surprising that so many explanations of his role offer themselves: to Anne Whitehead 'a distancing device from the traumatic content of the war material'; to Patricia Johnson 'an early-twentieth-century Renaissance man and symbol of Western civilization'; to John Brannnigan a detective investigating the patients' stories; and to Sharon Monteith a transitional figure between Victorianism and modernism—he remembers C. L. Dodgson (Oxford don and children's author 'Lewis Carroll', 1832–98) as a figure in his childhood family memories.[57] Or, to Dennis Brown, he is a 'postmodern hero' who 'appears, as in H.D.'s'—Hilda Doolittle (1886–1961)—'description of Sigmund Freud, the "blameless physician"—parental in nurturing, a saintly, disciplined, and notably patient individual. He is the lynchpin of the three novels'; in Margaretta Jolly's view, he offers his patients 'a kind of "epicritic" maternal relationship'.[58] 'Epicritic' is a neurological term explained by Rivers, referring to fine sensations and discriminations as contrasted with the 'protopathic'; Jolly is using it to refer to Rivers's sensitive way of treating his patients.

Some critics are more uneasy about Rivers. Knutsen identifies him as 'both a marginalized and an authoritative character. He is marginalized in his day due to his homosexuality'—a feature inferred by Pat Barker and rejected, in its application to the historical Rivers, by some—'and the fact that he is a noncombatant'. But Knutsen expresses some doubts about the complexities of Rivers's attitude to the war: this is one of the central figures of his own thinking, the recognition that his success—emotional rehabilitation of the traumatized officers—will return them to active service where they risk being killed: 'his initial pro-war attitude as the novel opens makes him seem marginal to many readers today who have e.g., internalized the anti-war view of most of the war poets and the later critics who have commented on their work'.[59] Of course, combatants like Sassoon and Prior were not uncomplicatedly 'anti-war', either, as the trilogy is at some pains to demonstrate.

Boyers, who is a critic of Pat Barker's political stance, expresses dissatisfaction with Rivers's complicity with the interests of power and with the changing dynamic of the conflict between him and his patient Billy Prior; he criticizes Barker's 'proceeding, as she does, by juxtaposing two such different central characters as Rivers and Prior without following out the differences so as to discover something she herself did not know'; he goes on to claim that, at bottom, the two are quite different; moreover, and disappointingly to Boyers, Prior and others come around to the Rivers position, so that 'Barker leaves us with his perspective as the sole dominant possibility in the novel.'[60]

Along with his role as a literary character, his fidelity to the known facts, his possible homosexuality, and other features, Rivers raises the issue of psychiatry and therapy, which will remain important in several other of Barker's books. At a trivial level the question is raised of whether a man like Billy Prior would have spoken familiarly about Freud in 1918.[61] Rivers is not exactly a Freudian; as Greif explains, 'while Rivers employed psychoanalytical techniques, his essential understanding was quite different to that of conventional psychoanalysis, taking its cue from the experiments on nerve regeneration he had conducted with the neurologist Henry Head [1881–1940, another historical figure, who appears in the trilogy alongside Rivers] before the war'.[62] He does, in a generally Freudian way, diagnose hysterical symptoms as a physical response to a traumatizing event's traces in the psyche, and uses something like a talking cure on his patients. In 'Pat Barker's *Regeneration* Trilogy: History and the Hauntological Imagination' (2003), John Brannigan connects the irruption of the uncanny in many of Barker's narratives to Freud, and declares that in 'the Regeneration trilogy (1991–5), in particular, these experiences of the uncanny occur in the context of a confrontation between the modern rationalism of psychoanalysis and the disorienting, traumatizing effects of war'.[63] In *Trauma and Survival in Contemporary Fiction* (2002), Laurie Vickroy aligns the representation of Rivers and his practice with 'contemporary theories that trauma establishes life patterns of dissociative defenses, repetitions, and rage'.[64] Waterman recognizes the centrality of Barker's theme of madness, but goes on to argue for the guilty complicity of psychiatry with the war-making power as it treats pacifism and nonmasculine behaviour as pathologies.[65] Of course, some of this nonmasculine behaviour is mutism, paralysis, inability to eat, not just timidity or unwillingness to fight.

SEXUALITY

One contemporary feature much to the fore in Barker's representation is sexuality. Sharon Monteith, as usual, is acute on this topic; she takes note of Barker's identification of war as an aphrodisiac and considers that one thing the trilogy does—like *Blow Your House Down*—is demystify sex. She particularly notes the brutal sexual encounter between Prior and a French boy in *The Ghost Road*.[66] Wheeler considers Prior a model of sexual transgression, a man who 'breaks down many of society's sexual taboos'.[67] In an interview with Francis Spufford, Barker was asked whether it was difficult to write male-on-male sex scenes as explicit as hers are in the trilogy; she replied that it was not, the key being to treat sex as an ordinary part of an ordinary day, to avoid adopting a special pompous language for its description.[68] Boyers criticizes the author for her 'illusionless handling of sex', or at least for priding herself on that handling, and says that she 'may be said to share with Prior an aversion to mere sentiment, a compulsion to call things by their rightful names, and a tendency to be offended when anything like a swerve into delusion is detected'.[69]

As for Rivers, whatever his sexual preferences, he is sexually inert as far as the narrative shows; he is also tolerant of the relatively open homosexuality of Owen, Sassoon, and Prior. Of these, only Prior, the imagined officer, is shown *having* sex, with the French boy, with an upper-class wounded officer named Manning, with a young munitions worker (female) to whom he becomes engaged, and even with an older woman with whom he has something like a foster-child relationship.

This is part of Prior's role as transgressor and agitator. Barker says she created him to oppose and irritate Rivers. What else does the construction of Prior add to the trilogy? Winter offers the suggestion that including a working-class officer, enlarging the demographic range, shows that 'trauma is democratic'.[70] Anne Whitehead claims, perhaps somewhat implausibly, that Prior was invented 'to parallel and contrast with the life of Wilfred Owen', and it is true that Owen is of a lower social class than officers like Sassoon and Graves—somewhere midway between Prior and Sassoon, perhaps—and homosexual like Prior though not defiantly so, but the contrast is muted in the book.[71] John Brannigan links Billy Prior to Paul Morel in Lawrence's *Sons and Lovers* and believes that one of his functions is to contest the idea of working-class solidarity—a myth that Barker has already subjected to scrutiny, for instance in *Union Street*.[72] Hitchcock identifies an 'alternative trajectory of regeneration and controversial vector of emergence' focusing on Prior and problematizing the concept of working-class masculinity.[73] And Richard Slobodin, in 'Who Would True Valour See' (1998), calls Prior, a bit breathtakingly, 'the most complete embodiment of what the author wants to say about the Great War'.[74]

Spufford's question about sex writing gets to Barker's style. In another interview, with Gillian Glover in 1995, she is impatient with the suggestion that she has a 'male voice', pointing out that nobody made that observation when she was writing about childbirth and women in the first two novels; only when she began to write about men and war did critics begin to call her tough and unsentimental style masculine.[75]

POSTMODERNISM

As is usual with Barker criticism, some of it is devoted to arguments for or against her postmodernism. These commentaries differ sharply from each other in part because their definitions of postmodernism do not coincide. Brown calls Dr Rivers 'a postmodern hero', though in clarifying that point—he is parental, patient, a sort of ideal physician—it is never clear why this is postmodern.[76] Brown goes on to argue that the Melanesian portions of *The Ghost Road* create 'a postmodernization of Barker's "Little England" realism'.[77] Realism and traditional organization of narration are, as usual, seen by some critics as disqualification for postmodernism. The matter of self-consciousness and reflexivity is important. Löschnigg, as we have seen, argues against reading the trilogy as postmodern because the novels seem to him to offer a transparent discourse meant to give onto 'an objectifiable historical reality'; and he distinguishes them from the very influential kind of 'historiographic metafiction' named by Linda Hutcheon because Barker 'neither foregrounds the difficulties involved in writing about the past nor is she concerned with poststructuralist tenets about the fictionality of our concepts of history'.[78] John Brannigan disagrees, suggesting that the novels are not in fact a transparent discourse of historical reality. The trilogy, he acknowledges, is not metafictional in the Linda Hutcheon sense (that is, parodic, flaunting its fictionality) but is postmodern in 'its critical attention to discourses of modernity, and the haunting of historical representation by its others'.[79]

Alternative views locate the postmodernism of the trilogy in its dialogism—that is, in Bakhtin's term, carrying on a dialogue with other works of literature (there is an obvious connection, or overlap, between this definition of dialogism and the elaboration, originally by Julia Kristeva, of the concept of intertextuality); Knutsen, for instance, defines Barker's work as dialogic 'because she represents a multi-layered spectrum of possible views of trauma, class, gender and psychology'.[80] She elsewhere calls it 'polyphonic in the Bakhtinian sense because it encompasses many discourses, and thus many versions of the traumatic events, yet no single discourse is allowed hierarchical authority [...]'.[81] The definition of postmodernism seems stretched unduly, however, when Knutsen goes on to cite free indirect discourse (a technique rendering a character's thoughts in the third person that blurs the distinction between the narrator's and the character's language and beliefs, common since at least Jane Austen [1775–1817] and perfected by Virginia Woolf [1882–1941]), which makes it difficult to discern any 'monolithic or hierarchical organizations of the discourses or dialogues', where free indirect style is not present.[82] Vickroy concurs on the dialogism, writing that Barker's style, while not experimental, and 'largely chronological', uses 'a dialogical approach'—especially by fluctuation between Rivers and Prior.[83] Paul, in a discussion of pastoralism, at least implies a dissenting judgement on the author's postmodernism in the phrase 'the basically naturalistic, semi-documentary approach that Barker shares with the other war novelists mentioned above'.[84]

A much more fruitful line of inquiry related to Barker's postmodernism is her use of intertextuality. Brown, for instance, calls the trilogy 'a tour-de-force of well-researched intertextuality [...]'.[85] Her intertextualities might be seen as taking a deep and a shallower version. The shallower one is what Vickroy calls 'an intertextuality of fact and fiction': that is, the use of real documents, real historical events, real case histories in her fiction.[86] Much of this is, of course, part of her historical research and is cited as such in the notes at the end of each of the novels. That she relied on primary texts, including books by Rivers and by the Canadian therapist Dr Lewis Yealland (1884–1954), or secondary texts including books about the front, is both obvious and, as the author explains, set out officially so that the reader might know what is historical and what is not. A slightly different kind of debt (also acknowledged in the 'Author's Note') is to Elaine Showalter's *The Female Malady*, a study of hysteria that shaped Barker's ideas about that disorder, her 'focus on psychosomatic symptoms', and probably also her ideas about masculinity seemingly threatened by male officers suffering from a 'female malady'.[87]

The deeper kind of intertextuality is that which links the novels of the trilogy to predecessor texts, without official acknowledgement by the author, through similarities of incident, attitude, or theme. Wheeler notes the use of a very important Great War memoir, *Undertones of War* (1928) by the English author Edmund Blunden (1896–1974), which, as both Sharon Monteith and Anne Whitehead also observe, seems to be the source of Prior's traumatic, silencing encounter with the human eye below the duckboard.[88] Other intertexts suggested, with greater or lesser degrees of importance or plausibility, include *Death of a Hero* (1929) by Richard Aldington (1892–1962) and Robert Graves's *Goodbye to All That* (1929)—both are fictional or nonfictional accounts of the war on the Western Front by men who served there, and Graves, of course, is a character in Barker's trilogy.[89] Sharon Monteith also links the figure of the war-damaged subaltern to Septimus Warren Smith in Virginia Woolf's *Mrs Dalloway* (1925), Chris Baldry in *The Return of the Soldier* (1918) by Rebecca West (1892–1983), and Lord Peter Wimsey, the aristocratic sleuth in novels by Dorothy L. Sayers (1893–1957), for example *Whose Body?* (1921).[90] Paul also mentions Woolf's and West's novels, both dealing with shellshock.[91] Monteith, interestingly, goes beyond the presence in *Mrs Dalloway* of a damaged war veteran—that is, an intertexuality of theme or character—to consider technique and link Barker's practice (somewhat loosely) to Woolf's famous explanation of her own technique using the metaphor of tunnelling; Woolf explained that she 'dug out' caves behind her characters—their pasts—and that these caves eventually connected.[92] Whitehead notes the names of battles, spoken with disgust by Prior; the intertext for this, though Whitehead does not name it, is clearly *A Farewell to Arms* (1929) by Ernest Hemingway (1899–1961).[93]

A bit more strained, perhaps, is Whitehead's linking of Orme's ghostly appearance both to Sassoon's autobiographical *Sherston's Progress* (1936) and to a remoter source: 'the description also alludes to the appearance of Cathy's ghost to Lockwood in the opening pages of Emily Brontë's [1818–48] *Wuthering Heights* [1847]'.[94] And Knutsen, whose interest in intertextuality accompanies a somewhat relaxed definition of it, points to intertexual relations to D. H. Lawrence, through the working-class connections of Billy Prior and Paul Morel (protagonist of *Sons and Lovers*),[95] and even to a perceived resemblance between Billy Prior and Billy Pilgrim in the novel *Slaughterhouse Five* (1969) by the American Kurt Vonnegut (1922–2007), built upon the loose similarity between Prior's trenches and Pilgrim's bombed-out Dresden, and the claim that both have come unstuck in time.[96]

CHAPTER FOUR

Regeneration (1991)

A s one would expect, reviewers of *Regeneration* took note of its difference from what had been expected of a Pat Barker novel. Peter Kemp, for instance, noted the move away from her established milieu and subject matter, in time, in class (i.e. upward), and in the gender of the main characters, but recognized the continuity of concern with violence and trauma.[1] And Justine Picardie, having summed up how Pat Barker was best known, remarked on the surprise of the new direction, which she identified explicitly as masculine.[2] The receptional change is touched on in Nick Rennison's *Contemporary British Novelists* (2005): 'Because [her earlier novels] centred on stories of working-class women in a very specifically realized part of the country (and a deeply unfashionable one at that), it was easy enough for metropolitan critics to ignore her work or to dismiss it as 'regional' fiction. ... All this changed with the publication in 1991 of *Regeneration* [...].'[3]

Having decided that her interest in trauma and memory, and even her interest in how men and women interact, could be best pursued by crossing all the aforementioned boundaries, Barker also turned to a more traditional 'historical novel'. That is, though she had used history in her earlier books, most notably in *Liza's England*; and though present-day history played a role in even her more contemporary novels, as in the echoes of the Yorkshire Ripper in *Blow Your House Down*; in *Regeneration* she produced a novel which both begins and ends in 1917, rather than coming up to date. Moreover, as historical novels often do, hers includes real people, about whom many biographical facts are on the record, in the persons of Siegfried Sassoon, Robert Graves, Dr W. H. R. Rivers, Henry Head, Lewis Yealland, and a few others. This limits the author's freedom to invent, as do the intractable facts of the Great War.

Barker's method of writing a Great War novel is indirect. Instead of showing battle directly she traces its effects on those damaged by it.

This necessarily turns the attention from the killed to the 'wounded' of various kinds. As Herbert Mitgang's review in the *New York Times* declared, the best war stories, ever since Homer, are actually anti-war.[4] This may be an oversimplification of what was, after all, a complex issue. Siegfried Sassoon was, in one man, both anti-war and pro-war; so, in a different way, was Rivers. That the novel produces an anti-war effect in modern readers is partly because the accepted view of the British effort in 1914–18 is anti-war and partly because of Barker's skill in showing its effects on fragile human flesh and nervous systems.

The story begins by reprinting 'Finished with the War: *A Soldier's Declaration*', the manifesto denouncing the way the war was going, written by Siegfried Sassoon in July 1917, with some assistance from Bertrand Russell (1872–1970) and John Middleton Murry (1889–1957), both associated with the 'Garsington group' around Lady Ottoline Morrell (1879–1938), and first delivered to his commanding officer to explain why he declined to return to the front, then published in newspapers and read out in the House of Commons. He objected both to the nature of the war—a war 'upon which I entered as a war of defense and liberation [which] has now become a war of aggression and conquest'—and to the complacency with which those at home 'regard the continuance of agonies which they do not share, and which they have not sufficient imagination to realize' (3). This gesture triggers the plot of the novel, since it creates for Sassoon and his supporters a crisis; a court-martial is almost inevitable (awkwardly for the authorities, given his distinguished war record and decoration for 'conspicuous gallantry') unless his action can be explained as resulting from some mental disorder. Robert Graves, Sassoon's friend, arranges for a medical board to refer him to a 'lunatic asylum' (7)—that is, Craiglockhart War Hospital. In one sense, at least, the framework of the novel has now been set. There will be a sparring match between two cultivated and sane men, both of whom have ambiguous and ambivalent attitudes toward the war; one of them is obliged to pretend to consider the other less sane than he actually is. Sassoon is a fire-breathing, risk-taking, war-making officer nicknamed Mad Jack who has been judged mentally or emotionally unbalanced because of his vehement public opposition to the war as it is being carried on. Rivers is an older man whose humane sympathy with the officers he sees at Craiglockhart is at odds with his professional responsibility to get them back on their feet and thus back into the killing zone.

Beginning the novel (and the trilogy) with Sassoon's statement also challenges Barker. The words 'agonies which they do not share, and which they have not sufficient imagination to realize' invite the author to imagine them, since it is no longer possible for anyone to share them, and then invite the reader to share the way the author has imagined those agonies.

Regeneration is far from being just Sassoon and Rivers; not only are there other patients including (the historical) Wilfred Owen (1893–1918) and some fictional cases; not only does Rivers leave Craiglockhart to visit colleagues, some of whom provide horrifying illustrations of alternative methods of treating war hysteria; but the presence of Barker's creation Billy Prior, a feisty working-class man, bisexually active, elevated into the officer ranks as a 'temporary gentleman' and suspicious of Rivers's aims, makes him in many ways the real counterpart to Rivers. He detects the class alignment between the doctor and most of his gentlemanly patients, which does not extend to him.

It might be said that *Regeneration* is more about Dr Rivers than about his patients, while the following two books move toward a greater focus on the damaged officers. *Regeneration* shows more of Rivers's life beyond the hospital in which he talks to Sassoon and Prior. It introduces Henry Head and Lewis Yealland, two figures from scientific and medical history, as something like the good and bad angels of Rivers's practice. Head, with whom he has a pre-war history in neurological research, is his humane colleague and friend. Yealland treats hysterical mutism with sadistic violence, though some success. When Rivers concludes gloomily that they are doing the same thing, Head reassures him: 'You and Yealland doing *essentially the same thing*. Good God, man, if you really believe that it's the first sign of dementia (240).'

Another episode away from Sassoon and Craiglockhart finds Rivers visiting Burns, a man whose disgusting encounter with a rotting German corpse has made him unable to eat. When Burns runs away in a panic attack, Rivers finds him, cradles him tenderly, and thinks '*Nothing justifies this. Nothing nothing nothing* (180).'

INTERTEXTUALITY

The Great War has been much written about in the decades since its conclusion and there is a large body of fiction (and nonfiction) on the subject; some of the best known work, written by combatants and participants, was published in the 1920s (1928–9 seemed the crucial period—perhaps a decade was necessary for reflection?). This body of work would include such British books, fictional and nonfictional, as *Death of a Hero* (1929) by Richard Aldington; *Memoirs of an Infantry Officer* (1930) by Sassoon; *Good-bye to All That* (1929) by Robert Graves; Edmund Blunden's *Undertones of War* (1928); and *Parade's End* (four volumes, 1924–8) by Ford Madox Ford (1873–1939). Contemporary (or nearly so) World War I books by women include *Testament of Youth* (1933) by Vera Brittain (1893–1970) and Rebecca West's *Return of the Soldier* (1918). And combatants from other countries contributed as well, adding such American titles as *The Enormous Room* (1922) by e. e. cummings (1894–1962); *A Farewell to Arms* (1929) by Ernest Hemingway; and *Three Soldiers* (1920) by John Dos Passos (1896–1962); *The Middle Parts of Fortune*, or *Her Privates We* (1929) by the Australian Frederic Manning (1882–1935); and *Under Fire* (1916) by the Frenchman Henri Barbusse. Books from the defeated side included the German novels *All Quiet on the Western Front* (1928) by Erich Maria Remarque (1898–1970); *Storm of Steel* (1920) by Ernst Jünger (1895–1998); and *The Good Soldier Svejk* (1923) by the Czech Jaroslav Hasek (1883–1923).

Later authors who lacked the living experience of the war nevertheless seized on it as a powerful subject; a very small selection of such books includes:

A Long, Long Way (2005) by the Irish novelist Sebastian Barry (1955–); *An Ice Cream War* (1982) by William Boyd (1957–); *Birdsong* (1993) by Sebastian Faulks; *A Soldier of the Great War* (1991) by Mark Helprin (1947–); *C* (2010) by Tom McCarthy (1969–); and, besides the remaining two novels in the *Regeneration* trilogy, Barker's later *Life Class* (2007) and *Toby's Room* (2012). Appearing while Barker's trilogy was in progress, Faulks's *Birdsong* is often linked with her work. In 'The Fog of War' (2005), Ann-Louise Shapiro also notes 'the importance in the 1990s of non-academic explorations of the effects of the Great War', mentioning novels, films and a Public Broadcasting System documentary.[5] As some critics have pointed out, by the time Pat Barker had begun writing about the Great War, it was the frequent subject of respectful treatment in fiction and nonfiction; but it had also been treated comically, as in *Oh! What a Lovely War*, a musical satire staged in 1963 and partly based on *The Good Soldier Svejk*, and *Blackadder Goes Forth* (1989), the final instalment of Rowan Atkinson's (1955–) BBC series of comic histories focusing on Edmund Blackadder, this time on the Western Front, which ends with Blackadder going over the top, presumably to his death.

Thus, though naturally the research underlying her fiction must include reliable historical accounts, it is unsurprising (particularly given her earlier practice) that Pat Barker's *Regeneration* shows intertextual relations to other Great War Books, and criticism of her work has often unpacked those relationships. Rudolf Weiss, for instance, comments in 'Mise en abyme in Pat Barker's *Regeneration*' (2004) on the high level of intertextuality and considers the 'essential concerns of the book' to be 'regarded as mise en abyme'—that is, placed in infinite regression, or endlessly duplicated, as in the reduplication of images viewed from a position between two mirrors.[6] Mark Rawlinson discusses the relationship between novelist and witness (i.e. nonfiction accounts by combatants) and the trilogy's 'promotions and demotions of the fiction and the real, and its refusal to observe the courtesies of attribution'.[7]

In 'Two Borrowings in Pat Barker's "Regeneration"' (2004), Alistair Duckworth comments on the links with Graves's *Good-bye to All That*, which is the straightforward source for the account of how Graves extricated Sassoon from the possibility of court-martial. He finds particular reference when Burns, another of the damaged officers, tells Rivers that you want to be wounded (something Graves writes frankly about); and he sees Blunden's *Undertones of War* as the source of the blown-up man whose eye Prior found under the duckboards in the trench, specifically because of the 'sequential specificity of the horrific details he provides', though Prior's initially casual reaction and comparison of the eyeball to a gobstopper are not indebted to Blunden.[8]

Discussion on *Regeneration* often slights Wilfred Owen in favour of the more dashing Siegfried Sassoon. Owen is, indeed, a less impressive figure—uncertain, deferential, not shown in conversation with Rivers. His importance is greater in *The Ghost Road*, but Kaley Joyes, in 'Regenerating Wilfred Owen: Pat Barker's Revisions' (2009), comments in greater than usual depth on Barker's use of Wilfred Owen, arguing, for instance, that 'in addition to writing Owen's persona and poems into her novel, Barker reworks two of his poems without identifying her source [...]. [She] destabilizes the authority of direct experience by emphasizing the accessibility of text.'[9] One intertext identified by Joyes is Owen's poem 'Disabled', written in 1917 but published posthumously, the source for an episode in which Sarah Lumb, visiting a hospital, sees terribly wounded and disfigured men and requires herself to look at them, against her strong desire to turn away. It is a powerful moment:

> ■ Simply by being there, by being that inconsequential, infinitely powerful creature: a pretty girl, she had made everything worse. Her sense of her own helplessness, her being forced to play the role of Medusa when she meant no harm, merged with the anger she was beginning to feel at their being hidden away like that. If the country demanded that price, then it should bloody well be prepared to look at the result. (160) □

There is this difference from Owen's poem—Owen has women's eyes passing from the disabled to the whole men, but Sarah actually understands that she should look at them—a more complex psychological point than Owen's poem makes, in part by the shift in perspective from a wounded man to a female noncombatant.[10]

The second Owen poem Joyes (and others) cite is 'Parable of the Old Man and the Young', also written in 1917 and published by Sassoon in 1920, a reworking of the Abraham and Isaac story with a twist: as the sacrifice of Isaac looms, an angel appears, to stay Abraham's hand and offer him a ram for a substitute sacrifice, as in the Book of Genesis, where God decides that his test of Isaac's father has been sufficient and replaces Isaac with an animal: 'But the old man would not so, but slew his son, / And half the seed of Europe, one by one.'[11] The connection with *Regeneration* comes when Dr Rivers contemplates a church window depicting Abraham and Isaac: 'Thus, as Barker revises Owen's poem through Rivers's thoughts, she confirms Owen's criticism of the war but alters the generational perspective. In Barker's version, the older generation, as represented by Rivers, is capable of admitting its betrayal and is therefore given the opportunity for contrition.'[12] Rudolf Weiss comments on the same relationship and says that the intertextual use of Owen's poem 'provides a chilling new version of the parable from *Genesis*'.[13]

In 'Britain and the Audit of War' (1997), Kenneth Morgan is interested in the changing attitudes toward the war, suggesting that acceptance or approval hardened into disapproval only after the armistice, when the 'horror of the trenches became the dominant cultural image. The literature, both poetry and prose, of the post-war years was almost wholly anti-war. This is epitomized by Philip [*sic*] Sassoon, whose encounters with the army psychologist, W. H. Rivers, provide the core of Pat Barker's *Regeneration* almost eighty years on.'[14] Though there is no doubt that some post-war revaluation may have made the writing about the war seem more oppositional, it is worth noting that Owen died in 1918, leaving powerful verses that display that horror; Henri Barbusse's *Under Fire* was actually published during the war, as was Rebecca West's *Return of the Soldier*. The patriotic war poems of Rupert Brooke (1887–1915), perhaps especially 'The Soldier', quoted in *Toby's Room*, were very popular, but there were anti-war voices raised even during the conflict.

Linkages to other World War I texts are the predictable kind of intertextuality. More surprising is Karin Westman's identification, in *Pat Barker's Regeneration: A Reader's Guide* (2001), of the influence of Angela Carter (in a way, Barker's mentor), especially in the 'more humorous scenes, with their gallows humor, earthy physicality, and vaudeville moments'.[15]

FIDELITY/REALISM?

History books are an obvious source, acknowledged in Barker's 'Author's Note', and the war looms large in the British public's historical register. This points to an interesting critical issue, which is the author's use (some critics would say, her misuse) of 'authentic history' in her history-based fiction. There are two related issues: one is how faithful to what really happened Barker's narrative is; the other is how successfully she conveys the sensation of reality, how well she makes readers *feel* as if this is reality.

On the latter question, there is some dispute. Paul Taylor's review in *The Independent* included the claim that the conversations between Sassoon and Owen, as Sassoon helps Owen to revise his verses, sounded like an Open University lesson; by contrast, Herbert Mitgang was powerfully impressed with the dialogue Barker created in its verisimilitude, saying that if not strictly accurate, still it gave the strong impression of accuracy in both serious and witty veins.[16] By contrast, the poet Lavinia Greenlaw claims that 'the dialogue seems disturbingly second-hand, as if, while written in one medium, it has been sieved through another—the book of the film of the war'.[17]

As for the use of 'real' history, Alistair Duckworth comments on the attraction for readers of the information Barker's novels provide 'on such topics as conditions in the trenches, treatment (or non-treatment) of shell shock, experiments in nerve regeneration, female employment in munitions factories, early twentieth-century anthropology, and homophobic paranoia during World War I', clearly endorsing the idea that readers might derive reliable information from them.[18] In 'Twentieth-Century Theories of Combat Motivation and Breakdown' (2006), Simon Wessely disagrees, particularly about the important central matter of war-caused psychiatric casualties. Barker is wrong, he suggests, to attribute to Rivers the insight that war itself disabled its psychiatric victims and that nothing essential distinguished those who broke down from those who did not; 'this is viewing history from our post-PTSD [i.e. post-traumatic stress disorder] perspective—Rivers himself said no such thing, and like most of his professional contemporaries, did not believe it'.[19] Dissenting commentary on Barker's representation of war neurosis seems to come from two directions. Some critics consider her writing unfaithful to Rivers, by making him either too Freudian or not Freudian enough. Others are uneasy with the influence of Elaine Showalter's *The Female Malady*, a 1987 feminist reading of the history of 'hysteria'. In '"Why Not War Writers"' (2008), Eve Patten takes up the question of Sassoon's throwing his Military Cross into the river and the ambiguity about whether it really happened (not an invention by Pat Barker, by the way), and uses it as an entry into 'this artful novel, with its complex interweaving of autobiography and memoir, historical document and imaginative fiction' toward a larger point, her 'review of some of the many hesitations surrounding war in general as a subject for narrative and representation'.[20]

In 'Compulsory Masculinity, Britain, and the Great War' (1998), Greg Harris addresses some other issues of historical fact and representation—the home-front battles against pacifists and homosexuals—and declares 'that ferocious climate of intolerance is depicted throughout

Regeneration' (though his conflation of Robert Ross [Oscar Wilde's Canadian friend and literary executor, 1869–1918] and Robert Graves is unfortunate).[21] Here *Regeneration* somewhat tentatively introduces a theme that will follow through the trilogy. In a conversation between Sassoon and Rivers, just after Sassoon reports that 'The pride of the British Army requires that absolute dominance must be maintained in No Man's Land at all times' (52)—a pompous official declaration from which he distances himself by adopting a public school accent—he turns to a discussion of Edward Carpenter (1844–1929), a pacifist, Fabian socialist, and homosexual activist; as Rivers is trying to change the subject, Sassoon says 'I read a book of his. *The Intermediate Sex*. I don't know whether you know it?' (53). Carpenter's book, published in 1912, is subtitled 'A Study of Some Transitional Types of Men and Women'. After a few lines he turns to Robert Ross, through whom he has first encountered pacifism, and then mentions Ross's connection with Oscar Wilde (which will become a topic through all of Barker's books about World War I). The payoff to the conversation comes when Rivers tells him that although 'there's nothing more despicable than using a man's private life to discredit his views', nevertheless it often happens (55).

Finally, the question of 'realism' and 'historiographic metafiction' is raised, though not in those terms, by Karin Westman, when she writes 'While some authors prefer to emphasize the act of historical appropriation, Barker does not do so in *Regeneration*,' inviting the reader instead to bring to bear on her fiction previous knowledge (or 'lack of familiarity') of Craiglockhart, Sassoon, Owen, and so on; and though she cites historical texts as warrant for her novel, Westman points out that she does so only in the 'Author's Note' which follows the narrative.[22] By contrast, Eve Patten does suggest that Barker 'allows her reader to see as part of her own textually self-conscious recreation of real events, the inevitable inadequacy of war's inscription'; the challenge to that adequacy for Patten is encoded in the scenes in which Sassoon helps Owen to revise his verses.[23] And in 'Stammering to Story: Neurosis and Narration in Pat Barker's *Regeneration*' (2001), Ankhi Mukherjee reads the novel as 'an allegory of the failure of the narrative project, which is at the same time, paradoxically, its greatest success'.[24]

Rivers

W. H. R. Rivers is one of the figures of real history enfolded in this novel (and the whole trilogy, of course). Many critics accept Rivers as the protagonist or the hero, and Westman cites Barker herself as calling him the main character, though other reviewers have assigned Sassoon that role.[25] Westman points out that Rivers challenges an essentialist view of gender when he links young officers to working-class mothers.[26] (He is also called maternal.) What is the main function of Rivers? In 'Scattering the Seed of Abraham' (1999), Catherine Lanone says that his role is 'precisely to read painful nightmares, to unravel the officers' traumatic web of images, to bring meaning back. As such Rivers ceases to be a doctor, he becomes a silent listener and a medicine man, a detective and a father confessor, sorting out tales of murder, pain and death.'[27] Clearly Rivers is conflicted. Though he believes in what he is doing, believes that it is right, he is also tormented by doubts. Sometimes these come out in dreams; as Lanone points out, his dream in chapter 22 requires Rivers to recognize the similarity between his practice and that of the brutal Yealland. In his dream he forced a horse bit into the open mouth of a patient. As the novel stipulates, in indirect free style: 'Obviously he and Yealland were both in the business of controlling people' (238). When he writes '[d]ischarged to duty' on Sassoon's file (the last moment of the novel), 'The pen', Lanone writes, 'has become the sacrificial knife, but no angel stays his hand.'[28]

This language connects the Yealland-like silencing with the Abrahamic sacrifice of the son, mentioned in Owen's poem and in the decoration of a church window, which Rivers observes with close attention. Patricia Johnson makes the same connection between Rivers, the sacrifice of Isaac, and Owen's 'bitter sonnet'.[29] Lanone ascribes to Barker's use of the myth the original idea of 'considering Abraham's plight—rather than Isaac's—as a gentle father figure who never loves his son more than when he picks up the knife'.[30] The Abraham–Isaac analogy goes beyond the question of sacrifice of the young to foreground the father–son relationship. Rivers himself links his own father with 'three types of patriarchal authority—family, education, church' and this connects Rivers senior with the older generation responsible for what the war is doing to young men.[31] There is another evident father–son relationship between the middle-aged Rivers and the young men he treats, perhaps most strongly between him and Sassoon.

This is the most important point about Rivers. Though he functions away from Craiglockhart and in roles other than as a therapist to damaged officers, his role is most importantly dialectical—in two senses: he counters other characters and he debates with them. Frances Stead Sellers attributed Barker's success to the way she balanced the two characters—Sassoon and Rivers—and Barker herself said that it was the Sassoon–Rivers relationship which 'was the genesis of *Regeneration*'.[32] In 'Analogy in *Regeneration*' (2001), Kenneth Pellow calls the Sassoon–Rivers relationship symbolically both a confrontation and 'a collaboration, between father and son'.[33] And Pellow goes on to say that this relationship, which occurs to both the men, separately, when they are apart, as the novel progresses, 'is observable—not always positively—to both of them'.[34]

Prior

Alongside Sassoon, the other major officer figure is the invented Billy Prior, who makes for a good contrast with Sassoon (different degrees of pugnacity; different life experience; different social class; different attitude towards sexuality). Kenneth Pellow, one of those critics who take Sassoon as the really important patient at the hospital, and thus see Prior as invoked primarily to clarify the outlines of Sassoon's character by contrast, writes, 'Rivers/Prior is a relationship that is interesting in its own right; but it is even more interesting for what it reflects of Rivers/Sassoon. The father–son connections, the distinct aspects of mentoring and nurturing, the competitiveness—all of these are the same only more so, with the result that we see them more pronouncedly in the main relationship for their analogous presence in the supporting one.'[35]

This relegation of Prior to the 'supporting' relationship is harder to understand when looking back at the trilogy through its second and third parts, but it is true that *Regeneration* begins with Sassoon's 'Declaration' and ends with his reassignment to duty. Prior's linkages with Rivers are important in their own right, as Karin Westman points out; despite the greater obvious differences (in class, most importantly) between Prior and Rivers, they are more alike than Rivers would want to admit, 'especially as Rivers contemplates his relationship with patriarchal authorities'—that is, they are both angry at authority, and their anger blurs the line—a line drawn by authority—between doctor and patient and between father and son.[36]

One obvious contribution Prior makes to *Regeneration*, and the evident reason for his inclusion, is to complicate the class picture. Rivers, Sassoon, Graves, and most of the Craiglockhart patients are 'gentlemen" as British officers were, almost automatically and unconsciously, expected to be. Prior is very different, an emissary from a world—northern, industrial, working-class—like those in *Union Street* or *The Man Who Wasn't There*. As Laurie Vickroy writes in 'A Legacy of Pacificism' (2004), he 'personifies conflicts between the state and the individual and between duty to authority and rebellion'.[37] Perhaps because his class distinction is so obvious, and so often insisted on by himself, there has been relatively little critical discussion of it. In *Pat Barker's Regeneration*, Karin Westman points out that the presence of Prior highlights Rivers's 'blind spot' about class, noting that his treatment of Prior is very different from that of Sassoon, though they are both second lieutenants. He calls Sassoon Siegfried but calls Prior *Mr* Prior, and sponsors Sassoon for membership in a golf club, a courtesy he never thinks of extending to Prior.[38] As Westman elsewhere observes, in 'Generation Not Regeneration' (2005), 'Cross-generational connections appear through the representation of social class in the novel...Rivers's friendship with Sassoon and his relationship with Prior reveal how class privilege is a recurring pattern of cultural experience across generations, not representative of one moment in history.'[39] The question of class is shaded, too, by the presence of Wilfred Owen. Owen is another lieutenant, but in his case a marginal member of the middle class; his family was poor, he was educated at a technical school, failed to earn a scholarship and thus could not enter the University of London. He was working as a private tutor when war broke out. By contrast Sassoon, a self-described 'fox-hunting man', was the child of privileged and wealthy people, and attended Marlborough College, one of England's leading public schools, and Clare College, Cambridge. Rudolf Weiss has commented on the hierarchical relations between the two men in *Regeneration*: the inequality consists of class, at least in part, though Owen's shyness and social incapability, and Sassoon's much greater self-confidence about his writing, play a role, too.

GENDER AND SEXUALITY

The turn toward male characters has been often noted—Karin Westman says that Barker was criticized for 'deserting the cause' of feminism—as well as Barker's sensible declaration that feminists need not write just about women, that feminism itself is not just about women.[40] Gender is very much a topic of *Regeneration*, despite the relative absence of women. Laurie Vickroy suggests that in Barker's view, 'War survivors' internal conflicts illustrated the gendered social contexts which cause and reinforce trauma: men are made helpless and terrified in war, and recovery from trauma is made difficult, when by encouraging his patients to express their fears and feelings, Rivers must contradict their upbringing as men.'[41] Harris, somewhat in contrast, suggests that Rivers is himself invested 'in those very notions of masculinity that he is trying to lead his patients to reject [...]'.[42] The gender-informed analysis of war, Vickroy adds, links Barker with Virginia Woolf, as both consider the continuance of war to be assisted, if not actually necessitated, by 'conceptualizations and language which are dissociated from human suffering'.[43] Anne Barnes, in a *Times* review, cited Sassoon's heroism and glamour which, she writes, were linked with other snobbish forces like chauvinism (presumably male chauvinism rather than extreme nationalism) and stereotyped manliness and, she argues, imposed myths responsible for unnumbered deaths.[44] Harris, quoting Samuel Hynes (the author of *A War Imagined: The First World War and English Culture*, 1992), writes that masculinity can be manifested in two ways: heterosexuality and war. 'It is no coincidence, then, that the most ferocious home-front battles were fought against pacifists and homosexuals and that soldiers receiving psychiatric treatment endured tremendous doses of guilt for not being men in control.'[45]

Failure of masculinity does not equal homosexuality; homosexuality is important in *Regeneration*, since both Sassoon and Owen were homosexual and the fictional Billy Prior is at least bisexual; but the fierce battles against homosexuals (and pacifists), though mentioned in this book, are much more important in the next novel, *The Eye in the Door*. Homosexuality, though present, is only rarely and superficially discussed, as the general cultural imposition of the time discouraged such discussion, but it appears in a variety of ways; and, as Westman goes on to argue, 'Rivers's unconventional theories about his knowledge of other cultures' sexual practices make him sympathetic to homosexuality in Britain.'[46] Barker has said that she suspects Rivers was himself a homosexual, though this is made explicit neither in the nonfiction accounts of his life nor in her trilogy.[47]

ANTI-WAR?

If war novels are usually anti-war novels, and *Regeneration* is anti-war, what sort of remedy or redress or solution or consolation is offered? None, really. Perhaps, as Owen said of his own work, the poetry is in the pity. There are some gains for the traumatized men, and critics have suggested several 'therapeutic practices' directed toward their amelioration. What, for instance, is the 'regeneration' of the title? As Karen Patrick Knutsen says in *Reciprocal Haunting: Pat Barker's Regeneration Trilogy* (2010), it is, on one level, a reference to the regeneration of nerve tissue, in an experiment carried out by Rivers and his friend Head, a procedure grounded in 'physicality and a scientific worldview'.[48] But, Knutsen goes on, '[a]s the narrative progresses, however, the trope becomes increasingly intertwined with abstract patriotic and religious ideas'.[49] This is hardly an uncomplicated regeneration, though in this case it comes through Rivers's re-enactment, through a talking cure, rather than as a result of cutting nerves. Another possible aid to regeneration, cited by Karin Westman, is imagination, as embodied, for instance, in the poems of Sassoon and Owen, and indeed in Sassoon's 'Declaration'. She suggests, as Sassoon would agree, that employment of the imagination could destroy complacency.[50] Elsewhere, comparing *Regeneration* with *Birdsong*, Westman writes that Barker's book—unlike Faulks's novel, which seems to suggest physical rebirth as the only repair for rupture—'asks readers to consider remembering as a form of healing, as a way to regenerate the bodies and the minds damaged by the body politic'.[51] Remembering, she goes on to say, offers a form of healing not just to the Great War generation but to Barker's own contemporaries.

FILM

Barker's *Regeneration* is exceptional in another way. Aside from the peculiar adaptation of *Union Street* into the Jane Fonda vehicle *Stanley and Iris*, this is the only one of Barker's books to be made into a film. Or, put another way, it is the only one to be made *faithfully* into a film. *Regeneration* appeared in 1997 in the UK, and in 1998 in the US, where it sometimes goes under the alternative title *Behind the Lines*. It received many favourable reviews on first screening, and the 2010 *Time Out Film Guide* echoes those reviews, calling it 'subtle, elegant and sharply intelligent' with 'marvelous performances all round'; the result is a 'profoundly moving film that never resorts to manipulative cliché'.[52] It was nominated for many awards under the auspices of the British Academy Awards, British Independent Film Awards, Genie Awards and Political Film Society in the US, including best performances, best film, best costume design, and best music score.

As Karin Westman points out, reactions differed sharply between the US and UK reviewers. She theorizes that the very recent phenomenon of *Saving Private Ryan* (the Oscar-nominated 1998 blockbuster directed by Steven Spielberg)—which, like *Regeneration*, began with a scene showing the horrors of war—warped the American reviewers' responses. Sara Martin's article on the film, 'Regenerating the War Movie' (2002), concurs on this point: the film 'appeared too formal, too restrained in comparison to the highly visual drama of, for instance, *Saving Private Ryan*'.[53] It also goes beyond the material of *Regeneration*, having the advantage of being filmed after the trilogy was complete: as Anne Whitehead notes in 'Pat Barker's *Regeneration* Trilogy' (2005), it shows Owen's death, one of the last events of *The Ghost Road*—though not the death of Prior—'in the interests of plot closure'.[54] Martin comments on the way that the process Barker developed through three full novels to reach 'the cathartic end of her trilogy' is telescoped into one film, forcing the 'audience to march at a more brisk pace toward a similar emotional effect [...]'.[55]

Both *Time Out* and the American film reviewers judged it within a context of film-making and other cinematic treatments of war. Karin Westman, in her chapter on the film, judges it by comparison with its source text and finds several disappointments. The film, she writes, has been simplified to focus on the theme of generational conflict; it is '[b]ereft of Barker's commentary on class, gender, and the shaping power of the imagination'; because it emphasizes generational conflict, it ignores Barker's cross-generational connections (such as between Rivers and Sassoon). In an apparent effort to 'open out' the narrative, the film relocates scenes from interiors to 'the lush grounds of Craiglockhart'—from private spaces to public, changing the dynamic of conversations between physician and patient.[56] Rivers, she asserts, is oversimplified; in making him a representative of the older generation the filmmakers turn him into someone comparable to Yealland, the sadistic therapist who 'cures' patients with a regime of almost unbearable cruelty; but the plot also requires Rivers to come around to agreement with Sassoon at the end and, according to Westman, because 'the hints in the novel that Rivers sympathizes with his patients must be absent from a script that asks Rivers to echo Yealland, Rivers's character must undergo a sudden epiphany as we reach the conclusion of the film'.[57] Finally, the novel's view of sexuality is also simplified as it is converted to cinema. 'The rescripting for the film of Sarah and Prior's heterosexual love-making, spliced at the end of the film with Owen's unrequited homosexual love for Sassoon, creates a composite scene that simplifies the novel's commentary on male–female relationships and dehistoricizes the novel's presentation of homosexuality.'[58]

Sharon Monteith offers a balanced assessment of the film; its shortcoming, she suggests, lies in its avoidance of the homoeroticism in the novel, but she contrasts it with a contemporary television treatment of the war, *Blackadder Goes Forth*, a dark comedy starring the English comedian Rowan Atkinson, which she says complicates tragedy in comedy.[59]

Films are not novels and, in fact, usually result from a simplification of fiction, so the changes Westman notes are perhaps to be expected from what is, after all, at least an *effort* to be true to Barker's vision. At least Pat Barker approved of the film and said, in answer to a reader's question, 'it was [a] relief to be able to say genuinely that I liked it'.[60] In an interview during the filming (while she was on set in Scotland) she amplified her approval, granting high praise to the intelligence of the script.[61] Some discontent with the film (for instance, that expressed by Karin Westman and Sara Martin) may arise simply from the way that films *must* deviate from their sources in narrative prose by the nature of the very different media.

Meanwhile, the novel itself ends less conclusively. Prior and his girl Sarah Lumb have had a deeper and more satisfying lovemaking; Rivers has been to London and observed Lewis Yealland torturing men back into 'health'; thinking back over his time as an anthropologist he comes to a tolerant breadth of judgement, clearly meant to apply back home as well: 'I suddenly saw that their reactions to my society were neither more nor less valid than mine to theirs' (242). Sassoon, who has finished his book of poems, *Counter-Attack* (in *The Ghost Road* the discovery that his new subordinate officer is reading this book will prove shocking to him), continues what the novel calls his 'straightforward, headlong retreat towards the front' (248) and is duly sent there; the date is 26 November 1917. After only a short stretch of narrative time Barker picks up these different narrative strands again in the next instalment of the trilogy, *The Eye in the Door.*

CHAPTER FIVE

The Eye in the Door (1993)

In 1993 the second novel of the trilogy, *The Eye in the Door*, appeared. This is a continuation of the story told in *Regeneration*, with many of the same characters as well as some new ones. It begins shortly after the end of *Regeneration*. The major change is in Billy Prior, who, unfit for service because of his asthma, has home duty as—in effect—a spy, investigating anti-war and otherwise 'subversive' citizens. This novel is the pivot of the three books in the trilogy, measuring the gradual replacement of Sassoon by Prior as the central officer.

Readers learn considerably more about Billy Prior, including his childhood molestation and later time as a young homosexual prostitute. His father and mother appear as characters: he and his mother share a fastidious disgust at his father's coarse habits—though Prior also recognizes that his mother's fastidiousness may be partly responsible for the coarseness. In conversation, his mother wishes to avoid all reference to the war or her son's current role in it, maybe because in his new position he must investigate and inform on old friends from his home town and social class.

The Eye in the Door enlarges on the references to Robert Ross, Oscar Wilde, and Edward Carpenter in *Regeneration* as they become part of an important theme: that is, the alleged role of the sexually different (including oversexed women as well as homosexuals) in encouraging defeatism. As a gay or bisexual man (alongside numerous others—his lover Lt Manning, a married man; Sassoon; Robert Graves, though he writes that he is moving in a heterosexual direction), Prior's relationship to this theme is ambivalent. And he is not alone, as his father is both anti-war and homophobic.

Prior remembers war experiences, as do others like Manning, but in *The Eye in the Door* his war is entirely prosecuted on the home front, a cause of conflict because that makes it so much harder to get a clear view of who is the enemy, and ultimately a cause of psychological dissolution.

Reviewers acclaimed it, mostly. It also won the *Guardian* Fiction Prize for 1993. In an article following that award, the novelist Philip Hensher called it Barker's most interesting book to date and cited other reviewers (including the judges of the award) who thought it better than *Regeneration*, as he also praised her for changing course drastically from her earlier books, whose subjects he claimed were suggesting a limited range. He went on to summarize some of the other reviews, with glowing phrases from *The Independent on Sunday*, *The Sunday Times*, and *The Times Literary Supplement*.[1]

Carl Macdougall (like many reviewers and critics before and since) began his review with a consideration of where Barker had begun and how she had changed after her earlier novels: citing approvingly what he considered her greater breadth in social coverage, including more than one class (i.e. more than just the working-class characters of her early books) and keeping politics implicit.[2] Similarly, Eileen Battersby claimed that her earlier books had been treated as if they were works of sociology rather than fiction (though that does not seem to be the keynote of most reviews or criticism of those books) but that her Great War novels were real historical novels, which Battersby praised for their muscularity and their storytelling.[3] She wrote this in an article about the Booker Prize shortlist, from which *The Eye in the Door* was omitted, she thought very unjustly.

PRIOR

There has been less later, systematic commentary written by literary critics on *The Eye in the Door* than on *Regeneration*. Perhaps this is because unlike the dualistic frame of *Regeneration*, with Rivers interacting with Sassoon, or with Prior, it focuses mostly on Prior himself; or at least he is the central character in a novel that has, depending on one's view, a more diffuse, less coherent structure or (looked at more positively) a broader canvas. And unlike *The Ghost Road* (and even, through flashbacks, *Regeneration*) it has almost no Western Front narrative. Instead the tension is mostly within Billy Prior. Still unfit for the front line, he has been given a position with the Ministry of Munitions that amounts to spying on the anti-war movement in Britain. His supervisor, Major Lode, is credited with the belief that 'This rag-bag collection of Quakers, socialists, anarchists, suffragettes, syndicalists, Seventh Day Adventists and God knows who else was merely an elaborate disguise, behind which lurked the real anti-war movement, a secret, disciplined, highly efficient organization dedicated to the overthrow of the state as surely and simply as Lode was dedicated to its preservation' (43). Lode's alarmist, not to say paranoiac, worries take in religious groups, radical trade unionists, and campaigners for votes for women. Prior takes a less hysterical view of the anti-war movement, if only because some of his old friends are in it, but does, in the end, serve Lode. His position is that the anti-war movement is harmful to the soldiers at the front. The result of that view, widely shared in a somewhat hysterical way by the government, is what Jessica Meacham, in 'War, Policing and Surveillance: Pat Barker and the Secret State' (2012), calls 'the rising hysteria of the domestic political, social and cultural situation during the latter half of the war,' resulting in the novel's 'preoccupation with surveillance' [...]'.[4]

The tension that in *Regeneration* existed between the traumatized officers and the doctor trying to heal them is, in *The Eye in the Door*, internalized into Prior himself. Here he is much more clearly revealed as a self-divided man. His sexuality is more evidently bisexual (though he is not tormented about this)—he has sexual relations with an upper-class officer, Manning, with his girlfriend from the earlier book, Sarah, and with an older woman back in his home town of Salford who, he realizes, had suckled him in his infancy. More important is the wrenching division between what he is and what he does, with the powerful emotional component it carries, and his emotional ties to Patrick MacDowell, an old friend now leading the anti-war movement, Beattie Roper, another figure from his past, imprisoned for trying to kill Lloyd George—that is, David Lloyd George (1863–1945) the Welsh prime minister during World War I—and her daughter Hettie. When he visits Beattie in prison, she says 'You were like a son to me' (40); and she calls him a 'greasy, arse-licking little sod' (31). She also divines his own confusion, asking him if he knows which side he is on. In a later conversation with MacDowell, Prior clarifies his position, declaring that he would turn in a deserter (because there are frightened conscripts who *don't* desert), and responding to MacDowell's class analysis with '"Well, let me tell you, Mac, the part of the proletariat I've been fighting with—the vast majority—they'd string you up from the nearest fucking lamp-post and not think twice about it. And as for your striking munition workers..." Prior swept the shed with a burst of machine-gun fire' (110).

Prior's self-division becomes realized in a dramatically divided condition of dissociation during which he loses consciousness of himself, having no idea where has been or what he has done until later reports give him glimpses of his other self. A fellow Munition Ministry worker, Spragge, turns up; when Prior asks why Spragge is following him, or what he wants, he is told that he is the one following Spragge. Once, drinking in a pub, he begins observing the light on the table; then 'He was back at his desk. No interval. One second he was in the pub, the next sitting behind his desk' (123). There are both symbolic markers of Prior's dissociation or doubleness ('Prior turned to face his doubled reflection in the window and thought he didn't like himself very much' [88]) and discursive, diagnostic ones, such as when Rivers tells Prior 'I think you found out how to put yourself into a kind of trance. A dissociated state. And then in France, under that *intolerable* pressure, you rediscovered it' (248). The dissociation from Prior's childhood presumably would be explained by events he wished not to experience. The reader is told that in the past he had been paid for sex; and he was molested, apparently, by a Catholic priest whom his mother had paid to offer him extra tuition. He also received a scholarship—became a 'scholarship boy'—apparently through the efforts of the same priest. In fact much of *The Eye in the Door* serves to fill in biographical detail about Billy Prior. He is from Salford, part of Greater Manchester, specifically Tite Street; his mother was, or wanted to be, 'genteel', while his father is coarser (the parental situation familiar from *Sons and Lovers*); he has been better educated than others of his class background. Richard Slobodin notes all these features of Billy Prior and concludes that he is the 'touchstone character' in the whole trilogy and that it is 'his multiplex elusiveness that makes him, in the mind of this reader, the most complete embodiment of what the author wants to say about the Great War'.[5]

The dividedness is not limited to Prior, though. Sassoon speaks to Rivers about his own feeling of being two people (anti-war poet and fiery warrior), and goes on to say, 'You know what finally put the kibosh on my Jekyll and Hyde performance, no, listen, this is funny. I got a new second in command. Pinto. Absolute jewel. But the first time I met him he was reading *Counter-Attack* [Sassoon's collection of anti-war poems published in 1918], and he looked up and said, "Are you the same Sassoon?"' (229) And Rivers generalizes this condition, thinking that most of us divide ourselves in order to survive, which he relates to the neurological experiments he and Henry Head had undertaken before the war, and two types of neurons with different functions, the 'epicritic grounded in the protopathic [...]' (232–3). Rivers goes on to reflect on his own duality, including as one of his selves the Melanesian one, the peacetime anthropologist.

Among the events in the 'larger world' that surround and emplace Prior's activities in this novel are the activities of opponents of the war, and the demonstrations of the suffragettes; a strange campaign by the homophobic conspiracy theorist and Member of Parliament Noel Pemberton Billing (1881–1948) against 'the cult of the clitoris', an alleged movement among women whose enlarged clitorises make them unsatisfiable by normal men, which somehow linked Oscar Wilde (1854–1900, hence dead 17 years), the Canadian performer Maud Allan (1873–1956), and 'the first 47,000'—an imagined threatening third column, made up of perverts, in danger of turning the country over to the Germans. Barker quotes one of the flyers—a historical document comparable to Sassoon's statement in *Regeneration*:

THE CULT OF THE CLITORIS

■ To be a member of Maud Allan's private performance in Oscar Wilde's *Salome* one has to apply to a Miss Valetta, of 9 Duke Street, Adelphi, WC. If Scotland Yard were to seize the list of these members I have no doubt they would secure the names of several thousand of the first 47,000. (22) □

Jessica Meacham comments on this reign of paranoia, particularly the so-called Cult of the Clitoris and the trial of its inventor: 'The trial does seem preposterous now, but in its role as a site for dispute over language and meaning it is indicative of the same slippage of representation found in the earlier relationships between William Le Queux, Erskine Childers and the War Office and MO5.'[6] Le Queux (1864–1927) and Childers (1870–1922) were novelists who encouraged fears of a German invasion.

The title of the novel is well chosen, with multiple resonances. It refers specifically to the eye which would be painted around the peep-hole in a prison (like the one where Beattie Roper is held and Billy Prior visits her), reminding the prisoner that she was under constant surveillance; it alludes to the eyeball Prior found under the duckboards at the front, which had the delayed effect of relegating him to Craiglockhart in *Regeneration*. This connection is made in Billy's mind in the prison: Beattie calls his attention to the eye painted on the door and its evident function of reminding the prisoner that she is being watched all the time. 'This eye, where no eye should have been, was deeply disturbing to Prior. For a moment he was back in France, looking at Towers's eyeball in the palm of his hand' (36). And it links to Prior's diagnosis of Rivers, based on a childhood event Rivers reveals, when Prior tells him 'You put your mind's eye *out*' (139). And Prior discusses a bad dream of his friends Mac and Beattie—now his quarry—and concludes '"eye" was stabbing myself in the "I"' (75).

VISION

Understandably, critics have commented acutely on the visual theme. John Brannigan writes, 'If *Regeneration* is a novel about violence and protest, figured through tropes of speech and silence, *The Eye in the Door*, as its title suggests, is a novel about visibility as a mode of knowing.'[7] Carl Macdougall seconds this identification of this novel as a text about varieties of sight and looking, including spying.[8] In 'The Eye in the Door' (1997), Anna Grimshaw also identifies 'vision and perception' as among the most prominent features, and links this to the title.[9] Sheryl

Stevenson, in 'The Uncanny Case of Dr Rivers and Mr Prior' (2005), notes Prior's own foregrounding of the pun that I equals eye, and writes that 'Ambivalence about seeing, even the impulse to blind oneself, is a response to threatening experiences exhibited by both Prior and Rivers [...]'; the blinding, in the case of Rivers, is the 'putting out the mind's eye' diagnosed by Prior.[10]

Prior is not only more central in this novel than in its predecessor; he is also more aware and insightful, even if at the same time more self-divided and conflicted. As Laurie Vickroy says in *Trauma and Survival in Contemporary Fiction*, he embodies conflict 'between the state and the individual and between duty to authority and rebellion'.[11] He also sharpens the class awareness, in something of a corrective, by Barker, to the idea of Great War literature as pastoral, a key theme addressed by Paul Fussell in his important book *The Great War and Modern Memory* (1975). For Prior comes from an urban background; as the author told Eddie Gibb in a 1996 interview, she presents Prior alongside the railway sidings in Salford because the literature of the Great War is usually about rural England, which is positioned as a contrast to the brutal, mechanized killing machine of the war; but for people like Prior, with backgrounds in the mechanized working class, the war is more continuity than contrast.[12]

DUALISM

This proletarian background is part of Prior's dualism, not just because the proletarian objectors to the war undermine the proletarian fighters of it, but because of Prior's ambiguous status as a temporary gentleman (an identification explicitly made by Manning). But the novel is suffused with similar dualism. In 'Pat Barker: *The Ghost Road*' (2005), Lynda Prescott gives a thorough account of the presence of this theme, or condition.

> ■ Prior's pathological condition [i.e. his dissociation and fugue states] is only the most extreme form of duality affecting many of the characters in the novel. Sassoon realizes 'I survive out there [in France] by being two people'...the anti-war poet and the efficient soldier. Many homosexuals, like Prior's friend Manning, lead consciously double lives. Prior's own bisexuality represents another kind of fracturing. And Rivers, struggling unsuccessfully to reconcile his academic English self with his recollections of life as an anthropologist in Melanesia, begins to wonder whether integration is actually possible.[13] □

Sheryl Stevenson adds another example of dualism by pointing out that the novel ends with paired scenes: Prior going back to Manning, Rivers saying to Sassoon 'let's go back'.[14] The division self-diagnosed by both Rivers and Sassoon redoubles that visible in Prior.

And this disintegration which, on the personal level, is a form of psychological disturbance, echoes or stands for a broader disintegration—'the social disintegration precipitated by war'; Grimshaw considers this the central preoccupation of *The Eye in the Door*.[15] That disintegration would be one element in the book's demonstration of the costs of war—that is, its anti-war effect. Readers may remember Rivers saying 'Nothing justifies this' in *Regeneration* (180); and at the end of *The Ghost Road* he will be saying 'It's not worth it' (274). Another element would be what Stevenson calls Prior's potential for violence and the 'intense hostility Prior expresses toward noncombatants, and particularly women'—though his fancy of machine-gunning striking munition workers is not specifically gendered, readers may remember his girl Sarah Lumb, who works in a munitions factory—which 'fits the First World War's paradoxical pattern of "the enemy to the rear," described by Paul Fussell and seen [in *No Man's Land: The Place of the Woman Writer in the Twentieth Century*, 1988] by Sandra Gilbert [1936–] and Susan Gubar [1944–] as a more persistent "battle of the sexes"'.[16] The real-life Sassoon wrote poems fantasizing about the slaughter of civilians and members of parliament ('Blighters', for instance, which fantasizes a tank assault on a civilian audience enjoying a music hall performance) and, on reflection, this attitude may not seem wholly paradoxical. Another illustration of the war's destructiveness (and *growing* destructiveness: this novel takes place in an environment of war-weariness) is what Sharon Monteith calls the 'ideological stranglehold' made up of paranoia mixed with, or possibly posing as, patriotism; among its manifestations is the attribution of cowardice to men who desert, or even show signs of shellshock.[17] And as courage is easily equated with manliness, cowardice with unmanliness or even womanliness, the suspicion of homosexuals, and even the weird campaign against women whose hypertrophied clitorises mean they can only be satisfied by bull elephants, become explicable as part of the same patriotic–paranoid phenomenon.

The Eye in the Door is a more sexualized novel than *Regeneration*. Billy Prior admits disgustedly to Rivers that he has been having nightmares of 'mutilation and slaughter' that were 'accompanied by seminal emissions' (71). In the first ten pages of the book he turns from one sex partner (Myra) to another (Manning), and (perhaps as a result of his time, lightly referenced, as a paid sex worker) knows how to make himself the sort of sex partner Manning will want—a working-class, that is socially inferior, 'sort of seminal spittoon' (11). Another view comes from John Brannigan, who considers Manning to be *Prior's* sex toy (100).[18] Ben Shephard refers to Prior's 'sexual confusion'—though his bisexuality is not presented as confused, so a better word might be multiplicity or versatility—and writes that it allows the author to 'dram-atize a moment of mass hysteria recorded at a crisis point toward the end of the war: a McCarthy-like witch hunt [i.e. like the investigation of suspected communists by US Senator Joseph McCarthy, 1908–1957] for those "of the homogenic persuasion," who formed part of what was seen as a dangerous and "unholy alliance of socialists, sodomites and shop stewards". The resulting climate of fear provides the book with its paranoiac title.'[19] Homosexual characters include not just Manning but Edward Carpenter, an important 'real' historical personage, linked to the Labour Party, the Fabian Society (the organization pursuing democratic socialism, founded in 1884), and modern pacifism, who was mentioned as an early contact of Siegfried Sassoon's in *Regeneration*; it is Lionel Spragge, Prior's fellow spy for the Ministry of Munitions (and something of an unwelcome *Döppleganger*), who identifies Carpenter as 'homogenic'. Even the American poet Walt Whitman (1819–92), dead longer than Wilde himself, is drawn into the controversy and assigned a share of the blame, as Spragge claims to have been introduced to him by Carpenter. Robert Ross, former friend of Wilde, and Lord Alfred Douglas (1870–1945), Wilde's former lover turned denouncer of sodomy, make appearances; Maud Allan, who performs Wilde plays and is somehow linked with the cult of the clitoris, is identified as a lesbian.

THERAPY

Sex is linked to war, again, via Rivers's discussion of the Freudian etiology of war neurosis (with Manning, who denies being a repressed homosexual). The practice of therapy, and the psychological theories that underlie it, are of course important in *The Eye in the Door* just as in *Regeneration*. John Brannigan links psychoanalysis and anthro-pology—Rivers's two professional interests—as two of the modern efforts to exert mastery over nature through human knowledge, though the historical Dr Rivers would probably disclaim any signal success in achieving this mastery.[20] His own dualistic thinking and feeling about war and about making men healthy so that they can be killed prevents him from being too complacent. Sheryl Stevenson has given the best critical account of how psychotherapy functions in *The Eye in the Door*, saying, for instance, that an unconscious compulsion, arising from the need to re-enact the past, 'could explain how Billy Prior gets himself into the stressful position of serving as an Intelligence officer assigned to spy on working-class pacifists whom he has known since childhood [...] [these relationships] uncannily reenact his childhood conflicts'.[21] Likewise Stevenson detects a Freudian transference—that

is, the process by which a patient redirects powerful emotion, sometimes onto the therapist—in the relationship between Prior and Rivers,
'who mirror each other's self-blinding and need for self-acceptance',
and identifies its concrete manifestation in the central chapter of the
novel, when Prior and Rivers exchange seats.[22] Before this point, Prior
has been able to disturb Rivers, but here he interprets Rivers's unconscious eye-shielding manoeuvre and gets the doctor to admit he has no
visual memory; Prior, in other words, begins to function as Rivers's
therapist, providing a psychiatric explanation for Rivers's loss of visual
memory.[23]

INTERTEXTUALITY

Pat Barker's fiction always involves intertextual relationships, some of
them of the obvious and necessary sort, seen in her usage of or connections with histories of the early twentieth century, memoirs and letters;
others more subtle. *The Eye in the Door* is unusual in Barker's oeuvre
in making its intertextual connection to one text so strongly evident,
rather than, as in earlier books, alluding to or echoing or paralleling
several but without any one becoming the Ur-intertext. Here the
connection with Robert Louis Stevenson's 1886 novella *The Strange
Case of Dr Jekyll and Mr Hyde* is both crucial and explicit (as in Sassoon's
citing his own Jekyll and Hyde performance, quoted above). It gives
literary shape to Prior's fugue states, during which he is violent (and
a reference to Jack the Ripper, the unidentified serial killer of prostitutes in London in 1888, adds suggestiveness to that violence); Sheryl
Stevenson points to a scene in which Prior and Rivers actually discuss
Jekyll and Hyde; Rivers discourages Prior from identifying with that
story but goes on to think about his own deeply divided nature: 'in
the central chapter of Pat Barker's *The Eye in the Door* (and thus at the
center of the Regeneration trilogy), this scene provokes our awareness
of reading characters who are engaged in analysis, both psychoanalytic and literary. They are simultaneously "reading" themselves as they
interpret a fictional text [...].'[24]

In *Reciprocal Haunting*, Karen Patrick Knutsen highlights the importance of Lt Manning, and not just because of his relationship with Prior
(and, elsewhere on the social scale, with people like Winston Churchill
[1874–1965, the Minister of Munitions in 1917 and hence Billy's ulti-
mate superior] and Edward Marsh [1872–1953, a longtime Churchill
associate also working in the Ministry]—in other words Manning
functions as a sort of intermediary between Billy Prior's working-class
status and the ruling men of the kingdom). Manning is also important because 'his surname connects him with another writer from the

Great War, Frederic Manning, who published one of the few fictional accounts of the war that centred on the experiences of the private soldier at the front rather than on the experiences of the subaltern or officer'.[25] Manning's book was originally published in 1929, anonymously and in a limited edition, with the title *The Middle Parts of Fortune*; in 1930 an expurgated version appeared, called *Her Privates We*. Both titles allude to the speech of Rosencrantz and Guildenstern in *Hamlet*, Act II, Scene 2, and turn on bawdy puns, particularly relevant in this case, the soldiers at the centre of the novel being privates. Moreover, Barker probably intends to echo 'privates' as genitals, since her trilogy not only includes much sexuality but much experience of, or anxiety about, castration or genital wounding, including at least one patient who fantasizes the theft of his penis. Stevenson also relates the Prior–Manning relationship to *Maurice*, a tale of homosexual love written by E. M. Forster (1879–1970) around the time of World War I but published only in 1971, after his death (and, it is worth noting, *Maurice* was considered to have been inspired by Edward Carpenter, a touchstone character in Barker's book).

Most assessments of *The Eye in the Door* have been strongly positive, some of them naming it Barker's best book. Some negative assessment comes from Jim Shepard, who critiques occasions when the novel's 'pedagogic impulse, usually smoothly subterranean, surfaces', times when characters seem pressed to represent classes or social movements, and the use of historical personages as 'celebrity walk-ons'.[26] Richard Bradford is suspicious of Barker's anachronism in attitudes:

> ■ One cannot wonder if she slightly overplays this opportunity for revisionism. Prior's alliance with the pacifists veers toward a heavy-handed polemic, constantly promoting the rubric that no-one wanted the war and, given the opportunity, most would have stopped it by refusing to participate. Persistent reference to Prior's sexuality gives one further cause to suspect that the novel is more a prismatic reconstruction of the period according to late twentieth-century expectations than a sympathetic attempt to recover the truth.[27] (101) □

And taking almost exactly the opposite tack, Robert Boyers challenges Barker's failure to do *more* with other anti-war characters, and declares that 'Barker draws these figures with characteristic vividness, but makes no effort whatsoever to get inside them or to account for their conviction. That they have conviction is clear; no one disputes their honesty or willingness to suffer for their pacifism. But it is also clear that Barker does not wish to take seriously their pacifism or to think through the political consequences of a principled opposition to this one war in particular.'[28]

Boyers seems to demand something that Barker has been quite explicit in rejecting—that she invent for her historical figures facts and beliefs that she cannot know about them. Different novelists observe different decorums in using real characters in fiction: in *The Public Burning* (1977), to cite an extreme case, the American novelist Robert Coover (1932–) turned American President Richard Nixon (1913–94) into a first-person narrator and involved him in a love affair with the atomic spy Ethel Rosenberg (1915–53), later executed. Barker is much more judicious in what she will do with her real personages, and her practice would preclude assigning them political convictions that history or biography does not justify.

Some of these cavils are like those that have been made about Barker's use of the War since she initiated the trilogy with *Regeneration*, especially the critique that she retrojects contemporary ideas, theories, and understandings—Freudian, feminist, postmodernist, or others— back onto the materials of 1917. But most reactions have been more in harmony with those of Eileen Battersby, the veteran commentator for *The Irish Times*, who insisted that each of the three novels should have won the Booker Prize, attesting to her satisfaction when that award did finally go to Barker for the final novel in the trilogy, *The Ghost Road*.[29]

CHAPTER SIX

The Ghost Road (1995)

The Ghost Road rounds out the *Regeneration* trilogy. It both continues the themes and narrative arcs of the first two volumes and differs from them in some very significant ways. Billy Prior is unmistakably the most important Old Craiglockhartean here, though of course Dr Rivers figures impressively, too. Siegfried Sassoon fades into a less important position, mostly seen in second-hand reports; Wilfred Owen becomes more central, in part because Prior and Owen serve in the same unit at the front, both take part in the same battle (the doomed attempt to throw a force across the Sambre–Oise canal, in November 1918, that is, just as the war is drawing to an end), and both die there: Prior witnesses Owen's death. Lt Manning, Prior's homosexual partner of *The Eye in the Door*, is here, too, as is Billy's girlfriend, Sarah Lumb, who has now become his fiancée. The reader sees Rivers involved in the treatment of various traumatized officers, suffering from complaints like hysterical paralysis or a belief, held by one officer, that his penis has been stolen; fortunately there is none of the harrowing electro-shock treatment by Dr Yealland, as presented at unsettling length in *Regeneration*.

What distinguishes this novel from its predecessors, aside from its relative finality (finality in encompassing the deaths of Owen and Prior; in bringing the war to a point where everybody knows it is soon going to be over; in delivering an ambiguous but vivid statement from a horribly wounded officer that 'It's not worth it')? One feature is a much greater interest in Rivers's anthropological work, including particularly his time in Eddystone, his companionship with a man called Njiru and his thoughts on death in Melanesia. These reveries, fuelled by a fever, inter-weave with the 'present day' events of the war and the treatment of its injured. The juxtaposition has clear thematic purposes: the Melanesian culture is a warlike culture, with deadly raids and headhunting consti-tuting important and possibly even health-giving aspects of men's lives. Their killing is 'normal', thus interrogating the normality of the war which is killing millions in Europe. There is also considerable attention devoted to Rivers's childhood and youth, including his family relationship with C. L. Dodgson ('Lewis Carroll'), already introduced in *Regeneration*, who tells the young boy that '*Boys are a mistake*' (26).

In part because of the greater proportion of the narrative devoted to Rivers's past, in part because of the determination to combine events on the home front with developments on the Western Front, in part because, as the final novel in the trilogy, *The Ghost Road* has some summing-up duties to take care of, it has a looser structure than its predecessors, especially *Regeneration*. This is partly owing to the incorporation of Billy Prior's diary, large stretches of which (written after he returns to the war) alternate with narrative portions mostly about Rivers. Prior, who has never been presented as any sort of writer before, comments on his own abilities; when the journal begins, in chapter 7, his first entry includes this comment: 'I bought it for the marbled covers and the thick creamy pages and ever since then the thick creamy pages have been saying, Piss off, what could *you* possibly write on *us* that would be worth reading?' (107). Yet he proves a very able writer, aided in part by Barker's giving him intertextual echoes of which he is presumably unaware—for instance, 'Facts are what we need, man. Facts' (107; echoing Dickens's *Hard Times,* 1854); 'Only the names meant anything. Mons, Loos, the Somme, Arras, Verdun, Ypres' (257; an echo of Hemingway's *A Farewell to Arms*); and an account of a gas attack, with men 'flailing about in green light' (180), that alludes to Owen's 'Dulce et Decorum Est' (a poem of 1917, ironically challenging a famous line from Horace's third ode, 'Dulce et decorum est pro patria mori' [Sweet and fitting it is to die for one's country]).

Barker provides Prior with copious self-consciousness in his role as writer, even a sort of metacritical awareness, as when he writes in his journal about the great number of writers among the officers:

> ■ I look up and down the dormitory and there's hardly a sound except for pages being turned, and here and there a pen scratching. It's like this every evening. And not just letters either. Diaries. Poems. At least two would-be poets in this hut alone.
>
> Why? You have to ask yourself. I think it's a way of claiming immunity. First-person narrators can't die, so as long as we keep telling the story of our own lives we're safe. Ha bloody fucking Ha. (115) □

Of course (as his mocking laughter reminds us) first-person retrospective narrators ordinarily do have this immunity, but narration through diaries, like narration through letters, provides no guarantee of the narrator's survival (as Prior's death reminds the reader).

The links between the Prior sections and the Rivers sections are multiple. Of course, Rivers has been Prior's physician. He immediately thinks, when he reads the newspaper headline 'SHEER FIGHTING. Both sides pay the price. Huns wait for the bayonet' (203), that Prior would have been in the battle. The book includes one letter from Prior to Rivers, written a day or so before his death, in which he refers to the central paradox of the warrior (something like the 'Catch-22' of the 1961 novel of that title by Joseph Heller, 1923–99): 'in my present situation the only sane thing to do is to run away, and I will not do it. Test passed?' (254). Prior's comment on the battle ground, 'Fifty years from now a farmer'll be ploughing these fields and turn up skulls' (240), links to Rivers's Melanesian experiences—for instance, 'They were invited to witness the placing of Ngea's skull in the skull house' (205)—and then to Rivers's shock when Hallet, mortally wounded, turns up in his hospital: 'A skull stared out at him' (230). Hallet himself links Prior and Rivers, since Hallet, who is in Prior's unit, is horribly wounded (shot through the face and cranium) in an attack; Prior helps to drag him back to the lines, though he knows his survival is impossible, and is recommended for the Military Cross. Back in England, Rivers provides the translation to Hallet's horrifying repeated outcry, as he is dying, 'Shotvarfet.'

The ending provides a splendid example of how Barker's braiding of the various strands works. Lieutenant Hallet, horribly wounded in the head, cries out 'Shotvarfet,' and Prior interprets this as 'It's not worth it' (274); with Hallet's father despairingly insisting that it *is* worth it, the process reaches its conclusion: 'And then suddenly it was over. The mangled words faded into silence, and a moment or two later, with an odd movement of the chest and stomach muscles like somebody taking off a too tight jumper, Hallet died' (275). Short break: then the scene at the Sambre–Oise canal, the battle on 4 November 1918, one week before the war's end, where the Manchesters have been mowed down and Owen and Prior have lost their lives, though they are unmentioned in this rather beautiful tableau: 'On the edge of the canal the Manchesters lie, eyes still open, limbs not yet decently arranged, for the stretcher-bearers have departed with the last of the wounded, and the dead are left alone' (275). After a bit more description of the scene—the sun is rising—the narrative turns to Rivers, presumably at the same time: 'Grey light tinged with rosy pink seeps in through the tall windows' (276), but though Rivers is physically in London, his spirit is in Eddystone, and he imagines Njiru advancing down the hospital corridor. The penultimate paragraph of the novel sweeps all these dead into one benediction: '*There is an end of men, an end of chiefs, an end of chieftains' wives, an end of chiefs' children—then go down and depart. Do not yearn for us, the fingerless, the crippled, the broken. Go down and depart, oh, oh, oh*' (276).

Other motifs link *The Ghost Road* back to the earlier novels—Oscar Wilde, for instance, is invoked when Prior tells his father that he is engaged; when his father expresses some surprise, apparently knowing of Prior's homosexuality, Prior reminds him that Wilde was married. Billy's molestation by Father Mackenzie, first referenced in *The Eye in the Door*, is more fully explored, including the fact that his rape took place under a picture of St Lawrence's martyrdom and that he soon began charging the priest money for sex, and later charged others. And Billy Prior's attendance, with his fiancée Sarah and her mother, at a séance (called a spuggy) links him with several of the earlier Barker books, particularly *Liza's England*, as well as to Rivers, who flashes back to a ceremony on Eddystone, which he calls a séance.

Lorna Sage commented on the relations between *The Ghost Road* and its predecessors: 'You can read it without having read *Regeneration* or *The Eye in the Door*, because these are novels that cover the same ground again, and again, like the battles their characters replay in memory and nightmares. This produces a powerfully ironic sense of imprisonment in the moment.'[1]

Pat Barker told one interviewer that *The Ghost Road* might well be her best book, though not the one she was fondest of; her favourite was *Regeneration*, which she clearly believed, despite good reviews, had been underappreciated, disappointing in terms of sales, and even unloved.[2] As the trilogy progressed, her books attracted many more and more enthusiastic reviews, as well as the recognition of being nominated for and winning prizes; *The Eye in the Door* won the *Guardian* Book Award, and *The Ghost Road* won the most prestigious fiction award available to a British author, the Booker Prize (originally the Booker-McConnell Prize and, since 2002, the Man Booker Prize).

Eileen Battersby, a veteran fiction reviewer, wrote about *The Ghost Road* twice in three days in *The Irish Times*, praising it at the same time for its vivid and harrowing qualities and for its lyricism. It was, she judged, a fine conclusion to the trilogy; she went on to declare her disappointment that *The Eye in the Door* had not won the Booker, and called *The Ghost Road* the year's outstanding novel. She predicted that it would not win the 1995 Booker Prize—Salman Rushdie's *The Moor's Last Sigh* was widely considered the favourite—but took the occasion to salute the three novels of the *Regeneration* trilogy as among the best novels of the twentieth century.[3] Kate Kellaway also looked back over the trilogy and called its concluding novel Pat Barker's best work. Her analysis of the structure compared it to a plait, in its weaving together of Prior's and Rivers's narratives.[4] Francis Spufford began his review by alluding to a Great War poem written by the Canadian Alan Seeger (1888–1916) and published posthumously, 'I have a rendezvous with death', and said that Barker had kept her rendezvous—presumably by completing the sequence, though Prior and Owen both keep their own rendezvous with death in the final novel. Spufford went on to praise the creation of Billy Prior for its ambiguity and his representation of traumatized masculinity.[5] Lavinia Greenlaw, who has a mixed judgement, overall, of the trilogy, calls *The Ghost Road* 'the most rewarding volume', because compared with its predecessors, it is 'altogether less emphatic, less given to bluster'.[6]

The award of the Booker Prize brought another round of commentary, including yet more praise from Battersby who had now decided that both its predecessors should also have won the Booker.[7] Kenneth Morgan notes that the Booker award to Barker 'emphasized once again how much the historical and cultural consciousness of twentieth-century Britain is dominated by ideas of war'.[8] George Walden (1939–), a Conservative Member of Parliament who chaired the judging panel that awarded her the prize, in his explanation of the decision in an evening newspaper the following day, cited the intelligence and clarity of the novel's style and called it (approvingly) uncomfortable because of its engagement with the terrible destructiveness of war. Like Battersby he recognized the author's ability to combine scenes of violence and suffering with moments of beauty.[9] Two days later Boyd Tonkin took issue with that justification in the *New Statesman*, not exactly denying Barker's suitability for the prize but suggesting that the Conservative politician Walden would have been less enthusiastic about Barker's earlier, pre-Trilogy novels, which by dealing with suffering in *contemporary* Britain would have been much more uncomfortable: 'Only when Barker made her peace with the "heavy industry" of period nostalgia that Walden so detests did the bookish powers that be salute her talent. Her trilogy grapples with just the sort of questions—about masculinity, violence and the [motives] of conflict—that animate her other fiction. But she had to make her own "flight from the present" to be noticed.'[10] Daniel Johnson's report touches on that uncomfortable quality, but instead of violence and destruction he finds the most troubling aspects to be the sex scenes, which he expected some readers to consider superfluous or even pornographic.[11] Derwent May had commented in his review not just on the inclusion of sex scenes but on the expertise with which the author imagines the activities and even sensations of the male member and follows it into surprising places.[12]

In her 2006 essay 'Dreams of Melanesia' Jennifer Shaddock was able to write that little criticism had been focused on *The Ghost Road* until that time.[13] This no longer seems the case, even if it was then. Some of the criticism is, indeed, cumulative or summarizing, treating *The Ghost Road* more as a portion of the trilogy than as an independent novel, but critics have addressed a number of important theoretical and critical issues the novel raises.

USES OF HISTORY

For instance (as in *Regeneration* and *The Eye in the Door*) there is the question of historicity, Barker's use of real history; though perhaps criticism has said much of what there is to say, in dealing with the first two novels. In 'Pat Barker, *The Ghost Road*', Lynda Prescott does approach *The Ghost Road* as a historical novel, and writes about the novelist's use of language: 'the historical novel involves a negotiation between the languages of past and present'.[14] She also notes—though not specifically in the context of the question, repeatedly canvassed elsewhere, of Barker's novels and whether they qualify under Linda Hutcheon's category of 'historiographic metafiction'—that 'Barker uses the terms "fact" and "fiction" in the ordinary, everyday way, as antonyms. However, in the context of written narratives the easy distinction between "fact" and "fiction" is more problematic, and especially so in the case of novels.'.[15] Katherine G. Nickerson and Steven Shea, who call Barker's use of real events a 'vertiginous blend of history and fiction', are less focused than many critics on the events of the war; instead (not surprisingly, as their article appears in *Literature and Medicine*), their focus is on Rivers.[16] They acknowledge the accuracy of Barker's depiction of Rivers in several dimensions, including the admiration he earned from patients and other physicians, but 'less is known about the personal and biographical events that shaped him'.[17] Nevertheless they find plausible Barker's attribution of his stutter, and possibly the repression of his visual memory, to childhood events connected with C. L. Dodgson; and they endorse Barker's suggestion that Rivers is suppressing homoerotic interests in Sassoon and Prior. Patrick Rengger's commentary on Barker's use of history is mostly about characters. He writes that all three novels shift their positions with reference to historical fact, incorporating real and historical characters as well as some whose fictionality is indeterminate, noting that in *The Ghost Road* the central position has been reassigned from the historical Siegfried Sassoon (in *Regeneration*) to the fictional Billy Prior.[18]

SEXUALITY AND GENDER

As for matters of sexuality and gender, *The Ghost Road* continues the examination of manliness, trauma, and hysteria undertaken by its predecessors. An officer afflicted with hysterical paralysis of the legs is troubled by Rivers's treatment—perhaps understandably. Rivers draws stocking-tops about his thighs, planning to move them down each day to restore sensation gradually. The officer, Moffet, finds the image not only feminine but erotic, obscene; the word 'hysteria' is also objected to because of its connection with the uterus. Prior's rapacious bisexual enthusiasm, noted by Eileen Battersby,[19] is shown by the fact that he lusts after an English woman on the second page of the novel (while thinking about Manning) and gives a brutal account of sex with a young French farm boy in one of his last diary entries. Critics have devoted more attention—perhaps disproportionate attention—to the sexuality of Prior, possibly because of his sexual ambiguity or dividedness. Shaddock, for instance, notes that 'Critics have speculated about the homoerotic connection between Rivers, who is single and seemingly asexual, and his bisexual patient, poet Siegfried Sassoon. Notably there has been no such commentary on his bi-racial relationship with the Melanesian Njiru, though the two share arguably the most intimate experience in the trilogy'.[20]

Karen Knutsen assembles the evidence for Rivers's homosexuality, despite his own and the novel's silence about his sexuality. She notes that he is understanding about homosexuality; he is the product of the same social system as the officers he is treating (actually more true of Sassoon than of Owen, who was not a student at a public school or an ancient university, and untrue of Prior); he admits to the suppression of emotion; in his field work he has realized how arbitrary are the conventions of his own society; and he talks about wearing a mask. Having begun with the likelihood that Rivers is homosexual, she then moves to certainty: 'Even though he himself is a repressed homosexual, he inspires confidentiality in his homosexual and bisexual patients Sassoon, Prior and Manning, as if they intuitively know that he, too, is attracted to men.'[21] She believes that Rivers is in love with Sassoon.

What has attracted some attention, including from a number of the book reviewers at the time the novel was published, is the treatment of the sex scenes. In the *New York Times Book Review*, Claudia Roth Pierpont sums up some of the commentary to the effect that the book could have been written by a man, not just because of the conventionally 'male' subject of men in war, but because of the scarcity of female characters, the inaccessibility of their interior lives, the unromantic quality of the many sex scenes, the male point of view from which they are rendered and the candid language with which the novel presents them.[22] As for creating sex scenes from the male point of view, Barker has denied that it presents a particularly difficult challenge to her imagination.[23]

TECHNIQUE

Those sex scenes are an aspect of technique, and much discussion of *The Ghost Road* has dealt with the author's technical choices—in structure, or language, or characterization. The most important structural feature is juxtaposition or alternation, which is more systematic and more noticeable in this book than in its predecessors. Sharon Monteith notes the move from encounters across class divides to encounters across very different cultures, observing how Rivers's memories of his time as an anthropologist, which have occupied little of his attention in the first two novels, loom much larger here, especially in the form of feverish dreams.[24] Patricia Johnson comments on the 'juxtapositioning of Europe and Melanesia' which produces 'some of its most disturbing effects, cutting through the outer surface of European civilization to suggest an inner core of connection in the rituals of headhunting'.[25] The point of this juxtapositioning is complicated; the suggestion that the Melanesians may be suffering from a shortage of opportunities for warfare and killing undercuts any plain anti-war message the book may have. More openly than before, Rivers seems to bring his anthropological training to bear on England, or at least wish to: 'It is difficult, Rivers thought. He could list all the taboo topics on Eddystone, but in his own society it seemed to him the taboos had shifted quite considerably in recent years' (225).

Nick Rennison, in *Contemporary British Novelists*, considers the plaiting unsuccessful: '[...] the irony of the anthropologists condemning the Melanesian tribesmen as "savages" for their headhunting practices when the Western society whose intellectual elite they represent is soon going to embark on mechanized butchery in the trenches seems too obvious [...]. As readers, we feel nudged too knowingly into making the obvious parallels and contrasts.'[26] Lorna Sage defended the technique of juxtaposition and foiling: 'You cut rapidly from document to dream to memory to dialogue. [...] The effect is of spread, not sequence.'[27]

There are other parallels and contrasts, of course, including those between Manning and Sarah, or France (the war) and England (the home front). Knutsen cites an interview in which the author revealed that 'she didn't want to turn the trilogy into a very simple antiwar message. She therefore juxtaposed Hallet's death scene with Rivers' memories from Melanesia'[28]—an explanation which suggests that Rennison may have misunderstood her aims. Shaddock sees the Melanesian scenes not so much as a contrast but as an opening out: 'critics have largely ignored the trilogy's progressively broadened geographical scope, which in the last novel includes not only Great Britain and France, but also Melanesia, one of Great Britain's colonial holdings'.[29]

Barker's mastery of language has been noted by many critics. Kate Kellaway writes at length about Barker's language. She begins by citing Wilfred Owen's famous assertion that 'the poetry is in the pity'—the famous declaration in the preface to his poems, now inscribed on a commemorative stone in Westminster Abbey—and amends it, on

Barker's behalf, by replacing poetry with prose and, more importantly, pity with disgust. In Kellaway's account, Barker's lack of sentimentality precludes pity.[30]

She goes on, as most critics do not, to write that Barker's books also contain comedy. Francis Spufford similarly notes her wit, its accuracy and candour and its combination of horror and paradoxical pleasure;[31] elsewhere he links it to the wit of the war poets, and through them to the frankness of the young officers, for whom avoidance of euphemism or sentimental rodomontade is a gesture against the language that served to hide the realities of the front.[32] Lynda Prescott has written one of the most thorough analyses of *The Ghost Road*. She relates it both to one of Wilfred Owen's letters to his mother, in which he describes a 'strong poetical experience in a wrecked garden', which reminds him of a poem by Percy Bysshe Shelley (1792–1822) called 'The Sensitive Plant', and to Shelley's poem itself, with its 'dark, melancholy mood'. She uses this grounding to address one passage at length, when Hallet, as yet unwounded, undresses in the garden.

> ■ In one arresting phrase—he stepped out of his drawers and out of time—Barker yokes together, through the grammar of her sentence, the prosaic and poetic elements of this scene. So, without ever jeopardizing her down-to-earth novelistic realism, she also manages to incorporate into this passage the 'strong poetical experience' Owen felt, with hints of the mythic qualities of Shelley's poem.[33] □

John Harvey also comments on Barker's style, concentrating on tense. Near the end of the book—and at the end of the lives of Billy Prior and Wilfred Owen—their last battle is narrated. 'This battle, like the whole novel, is narrated in the past tense—but a past tense that is itself *tense* with presentness'; after quoting a paragraph of vivid scenic language, including 'He saw Kirk die. He saw Owen die' (273), he turns to two present-tense paragraphs, beginning on page 275 of the novel: 'On the edge of the canal the Manchesters lie, eyes still open, limbs not yet decently arranged, for the stretcher-bearers have departed with the last of the wounded, and the dead are left alone,' Harvey explains:

> ■ In context this passage is emotionally touching, and part of the movingness comes from the shift to the present tense. They died—they are dead, we see them in front of us still in death (again the visual emphasis). But though they are still the picture moves [...]. In death, the tense of the present instant becomes also the grave tense of the permanent present. Stillness: slow movement: grief: a beauty—the passage demonstrates that a change of tense can speak not only from, but to, the heart.[34] □

Another authorial decision about structure is the use of Billy Prior's diary. This is partly a tactic to permit him to speak in the first person while at the same time not ruling out his eventual death within the pages of the novel. But there are other consequences. Lynda Prescott considers the material character of his diary important: Barker 'goes to some lengths to establish the material form of Prior's diary, written on "thick creamy pages", which will later be shared with his companions when the front-line paper shortage—something Owen mentions in his letters—threatens to interrupt the steady flow of soldiers' writing'.[35] When Prior says that he does not have many pages left, but he has enough, the novel provides a grim foreshadowing of his death. Knutsen makes something different of the diary: 'This foregrounding of a seemingly unmediated, personal voice in diary form offers an alternative reading of the past to the diaries and memoirs of the middle- and upper-class war poets,' but Prior's voice also 'continues to reverberate dialogically with other literary voices'.[36] His self-deprecation, his sarcasm about a hut full of would-be writers, may put some ironic distance between him and the other war writers, though he is serious about his writing, despite his observation that only the names of battles matter.

Twelve years after she completed the *Regeneration* trilogy, after her efforts had been rewarded with the Booker Prize, when she had unmistakably placed herself among the foremost living novelists in Britain, Pat Barker returned to the era of World War I with *Life Class*. At that time she admitted to an interviewer that simply hearing the words 'first world war' usually made her groan.[37] But between 1995 and 2007, she turned away from history to the present day, while continuing to explore important issues of violence, trauma, memory, and inexplicable suffering, starting in 1998 with *Another World*.

CHAPTER SEVEN

The Violence Around Us

ANOTHER WORLD (1998)

When Pat Barker followed the completed *Regeneration* trilogy with *Another World*, it was predictable, indeed inevitable, that her new book would be read and judged in the light of the previous three highly, and increasingly, acclaimed books, the final one of which had won her the Booker Prize and shed unprecedented critical light on her career and interests. She told Elizabeth Renzetti in a 1998 interview that she had worried about becoming stereotyped as a novelist who wrote only about World War I, just as she felt that, before the trilogy, she had been in danger of being stereotyped by her feminist and working-class concerns.[1] And in fact *Another World*, though set in the contemporary world, does not entirely turn away from the war, since one of its three main narrative strands has to do with Geordie, a 101-year-old veteran of the Great War, now dying, and with his memories of the war, and what the war did to him and his companions. There is a broader canvas, or perhaps a triptych, of which Geordie's story forms one wing; in the centre is the story of the uncomfortably blended family of a married couple, Nick and Fran: Nick's daughter Miranda, Fran's son Gareth, and their joint son, two-year-old Jasper. Fran is also pregnant again. The stresses on their family come from the pregnancy and Fran's irritation about it, a move into a new larger home, Gareth's mental instability (wanting only to play video games, terrified of being bullied at a new school, resenting his baby brother to the point of near-murderousness), and Miranda's own unsettled and resentful condition, as her mother (Nick's ex-wife) has been hospitalized for depression. Every member of the family save Jasper is touchy and resentful. Nick is drawn away by the impending death of his grandfather, Geordie, with whom he soon has to begin spending his nights once the old veteran has been sent home from the hospital, clearly to die of the bowel cancer he cannot acknowledge (he believes he is dying of his bayonet wound received on the Somme).

The third wing of the triptych is provided by the turn-of-the-twentieth-century Fanshawe family, who owned the home into which Nick and Fran are moving. The Fanshawes link to the Great War. Their son died at the Somme, which is a byword for pointless carnage, the battle lasting from 1 July to 18 November 1916 and costing some million casualties. And they add to the theme of child-murder, as Nick discovers by reading a book about local crime. The Fanshawes' eleven-year-old son and thirteen-year-old daughter (the ages of Gareth and Miranda) killed their younger brother James, were tried for it and acquitted, but seem nonetheless to have later acknowledged their guilt. Gareth's easy violence against helpless, much younger children parallels the Fanshawe murder; though he stops short of homicide, this is partly just good luck; and Geordie is tormented by the knowledge that he killed his brother Harry—in wartime, it is true, in No Man's Land, while Harry screamed with pain from his disembowelment—but Geordie is haunted by the fear that he may have been moved by envy and resentment of his brother, the favoured one in his family.

Reviewers greeted *Another World* somewhat warily. Eileen Battersby, who had claimed that each of the *Regeneration* trilogy should have won the Booker Prize, wrote that on the evidence of *Another World* Barker was not very imaginative and, while granting her honesty, pointed to moments in the novel where, according to her diagnosis, the author's intelligence outran her artistic ability.[2] Michael Arditti, in *The Independent*, acknowledged the raw emotion of the novel but judged that the different parts remained too unharmonized, and Natasha Walter, in a mostly negative review, agreed that the strands failed to cohere because of the artificiality of the parallels, going on to criticize the plot for clumsiness and the language for lacking energy.[3] In the *New York Times*, Barry Unsworth (1930–2012), a fellow novelist and fellow Booker Prize winner, alongside some perceptive comments on the technical artistry of the novel, complained about what seems Barker's gloomy foregrounding of desolation, which Unsworth appeared to consider the result of contrivance on the author's part to give everything as dismal an aspect as possible.[4] Perhaps Barker was right to be uneasy about the successor to the trilogy.

The connection between *Another World* and the trilogy is a frequent topic in the criticism of the novel. Anne Whitehead identifies it as a transitional book, linking the Great War interests of the trilogy with the child-murderer theme of the following book, *Border Crossing* (129), and she points to the resemblances between Geordie's conversations with Helen and Billy Prior's with Rivers.[5] John Brannigan goes so far as to call it almost a supplement to the trilogy, because it continues exploring the war's residual trauma, though he goes on to point out that it is less interested in psychoanalysis.[6] Katie Trumpener finds another connection: 'Another World (1998) is conceived at once as a modest, private, domestic drama and as a metacommentary on the reconstructive, memorializing project of Barker's earlier novels. [...] [It] is set in the present but haunted by a dying World War I veteran, for whom the traumas of battle are still vividly present.'[7]

Other critics connect it with earlier works in the Barker canon. Sharon Monteith links Geordie to Frank in Liza's England but notes the difference that Geordie has no belief in religion or even spiritualism to console him.[8] Nick Hubble also makes the connection with Liza's England. In that book, Stephen recognizes that the big house in which he rents a small flat is the former home of the capitalists for whom Liza worked: 'This same idea, of a Victorian past underwriting a modern present, was treated rather differently by Barker 12 years earlier'— perhaps because there it was an interesting fact but in Another World, with the house's legacy of fratricide and obscene painting, it stands for more. Hubble also connects Nick's visit to the battlefields of the war alongside Geordie, which the novel calls Geordie's attempt 'to graft his memories onto Nick' (74), to the 'inter-generational transition' that occurred between Liza and Stephen in Liza's England.[9]

History

Analysis of the novels of the trilogy often focused on Barker's use of history, her representation of 'real' events, the question of how accessible objective truth is for the artist. Though the facts of the war are less important here, aside from the sheer mad destructiveness of the Somme—a regular trope in much English writing that includes or even just mentions the war—and Geordie is an imaginary character, there is still a relationship to history, in this case contemporary or very recent. A number of critics have touched on the connection between this book and real murders. Heather Nunn and Anita Biressi, in 'In the Shadow of Monstrosities' (2005), connect it to

> ■ iconic figures—[Mary] Bell, the young girl who killed two small boys in 1968; Sutcliffe, the serial killer of women in the 1970s and early 1980s [i.e. the Yorkshire Ripper, part of the background to the fictional Blow Your House Down]; the boys Venables and Thompson, who were filmed leading two-year-old James Bulger to his death in the early 1990s; and the Wests, whose systematic sexual abuse and serial killing of young women came to light in the early 1990s [...].[10] □

Many critics remark on the connection with the Mary Bell and Jamie Bulger crimes. Suzie Mackenzie, who writes about the inspiration of the Bulger murder and even more those committed by Mary Bell, paraphrases Pat Barker on truth and objectivity, their crucial but problematic status. The author maintains that objective truth exists—somewhere—and that you must seek to capture it, since human beings can only build an identity on the past, and therefore on an objective perception of the past. She acknowledges how difficult if not impossible it is to obtain secure knowledge of the past, against the obstacles presented by forces which busily distort it.[11]

All these violent events from late twentieth-century history are specifically (though impressionistically) invoked in the beginning of the novel, when Nick tries to persuade himself not to worry about Miranda:

■ But then, like everybody else, he lives in the shadow of monstrosities. Peter Sutcliffe's bearded face, the number plate of a house in Cromwell Street [the home of Fred and Rosemary West, where they murdered ten girls], three figures smudged on a video surveillance screen, an older boy taking a toddler by the hand while his companion strides ahead, eager for the atrocity to come. (3) □

Beyond the murders, Anne Whitehead has identified the original inspiration for the Fanshawe family, which she says is 'loosely based' on Lord Armstrong, a munitions manufacturer who retired to Cragside House, a stately home echoed in Fleete House, to which Nick and Fran take a family outing in the novel.[12] As many critics have noted, and the author has stated, her novels are about the way the past haunts the present; that the past is in some ways inaccessible, that many forces make it difficult to attain objective knowledge about the past—for instance, Geordie cannot know if he killed Harry selflessly or selfishly—makes the need terrible. John Brannigan, who identifies the subject of the novel, like *Border Crossing*, as the Bulger murder, has a different view of Barker's realism, which he sees as greatly complicated by her use of symbolism, and he goes on to compare her to Joseph Conrad (1857–1924) and Kate Chopin (1850–1904), two of the best known early twentieth-century practitioners of symbolist fiction.[13] He continues by arguing that representation is an aesthetic as well as an ethical problem even more than in earlier novels.

Technique

Brannigan's observations on Barker's use of symbolism, including 'neo-modernist symbols and devices' foreground the author's technique.[14]

Critics have been divided on its success, particularly the braided stories and the style. Michael Arditti complained that the strands remained too incoherent, and Eileen Battersby makes a similar objection, arguing that the Geordie strand dominates the others and once his story begins it redirects the reader's attention from the problems of Nick and his family.[15] By contrast, Nunn and Biressi appreciate the artfulness of the combination of strands, though they change the metaphor: 'different temporal worlds overlap like the circles in Venn diagrams producing strange spaces of convergence, echo, and repetition', inviting readers to recognize 'the almost inexpressible connections and tensions between cause and effect, determinism and individual agency, and contingency and predestination'.[16] They consider that the novel's coincidences link 'the Fanshawes, the Bulger case, and the contemporary dwellers of Lob's Hill'—that is, the former Fanshawe home, the house into which Nick's family has moved.[17] And Anne Whitehead acknowledges that the book can be accused of failure to integrate the World War I story with the 'theme of child murder. However, the concept of dissociation provides the unifying subject matter of the novel.'[18] And Catherine Bernard relates the present and past narratives through the exposure of the past as Nick and his family peel off wallpaper and expose the family portrait of the Fanshawes: 'For a brief, uncanny moment "the living stand and gaze at the dead". The trauma of the First World War inverts that relation. The dead stand and gaze at the living.'[19]

Beyond symbolism, to which Brannigan devotes considerable attention, critics notice the narration of the story—that is, the main story, exclusive of the interpolated texts like Geordie's recorded memoirs and the printed story of the Fanshawe murder—in the present tense. To what effect? Eileen Battersby thinks that it works to intensify the tense atmosphere; Barry Unsworth calls it vivid but considers it less adequate to moments of reflection than of action; Sharon Monteith links it to Geordie's being arrested in time and cites it as a cause of the disturbing atmosphere of the novel.[20]

Intertextuality

As is usually the case with Barker's novels, there is an intertextual dimension or layer alongside the incorporation of historical fact. The most frequently cited intertext is Henry James's novella *The Turn of the Screw* (1898), which, like *Another World*, features ghostly apparitions and ambiguous childhood evil. The novelist Julie Myerson named James's novel as a way of identifying Barker's artistic territory and specified thematic links including irresponsible children and threat.[21] In 'North-East Gothic' (2007), Sarah Gamble quotes a passage in which Gareth stares down from an upstairs window of Lob's Hill and comments: 'Although this latter allusion is not as obviously marked, this evokes the spectre of another Gothic text, Henry James's *The Turn of the Screw*—a text, it is worth noting, published in the same year as Lob's Hill was built, and one which forms a cornerstone of Barker's own narrative construction,' including Gareth's re-enactment of the surveillance central to James's story.[22] Anne Whitehead adds another intertext: Freud's '"Beyond the Pleasure Principle" [published in 1920], a key moment in the theorizing of trauma, for her portrait of Geordie [...]'.[23] In 'Memory and Literature: The Case of Pat Barker's *Another World*' (2005), Maria Holmgren Troy also credits Freud, though more generally, particularly on the psychological theory of memory. Later she invokes Nick Carraway, the narrator of *The Great Gatsby* (1925) by F. Scott Fitzgerald (1896–1940), triggered by their identical names, though when she goes on to reason that because Nick Carraway is an unreliable narrator then Barker's Nick is also possibly unreliable, the parallel suffers since this Nick is not a narrator.[24] Another connection is with the Gothic novel, via the mechanism of ghosts and the disturbing large house. James's story is a Gothic construction. Others noticed are *Jane Eyre* (1847) (by John Brannigan) and *Wuthering Heights*, according to which Anne Whitehead finds Miranda's assimilating a carving above the lintel of Lob's Hill to Brontë's novel a sign of hauntedness. In 'It Happened Once... It can Happen Again' (2011), Judith Seaboyer considers that the last lines of *Wuthering Heights*—which predict no further trouble from two troubled but now dead lovers—'parallel those of *Another World*'.[25] As for the meaning of these Gothic resonances, most critics take them as deepening the mood of evil, of hauntedness, though John Brannigan believes that the analogies which are evoked by the Gothic plot elements are in fact false and, in a metafictional move, redirect the reader to the qualities that make *Another World* a historical novel.[26] And Sharon Monteith calls attention to Fran's saying 'it's nobody's fault' and detects there an intertextual reference to Dickens's *Little Dorrit* (1855–7), whose original title was *Nobody's Fault*.[27] Two further intertexts deserve mention: one is William Faulkner's Nobel Prize address of 1949, which is echoed in the statement that 'Geordie's past isn't over. It isn't even the past' (241) and in Wilfred Owen's 'Dulce et Decorum Est', unmistakably invoked when the dying Geordie grapples with Nick: 'He's floundering like a man in mud or fire' (161).

Class

Another feature to be sought, and almost always found, in all of Pat Barker's novels is a commentary on class. On first glance, *Another World* seems unpromising in this respect, since all the important people except

Geordie are solidly middle-class: Nick is an academic and his family is prosperous enough to buy the former home of an industrial magnate. Judith Seaboyer, however, relates it to other Barker novels as a 'tale of transgressive border crossings'' and continues that Barker's 'critique of class and gender and twentieth-century Britain is as realist as it is materialist'.[28] This may slightly resemble the effort of Helen, Nick's historian colleague who takes Geordie's testimony, who tried to get him to talk about class, justice, privilege, profiteering, and homoeroticism: 'She tried to get Geordie to frame his war experience in terms of late-twentieth-century preoccupations. Gender. Definitions of masculinity. Homoeroticism. Homo-*what*? asked Geordie. Helen, with her Oxford first.' (83). Indeed this list of contemporary preoccupations back-dated to World War I sounds wittily like some of the criticisms of Barker's trilogy. In fact the class analysis of the novel gets not much further than the discussion of profiteering by the rich, and suffering and dying by the poor. Brannigan contrasts the novel with the class analysis of more politically engaged writers, who typically assign blame to those who send the soldiers to fight and die rather than to the soldiers themselves (an analysis dating back to Sassoon and Owen). This theory is partially supported by Barker's ascribing to the older Fanshawe the use of the bitter lines '*If any question why we died, Tell them, because our fathers lied*' (277), written by Rudyard Kipling (1865–1936) after his son was killed at the battle of Loos, but since they mark the graves of both Robert Fanshawe, killed at the Somme, and James Fanshawe, killed by Robert and his sister, the lesson is complex. Brannigan points out that the guilt goes beyond the masters of war. Anne Whitehead endorses the traditional engaged belief, saying that (in Barker's implication) Geordie is less guilty of Harry's death, though he killed him, than are the munitions makers, like Fanshawe.[29] The Kipling lines bring in the theme of filicide and are thus linked to Rivers's meditations on Abraham and Isaac in *Regeneration*; as Gamble says, the book provides 'a phantasmagoric haunting along the lines proposed by Abraham, the result of which is the "endless repetition" of the same crime down the generations', though filicide is varied with fratricide and approaches to it, as well as thoughts of patricide and matricide.[30]

Gender and Sexuality

More promising than class, perhaps, is the treatment of gender and the larger matter of the family. The somewhat surprising feature of gender is the imbalance between male and female characters. Sharon Monteith comments on the removal to the background of Fran, Barbara, Miranda and Frieda, whom one might expect to find at the centre of a family drama.[31] Gamble similarly comments on the focus on male characters, ranging from young to old (Gareth–Nick–Geordie) and explains them as representatives of the 'late modern family, in which masculine identity and authority are placed under threat both inside and outside the house'.[32] Presumably this refers to Nick's somewhat baffled relations with his pregnant wife, as well as Gareth's being beaten up and sexually humiliated by a group of older girls. Margaretta Jolly does comment on the significance of Fran's pregnancy, which she finds similar to Geordie's death: 'It is no surprise that Barker portrays the pregnancy in witheringly unromantic terms: ugly, painful, even morbid, her stomach "a bag of drowning kittens"' [...] Significantly, the one difference between the uncanny mural of the Victorian family and their modern-day counterparts is that the ghostly mother is not pregnant.'[33] The mural is uncanny because it seems to depict the current occupants of the house in an upsetting way. And Miranda's importance is insisted on by David Waterman as she links to Muriel Fanshawe, sees ghostly apparitions and apparently tries to smother Jasper.[34]

What of the family? Sharon Monteith argues strongly that the novel is a reply to modern right-wing celebrations of the family, insisting—in the face of the Christian right—on its revelations of cruelty and violence.[35] Powerful diagnoses of what *Another World* tells about the family include Anne Whitehead's somewhat chilling declaration that in this book Barker 'confronts the reader with the cruelty of all children, and the violence that makes up the "dark centre" of every family' and Nunn and Biressi's statement that the family is 'depicted as a space of potential violence, abuse and seething malevolence'; and that children are by no means exempt from responsibility for that malevolence is further explained by Anne Whitehead as follows: 'Through Gareth's violence toward his young brother and his experiences of beatings and humiliations at the hands of other children and through Miranda's nascent sexuality and precocious seriousness, *Another World* reveals children as ambivalent figures, increasingly straddling the child and adult worlds.'[36]

Family violence is inextricably linked to memory, and memory to trauma, in a connection familiar to readers of previous Barker novels, not just the *Regeneration* trilogy but as far back as Kelly Brown's story in *Union Street*. Mike Hepworth refers to this as 'generational consciousness': 'the subjective awareness of the central character of having lived through a series of cataclysmic sociopolitical events', the example of which, in this novel, is trench warfare.[37] But traumatic memory may be less influential on Geordie, despite his brooding on his killing of Harry, than on others who lack his lived experience of cataclysmic events. In 'The Novelist as an Agent of Collective Remembrance' (2007), Maria Holmgren Troy lists a number of earlier books in which memory is an important thread and, though focusing on *Another World*, insists that 'in most (if not all) of Barker's novels, memory and trauma are central; they are linked and interlinked to different kinds of socio-cultural oppression, familial concerns, neglect, abuse, rape, murder, and war'.[38] Memory is embodied in the family portrait at Lob's Hill, though none of those viewing it has any actual memory of the people depicted or the lives they led; Troy suggests, then, that 'the portrait represents a collective of cultural memory that exhibits traumatic aspects of the patriarchal middle-class family'.[39] Nick recognizes Geordie's effort to graft his own memories onto his grandson. Troy comments on the unhealthiness of Nick's building his identity on his grandfather's shaving mirror and finds his inability to recognize himself in it as 'not a sign of illness, but of recovery', a relinquishing of the 'founding trauma' of the war.[40]

This sounds hopeful, and raises the question of the overall direction of the novel. Most critics find it dark, suggesting the eternal recurrence of patterns of violence through generation after generation. John Brannigan says the repetitive structure of trauma implies '*it happened once, therefore it can happen again*'.[41] It is true that the last pages provide a quiet and very partial suggestion of resolution. And Nunn and Biressi provide the most optimistic reading—arguing, more or less, that it happened before but it *need not* happen again: 'the resolution [...] attempts to refute any deterministic model of familial betrayal and violence, insisting on individual autonomy and the adoption of personal responsibility for actions undertaken'.[42]

BORDER CROSSING (2001)

In her next book Barker created what Mark Greif, in 'Crime and Rehabilitation', interestingly called the 'social services procedural': 'a rich rewrite of the police procedural, one of the classic subgenres of the detective novel, in which the novelist renders the nitty-gritty details of police practice and we see how detection is done. [...] Here, in *Border Crossing*, Barker shows the opposite: how the state can work to save a person, to release (rather than catch) a human being.'[43] It is no surprise to readers of Barker's work that *Border Crossing* features crime and cruelty and suffering at its heart. It centres on a *pas de deux* between two men: one, Tom Seymour, a clinical psychologist, the other, Danny Miller (now called, under a new name assigned to him on his release from incarceration, Ian Wilkinson), a young man who at ten years old murdered an old woman. The theme of murderousness in youths is recurrent in Barker's later works: Gareth, in *Another World*, could easily have killed his brother, and a character in the next book, *Double Vision*, also killed as a child and is, in fact, possibly the now adult Danny Miller, provided with another new name. In *Border Crossing* another murder by young boys once again shines the public light on Danny Miller's case. The growing danger of the world—whether a real danger, or more a subjective quality of fearfulness in the public—is tangible in these books. Sharon Monteith's phrase is 'the death of safety in contemporary society'—a phenomenon she connects to the Bulger case.[44]

The title *Border Crossing* (which finds its place in a series of symbolically freighted two-word titles—*Another World*, *Double Vision*, *Life Class*, *Toby's Room*—for Barker's novels since the completion of the trilogy) alludes most centrally to the therapeutic situation and Tom's inability to preserve his boundaries. His guilt—because he testified at Danny's trial and both he and Danny believe he helped the jury decide to convict, though Danny denied the crime—leads him, once they meet again at the beginning of the book, to try to help Danny. (He is also writing a book on children with conduct disorder, but his motives for helping Danny, while confused, seem largely unselfish.) The narrative rather insists on the repeated border crossings; Danny's parole officer, for instance, reflects on her indecisiveness about his rehabilitation: 'As they waited for the car to pass, she was aware that a line had been crossed in her thinking about him' (69). Tom learns that a teacher in Danny's school had become over-involved (in love with him, even) and had to be dismissed: the head reports 'He was ... totally committed. Good degree, good references, but no experience, no ... sense of danger, I was going to say, but that's not the right word. [...] He ended up poddling about in things he wasn't qualified to deal with' (126). Late in the novel, as Danny's newly assigned disguise is being penetrated, he comes to Tom's house for help, 'and yet Tom was aware of a line being crossed' (165). One of the reviews, written by the physician Dr Harvey Bluestone, expounded on all this crossing:

> ■ A plethora of borders are crossed in this book: the border between illness and evil, or 'mad or bad'; the border between classes; and the ocean between practice in England and the United States. However, the most troublesome borders crossed are those of the therapist Tom and his patient Danny. [...] he uses Danny to fill the loneliness in his life caused by the end of his marriage, and to try to work out his own problems, and he makes little effort to separate his personal life from that of his patient.[45] □

Dr Bluestone goes on to note with disapproval that Tom more than once gives Danny alcohol. In an interview Barker revealed that she saw Tom, and her other therapists, as representatives of the novelist, since both professions—therapy and fiction-writing—require their practitioners to maintain a balance (or perhaps a border) between too much involvement and too much detachment, adding that mediums, of which her fiction contains many, also stand for the novelist.[46]

Bluestone is astute on most of the borders he mentions, but the point that he makes about classes is odd, in that almost all the people in *Border Crossing* are middle class—professionals, like Tom, his wife Lauren (an art teacher in London), various hospital and legal administrators, and even, arguably, Danny Miller, who, though he lived on a chicken farm, is the son of an army officer and in the present day of the book is reading English at a university. The setting—Newcastle, much of it in decay—is reminiscent of earlier works like *Union Street*, but far from being populated mostly by working-class men and women, this novel features very few. In 'Fire and Water in *Border Crossing*' (2011), Mary Trabucco finds the setting significant, in that 'the derelict urban landscapes of post-industrial England are a kind of traumatic blockage that cannot be narrativized'.[47]

Therapy

Analysing the novel by reference to the trilogy, Julie Wheelwright contrasted Tom with Dr Rivers, unfavourably, in that Tom lacks distance and, unlike Rivers, cannot maintain what Tom himself insists is necessary: 'the clinician's splinter of ice in the heart' (12), that is, detachment—in other words, observing borders.[48] Mary Morrissey considered *Border Crossing* the obverse of the *Regeneration* trilogy, insofar as in the trilogy Barker shone light on Dr Rivers's humane treatment of traumatized men despite the opposition of the medical profession, while in *Border Crossing* Barker raised questions about the professionalizing of both therapy and the criminal justice system.[49] Richard Eder also used the *Regeneration* trilogy as a touchstone, declaring that *Border Crossing* was a lesser work, in part because of its greater bleakness. Anna Burnside seems to concur, calling both *Border Crossing* and *Another World* inferior to *Regeneration* in breadth, though she goes on to cite similar themes and the author's fearlessness.[50] Trabucco relates it, via 'the interaction between language, psychoanalysis, and history', back to both *The Eye in the Door* and *Liza's England*.[51] And Sharon Monteith connects the murderousness of Danny Miller to the disturbing incidents of Barker's fiction in books beginning as early as *Union Street*.[52]

In her *New York Times* review, Michiko Kakutani acknowledges the author's absorption in what people make, or mismake, of history and the hold the past exerts on the present, but is unimpressed with *Border Crossing*, writing that Barker takes her plot from the thriller genre, but does so inartfully—that her manipulation of the parallels between Tom and Danny is forced.[53]

As Tom's profession, the mainspring of the plot, and Barker's comments make clear, she is concerned here, as in some previous works, with the theory of therapy. As Sharon Monteith cautions, she is 'interested in therapy but refuses to represent it as a panacea for society's ills'.[54] In fact, whether Tom's therapeutic attentions to Danny Miller have any palliative effect at all is unclear. Mary Trabucco mentions the 'tarnishing of sympathetic imagination by complicity'[55]; and Richard Restak, himself a psychiatrist, sums up what seems to be its failure: therapy should seek to change the patient—in this case, Danny Miller—but the process in *Border Crossing* seems reversed, since Tom, not Danny, is the one who changes. This replicates the situation in *The Ghost Road*, where Rivers seems to change more than his ostensible analysand, Billy Prior. Restak diagnoses the reason, which is that Danny has created a situation in which, if Tom refuses to bend the rules—to cross sensible boundaries—on Danny's behalf, this is construed (by them both) as 'betrayal'. But this ignores Danny's own earlier, much more serious betrayal—killing Lizzie Parks, the murder of which he is guilty, but which somehow keeps being elided in the therapeutic transaction.[56]

It should be noted that in addition to Tom Seymour's professional inclination toward sympathy, and his guilt over what may seem a past betrayal, there may be other reasons for his over-involvement in Danny's life and what is ostensibly, at the most optimistic interpretation, his 'recovery'. Tom's mistake, if that is what it is, derives at least in part from his belief in the possibility of rehabilitation (presumably a belief without which his profession would be pointless). But does rehabilitation work? Sharon Monteith's pessimistic reading of the end of the novel (in which Danny, renamed again, is studying English at another university and enjoying the companionship of friends who have no idea what he has done) is starker than John Brannigan's and perhaps Mary Trabucco's, who at least considers it a 'radically open-ended' resolution; among the possible readings is that Danny has 'managed to turn [Tom] into an accomplice through a symbolic transfer of guilt'.[57] The last page of the book, after all, has Tom looking at the new Danny Miller and telling himself 'He was looking at success. Precarious, shadowed, ambiguous, but worth having nevertheless. The only possible good outcome' (214–15); but in the next two paragraphs, he thinks about Lizzie Parks, the old woman Danny killed. Is this a good outcome? Mark Greif discusses this at length, insisting that 'The principles most at stake in *Border Crossing* are the liberal belief in rehabilitation and in what is called "moral perception".'[58] He goes on to describe what he calls the 'liberal conception of the criminal', one in which there are bad acts but not bad people (a formulation Tom Seymour himself employs), crime is produced by environment, and hence treatment is preferred to punishment. Waterman explains, 'If Tom distinguishes between different forms of guilt, qualified levels of innocence, he is only doing what is considered normal in modern Western society.'[59] But Greif considers that too simple: 'the novel's complex take on bad deeds and a "bad" self also makes successful rehabilitation—especially after the most brutal, baffling, and unmotivated of crimes—that much harder to imagine'.[60]

By contrast with previous books, not much criticism of *Border Crossing* has focused on Barker's technique—Kakutani's complaints about plotting aside—or on the question of the real and representation. Richard Eder did praise the novel for the exciting quality of its prose and for investigating serious moral issues;[61] and in 'Family at War' (2005) Eluned Sumners-Bremner, somewhat obscurely, judged that both *Another World* and *Border Crossing* border on what critics have not quite found the courage to call, in the work of a Booker Prize-winning author, a sort of realist failure.'[62]

DOUBLE VISION (2003)

In an interview given on the publication of *Border Crossing*, Pat Barker told Elizabeth Grice that her next book would be about child evac-uees of the Second World War.[63] Whatever came of that idea, the next book did deal with areas of extremity and with war, but it was set in a contemporary milieu, in northern England, and had as its two main characters Kate Frobisher, a female sculptor whose husband Ben, a war photographer, has recently been killed, and Stephen Sharkey, a war reporter who was Ben's friend and colleague in covering wars and disasters. Even more than in her earlier books, *Double Vision* surrounds the main characters (who live in an apparently peaceful rural area) with violence and monstrosities. The 'cull' of animals required by the 2001 epidemic of foot and mouth disease is going on—they are killed, then burned on all sides of the village—one of the characters has lost her beloved sheep to it and there are visible pyres all around. The 11 September 2001 attack on the World Trade Center is featured, since both Ben and Stephen were in New York and Ben faced an ethical crisis about representing what he saw. The trial of Slobodan Milosevic (1941–2006, former president of the Republic of Serbia) for war crimes in Bosnia during the war of 1992–5 features, since Stephen goes to the Netherlands to cover it, as he has covered the war itself; Israeli tanks are bombarding a Palestinian town; and one of the main characters is herself subjected to a violent attack, while another is a former child murderer, possibly Danny Miller. Symbolically broadening the canvas is a discussion of Goya's 'Disasters of War' prints of the 1810s, one of which is in a museum nearby; more important than what they show is what Goya's language, in the titles he gave some of the most vivid prints, says: 'One cannot look at this', 'I saw it', and 'This is the truth' (100). These words also constitute the epigraph of the novel.

As in *Border Crossing*, Barker has turned her attention to middle-class characters: a reporter, a sculptor, a vicar, a physician, his wife the hospital administrator; there is also a mysterious man named Peter Wingrave, more unplaceable, like Danny Miller. And much suggests that he *is* Danny Miller, now given another new name. He read English at a university (which Danny is doing at the end of *Border Crosing*); he did a creative writing course, like Danny Miller (some of his fiction is shared here, and it is chilling); he has been in prison and is now on a rehabilitative scheme. His crime, which for some time is kept secret as part of the non-judgemental reclamation process, is revealed to have been the murder, when he was ten, of an old woman who surprised him as he was robbing her house. Though Maya Jaggi simply identifies Peter as Danny with a new identity, Ellen Warner more cautiously writes only that he *seems* to be the same person—though she compares him to Billy Prior, who is a recurrent character—and the novel leaves this question (like some others) unanswered.[64]

Neil Gordon's review of the novel placed it in a summary of Barker's career. He described the movement, in her ten novels (to that date), from the slums of north-western England (actually north-eastern) to the educated professionals who populate her later novels. Gordon argued that this moved from the sufferings and violence consequent on poverty to the sufferings of the class to which she had turned, but whichever demographic population she wrote about, her books described a world rich in violence and injury.[65]

Maya Jaggi, like Neil Gordon and many reviewers and critics, used the new novel as a way of summing up its author's career to date and listed, as pervasive themes, trauma and redemption; and the past and its influence, usually baleful, on the present. Rosemary Goring, similarly retrospective, referred to the *Regeneration* trilogy and the struggles of its soldiers, and to *Border Crossing* and the Danny Miller crime, and wrote that *Double Vision* linked together these two fictional realms—that is, war, and the (peacetime) phenomenon of people who kill for no apparent reason.[66] The novel may be said to inquire into whether any reason is sufficient, or what permits people to decide that there *is* a sufficient justification. In 'Double Vision: Regeneration or Traumatized Pastoral?' (2005), Sharon Monteith and Nahem Yousaf also link *Double Vision* with its predecessors, saying that it is 'both a departure and a return'; it is a return insofar as the war reporter now stands in for the soldier-poets of the trilogy; it is part of a new strain insofar as, they write, her later fiction recurrently focuses on marriages.[67] (Stephen's marriage has ended, the vicar's wife has left him, and Stephen's brother-in-law Robert is in a tottering marriage.)

Double Vision is another ensemble fiction. It has major and minor characters, but there is no single narrative arc that connects them, and in fact some critics were disturbed by the way it begins with Kate Frobisher but allows her to slide into the background. What links the characters?

Vision

One thing is vision, as the title suggests. Kate and Stephen are both artists—he a writer, she a sculptor. He has seen more, and more troubling, things though she, as the keeper of her husband's photographs, has shared the vision at one remove. One of the novel's most striking moments comes when, looking through Ben's photos, Stephen comes across a picture of a dead rape victim that the two of them had seen in Sarajevo, the capital of Bosnia and scene of some of the worst horrors of the war; her situation has haunted Stephen ever since, and finding that Ben had returned the following day (after they had jointly decided that photographing her would be too intrusive and callous) and taken her photo raises the same questions of what it is permissible to represent that have, in part, ended his reporting career, once again evoking Goya's 'paradoxical' words from 'The Disasters of War'. In 'To See and To Know' (2011), John Brannigan relates this book to its successor, *Life Class*, as an engagement with 'the ethics of vision [...] the violence of seeing [...] the ethical demand to see';[68] Barbara Korte, in 'Touched by the Pain of Others' (2007), makes incisive connections between this novel and the ethics of representation, particularly in the media.[69] Brannigan has also linked the various components of a novel that, in an approach common to many of Barker's novels, employs multiple omniscient views into one consciousness after another through the problem of 'how the subject attends to the other as a subject'.[70]

Violence

The different strands are also linked by the fact or threat of violence, which is all around us, from many sources including terrorism and war as well as crime.[71] And, as Wendy Smith points out, Barker approaches violence and trauma in this novel from 'an intriguing new angle'—'the impact of violence on those who observe it, in particular of those who depict it'.[72] Stephen shrinks from the violence he has observed—an overload of it has caused him to abandon his career as a war reporter—and yet in a crisis, he is capable of employing violence himself. When he interrupts an assault on his young girlfriend Justine, he batters one of the criminals with a statuette, and admits that he tried to kill him. From the other perspective there is Peter Wingrave, released and possibly reformed child murderer. His behaviour in the novel—sneaking into Kate's studio after hours and wearing her clothes while he mimes her sculpting; possibly witnessing her car crash without any effort to help her—makes him a mystery. The novel asks whether Peter is guilty, possibly evil, and if so what makes him so. Even experts cannot say. As Peter tells Stephen, when they discuss his disturbing fictions, 'We all have a dark side' (167). Stephen's nephew is diagnosed with Asperger's disease, or syndrome, a form of autism limiting social interaction; this is described as a failure of empathy, an inability to see other people's personhood, and the novel implies that Adam stands for violent people everywhere, who can commit shocking acts like the rape–murder in Bosnia Stephen keeps remembering, or perhaps the attacks on the World Trade Center, because they cannot empathize.

One dimension to the question of guilt and innocence is its gendered formulation. This is the explicit focus of Marie-Louise Kohlke, who writes, in 'Pathologized Masculinity in Pat Barker's *Double Vision*' (2011), that Barker's 'proliferating limit-cases of extreme male violence, spanning different periods and cultures, come close to demonizing masculinity, imbuing it with an inhuman—or anti-human—diabolical urge to kill and destroy'.[73] Peter's capacity for violence, then, is the demonstration that the only difference between the violent capacities of 'good' and 'bad' men is 'superficial'; Peter stands for all men who can be violent on occasion.[74] Kohlke does conclude, however, that Barker is sympathetic to violent masculinity, which 'poses itself as a kind of unsolvable riddle of alterity'.[75]

One sharp distinction between *Double Vision* and at least the *Regeneration* trilogy is its closer attention to intellectuals and artists. John Brannigan in particular sees it as raising questions about the role of intellectuals and the danger of depending on rationality.[76] Reason is unable to cope with the violence and threat of life; moreover, like so much of Barker's fiction, *Double Vision* includes the irrational or at least the threat of the irrational, in the form of ghosts—or 'ghosts'—which, in Nick Hubble's view, recall the ghosts of past and future that appear to Owen and Sassoon in the trilogy; Brannigan also notes the challenge to rationality presented by hauntings and apparent synchronicities.[77] There are also ghostly apparitions in *Another World*, of course. Also complicating rationalism is the role of religion. This is not a 'religious' novel, but it does have a priest in a prominent role (that role is ineffectual and not very spiritual, but he is a clergyman) and Kate's project throughout the novel is sculpting a Christ for the nearby cathedral. Brannigan identifies the religious themes in the book—including salvation and redemption, the possibility of saving human beings—but clarifies that they are 'understood in thoroughly historicist and humanist terms'.[78] And in another spiritual but not particularly religious manifestation, Stephen and Justine have a strong relationship that is fuelled by good sex. Rosemary Goring comments on this, calling the sex spiritually renewing, and invoking D. H. Lawrence, presumably his *Lady Chatterley's Lover* (1928) in particular.[79]

Critics have paid only modest attention to the form of the novel, aside from noting its movement from one consciousness to another. Monteith and Yousaf do link the alternating perspectives of Kate and Stephen to many previous examples of doubling, including 'Liza and Stephen in *Liza's England*; Rivers and Njiru in *The Ghost Road*; *The Eye in the Door* with *The Strange Case of Dr Jekyll and Mr Hyde*', all of which are 'dialogic exchanges'.[80] There is some of the sort of intertextuality characteristic of the author, though Mark Anthony Jarman may overstate his case when he identifies allusions and symbols linking the novel to *The Waste Land* (1922) by T. S. Eliot (1888–1965), *From Ritual to Romance* (1920) by Jessie Weston (1850–1928), Conrad, Hemingway, A. E. Housman (1859–1936), and the Brontës.[81]

Finally there is the question of the ending of the novel. Wendy Smith quotes the author as saying 'I was hoping for a happy ending, because the book is really about looking at the worst people can do and yet not allowing that to overpower you and distort your life.'[82] As the book ends, Stephen and Justine are on a visit to Holy Island, off the Northumbrian coast. Stephen has been thinking about the death of Ben Frobisher in Afghanistan, and they have been briefly threatened with capsizing in a small boat in the turbulent North Sea—so it is hardly a moment of idyll—but in the last pages the two stand together, skipping stones into the sea.

■ 'There,' he said. 'You see?'
   Then he put his arm around her shoulders and they walked on, half in the water, half on land, while behind them the sun rose above the dunes, casting fine blue shadows of marram grass onto the white sand. (238) □

Unless the throwing of stones at the seaside is meant to arouse troubling memories of Gareth stoning his little brother, at another beach, in *Another World*, this is a quietly positive conclusion, and, as Monteith and Yousaf write, 'key characters have gained distance and perspective on themselves and on the events that have shaken them. Finally it is not redemption or regeneration but self-preservation and adaptation that count in *Double Vision*.'[83]

Violence, trauma, and the threat they pose to persons and psyches are never far from Pat Barker's concerns. Even in the three present-day novels published after the completion of the trilogy, the violence of war is never far away; Geordie's horrific memories in *Another World* were of the Somme and the Western Front in the First World War; Stephen Sharkey lives in the twenty-first century, but has experienced wartime horrors in Bosnia and elsewhere. Only *Border Crossing* has no war. With her next novel Barker would return to the Great War, perhaps the historical period that most energizes her writing, and, in a continuation of the focus on art and representation in *Double Vision*, to art and artists in a time of crisis.

CHAPTER EIGHT

Back to the Front

LIFE CLASS (2007) AND TOBY'S ROOM (2012)

In 2001 Pat Barker told Anna Burnside that she wanted to write another historical novel, but not develop it into a trilogy.[1] She had also expressed some weariness with the subject of the First World War, especially with her own identification, in the public mind, with that subject matter. The historical novel she mentioned to Burnside appeared in 2007, in the form of *Life Class*, which returns to the era of the Great War. And, with its successor *Toby's Room* set in the same period and including the same characters, there is reason to believe in the possibility of another World War I trilogy. Similarities between these two novels and the *Regeneration* trilogy are not hard to find: the obvious one is the war itself, though oddly (since *Life Class* and *Toby's Room* focus on painters, some of whom remain in England and have nothing to do with the war) there is a more harrowing presentation of the horrors of war than in all the trilogy. Again there is a mixture of historical personages and fictional ones. Lady Ottoline Morrell figures here, as she did less prominently in the trilogy, and her visit to Sassoon at Craiglockhart is mentioned; Virginia Woolf and her sister Vanessa Bell (1879–1961) play significant roles; Oscar Wilde (already, or still, dead, of course) is mentioned in connection with the homosexual panic which circled around his name, particularly in *The Eye in the Door*; the historical Welsh artist Augustus John (1878–1961) appears in the historical Café Royal, which was a famous meeting place in Regent Street for artists and celebrities, especially between about 1890 and 1920. Playing a role reminiscent of that enacted by W. H. R. Rivers in the trilogy is Henry Tonks (1862–1937), a surgeon and artist who, in the pre-war scenes, is teaching the life class to students at the Slade School of Art, and then, once war begins, is involved in plastic surgery on mutilated men, as well as drawing pictures of horrible facial injuries for posterity.

The fictional group comprises, most centrally, Elinor Brooke, Paul Tarrant, and Kit Neville, all artists and current or former students at the Slade. Tarrant is like a visitant from early Barker, though with a difference; he is from Middlesbrough, an industrial city on Teeside, near Thornaby-on-Tees where Barker was born, and of the working class, a grammar school boy; but his grandmother's earnings as a grasping slumlord have enabled him to escape his environment to study art. Both Elinor and Kit are from a more privileged station in life, living in large houses in the home counties. Various ironies arise, including the fact that the working-class Paul Tarrant becomes an officer, the gentlemanly Kit Neville an enlisted man; as Kit tells Paul, 'You're a temporary gentleman, I'm a temporary non-gentleman' (*Toby's Room*, 133). Moreover, though Paul is very glad to escape from the industrial north-east—'of course he wanted to be an artist. It was the opposite of the life he'd lived in the shadow of the ironworks that gobbled men up at the start of a shift and regurgitated them twelve hours later fit for nothing but booze and sleep' (*Life Class*, 37)—he is uneasy with those from a more assured, privileged background. While Paul escapes to the south and the bohemian middle class, Neville, who is something of an Italian Futurist in his artistic credo, glorifying modernity, youth, mechanism and speed, is painting Middlesbrough and the machinery from which Paul escaped.

The interest in art and artists that Pat Barker demonstrated so handsomely in *Double Vision* continues in *Life Class* and its successor. There is the question of what art may legitimately represent: and the harrowing scenes Paul and Kit experience give literal solidity to the 'Disasters of War' category—paintings Goya executed of Napoleon's invasion of Spain—cited in *Double Vision*. The decorum, or adequacy, of painting the war is argued between Paul and Elinor, though the argument is oddly tilted toward aesthetic considerations. Paul tells her that he draws patients in the hospital, even though he doesn't expect his work to be shown, but 'Because it's there. They're there, the people, the men. And it's not right their suffering should just be swept out of sight' (*Life Class*, 220). (His argument is somewhat equivalent to Sarah Lumb's determination to look at the mutilated men in hospital, in *Regeneration*.) Elinor's response is that she must ignore the war: 'Totally. The truth is, it's been imposed on us from the outside. You would never have chosen it and probably the men in the hospital wouldn't either. It's unchosen, it's passive, and I don't think that's a proper subject for art' (*Life Class*, 221).

Life Class begins in 1912 and is mostly concerned, for a while, with the artistic studies and ambitions of the three central characters and their romantic entanglements, two categories that sometimes become intertwined. As artists, Paul and Elinor are somewhat frustrated, particularly Paul, whose drawing comes under savage criticism from

Professor Tonks; for instance, '"Is it a blancmange?" had been one of his comments on Paul's early efforts. Tonks had trained as a surgeon and taught anatomy to medical students before Professor Browne invited him to join the staff at the Slade. His eye, honed in the dissecting room and the theatre, detected every failure to convey what lay beneath the skin' (*Life Class*, 4–5). Later he is even more brutal, telling Paul that his painting is without feeling and 'You seem to have nothing to say' (37). Neville, older and now finished at the Slade, oozes self-confidence, well-deserved, it seems, on the basis of his early success; on his first appearance (at the Café Royal), the narrator introduces him with 'He was starting to be famous, a circumstance that some people attributed to a talent for painting and others to a talent for self-promotion' (18). Neville is a practised seducer, as well—perhaps through a combination of talent and self-promotion—but he has no success with Elinor, while Paul, much less confident, has an affair with an artist's model while gradually falling in love with Elinor, and becoming her lover when she visits him at the front. She seems to play the two against each other, inviting them both for a country weekend, for instance, while declaring her indifference to marriage. As Neville explains, 'For Elinor men come in twos. Always did,' and he goes on to toast her as 'Elinor. Our Lady of Triangles' (*Life Class*, 259).

The depth of her triangularity becomes clear only in *Toby's Room*, when her attachment to her brother is fully revealed. She is something of a 'New Woman', with cropped hair, an independent life in a London flat, and contempt for her conventional married sister. The war changes everything; both Neville and Tarrant enlist in the Belgian ambulance corps and see action at Ypres; later Paul joins the infantry and Neville continues as a stretcher-bearer. Both are injured—Paul twice in the same leg, Neville with part of his face torn away by shrapnel (in *Toby's Room*). Elinor rather unrealistically insists that the war changes nothing, that it is a bully dominating life, that she need make no accommodation to it (neither changing her art nor doing 'war work' like knitting socks for the soldiers). Her social milieu includes famous pacifists like Lady Ottoline, who has war resisters doing farm work at Garsington, her Oxfordshire estate. The inclusion of Lewis, a Quaker pacifist who nevertheless treats wounded men at the front alongside Paul Tarrant, and loses his life there, may be designed as a comment on the easy pacifism of the Ottoline circle. From time to time both novels introduce sharp notes that complicate any simple dichotomy between male violence and female sensitivity, or between benevolent pacifism and thoughtless bellicosity. Elinor ponders the fact that medical students have had to be issued with uniforms because they were being harassed by women who handed them white feathers, signs of cowardice, which causes her to reflect, '*It pains me to say it, but the one thing this war has*

shown conclusively is how amazingly and repulsively belligerent women are.
Some *women*' (*Toby's Room*, 71). Later, Elinor tries to invoke Paul's
sympathy for Olive Schreiner (1855–1920), a South African writer who
had been asked to leave a hotel because the other guests might think
she was German:

■ 'Paul? What are you thinking?'
  'I'm thinking there are worse things than being chucked out of a hotel.
  Like ending up in a hole in the ground with your guts draped round your
  neck.' (173) □

The complicating factor to everything, rising to prominence in the
second novel though mentioned in the first, is Elinor's brother Toby.
The two of them have always been close—are often mistaken for twins.
Paul reflects on his own rather slight acquaintance with Toby: 'Paul
probably wouldn't have noticed him at all, if it hadn't been for his
extraordinary resemblance to Elinor. Curiously, Toby had been beautiful, whereas Elinor, even at her best, just missed beauty, though Paul
found her more attractive because she didn't have that final, daunting
perfection' (*Toby's Room*, 102). Their extraordinary closeness is more
than just sympathy or resemblance, as, it is revealed in *Toby's Room*,
they have committed incest, for which both feel some guilt. This act
seems to determine Elinor's complicated attitude toward sex, as first
revealed in *Life Class*. Toby, a medical student, goes on to become a
medical officer on the Western Front, where Kit Neville serves under
him, retrieving the wounded. He is a reckless man who exposes himself
(somewhat like 'Mad Jack' Sassoon)—and, more controversially, his
men—to unnecessary dangers, bringing back dead bodies under fire
and even going back out to hunt for identity tags, so the families will
have some resolution. When Kit Neville discovers a shaming truth
about Toby, that he is having sex with a stable boy (an act that adds
to homosexuality an exploitation of hierarchical power, since the boy
could hardly refuse a superior officer), Toby tries to get himself killed
rather than face disgrace, and ultimately commits suicide.
    This is one of the secrets of *Toby's Room*. The first, of course, is the
incestuous past of the siblings, which remains their secret. The second
secret, of what happened to Toby, is something of a suspense-builder in
Toby's Room. The Brooke family knows he is missing, presumed dead
(probably meaning dead, but with no recoverable body remaining), but
all efforts to find out any further details are futile; when Elinor discovers
a scrap of paper in his uniform predicting that he will die and blaming
Neville, she insists on finding out the truth and, with the help of Paul
Tarrant, does so. She seems to achieve some resolution—there has been
a slightly creepy maintenance of his belongings and, having placed Paul

in Toby's room, where his uniform is still hanging, still retaining the smell she has relished, she steals in to have sex with him. Paul's reflection, as Elinor slips in—a line from the frustrated love poem 'They Flee From Me' by Thomas Wyatt (1503–42)—introduces an uneasy note of power and dispossession, and when, the next day, they exchange a 'sexless, almost brotherly kiss', (112) there is still some confusion. But the last line of the novel reads: 'She waited for his knock, and then, briefly aware that she was leaving Toby's room for the last time, ran downstairs to let him in' (*Toby's Room*, 263).

Not surprisingly critics linked *Life Class* (and *Toby's Room*, later) to the trilogy; Susanna Rustin said that Barker was returning to the matter of her best work and called *Life Class* a postscript to the *Regeneration* trilogy, a belittling judgement that does not do justice to the independent qualities of the novel.[2] Alan Cumyn considers it auspicious that the novelist returns to the war, and particularly approves her turning to the *beginning* of the war: in other words, long before the despairing period in which all the novels of the *Regeneration* trilogy are set, in 1917–18.[3] Cumyn goes on to suggest that Barker is trying to balance the war against the peacetime scenes, but, like Elinor, finds war a 'bully'. One linkage to the earlier books is the motif of Oscar Wilde, whose presence has loomed so vividly over the trilogy, especially *The Eye in the Door*; Kit Neville, as a painter of a somewhat Futurist bent, writes articles 'full of the need to stamp out the effeminacy of the Oscar Wilde years. You'd think, the way Neville wrote about it, that the Wilde trials had taken place last year, not a generation ago. What a shadow it cast' (*Life Class* 52).

By contrast, others, including the novelist herself, see the connection as being with *Double Vision*, the novel published just before *Life Class*; she told Alden Mudge, 'I feel this book is not linked to the trilogy so much as it's linked to *Double Vision*', because of the ethical questions posed there about the representation of horrors.[4] Just as Stephen Sharkey wondered about whether it was right to photograph (that is, make art of) dreadful scenes, so Paul Tarrant and Kit Neville wonder the same thing; both want to paint the war, but are constrained by the official ban on depicting the dead or even real wounds. In *Toby's Room*, Paul has been accepted as a 'war artist' but wonders what that means. In 'To See and to Know', John Brannigan writes that the 'preoccupation with the relationship between ethics and vision continues [from *Double Vision*] in *Life Class*, and these three words—"There. You see?"—are repeated in two scenes in the novel' (they come from the last page of *Double Vision*). He explains, 'In both instances, the words call for an act of witnessing, of submitting oneself to the unimpeachable veracity of what is "there", before one's eyes.'[5] Naturally the question of the representability of dreadful scenes that applies to artists in 1917 also applies to Pat Barker, who must represent them so that a reader may see how dreadful they are. Is this ethical?

Pat Barker told one interviewer, Peter Kemp, that she returned to the period of the Great War not because of the war as such, but because of her interest in the early twentieth-century artists who studied at the Slade School of Art in London, among whom were Christopher Nevinson (1889–1946), Mark Gertler (1891–1939), Paul Nash (1889–1946), and Dora Carrington (1893–1932).[6] And it is true that in her later works she turns more and more to artists as subjects. Michiko Kakutani, never a great admirer of Barker, also identifies some of the originals of her characters and welcomes the return to the wartime era; she writes that *Life Class* has the narrative power lacking in Barker's books with contemporary settings, but finds the characters unsatisfactory, Elinor guilty of selfishness and Neville close to war profiteering, and, all in all, self-centred men and women who have (Kakutani suggests) cultivated an unjustified withdrawal from real life in the interests of their art.[7] This may be an analogue of the 'splinter of ice in the heart' that Tom Seymour considers essential for the therapist—or even the novelist? (Barker has said that the painters in the novel are standing in for writers.[8]) As for Tonks, whose personality is well attested in the artists' memoirs she cites in the Acknowledgements, Simon Avery has this to say in 'Forming a New Political Aesthetic' (2011): 'he is established as both the embodiment of the dominant system and, in a very Foucauldian sense [i.e. as explained by Michel Foucault (1926–84), a French theorist of power], its structures of power, judgment and surveillance'.[9]

Technique

Technically both *Life Class* and *Toby's Room* show some interesting means of coping with the diverse materials and the multiple consciousnesses. *Life Class* has substantial portions narrated through letters between Paul and Elinor; *Toby's Room* makes a similar use of Elinor's journal, in part because, for reasons she can never explain, she has stopped writing back to Paul. And, as always, Pat Barker shows a brilliant skill in using free indirect style. There are shifts from past to present tense for emotional impact. The imagery, naturally, is very vivid: as Avery writes,

■ As with the Trilogy, Barker captures the horrors of war through a series of particularly poignant images centred principally on damaged bodies—a mother suffocating her hideously disfigured son; a man cradling his intestines; a soldier whose penis has been severed by shrapnel; another with one eyeball hanging out; a doctor kicking an amputated foot across the operating room [...].[10] □

Toby's Room has more scenes back in England than *Life Class*, but they are in their way just as terrifying on the costs of the war, particularly to men who have lost their faces to it. Kit Neville sardonically responds to a cabbie who quotes Rupert Brooke's early, sentimental sonnet 'There's some corner of a foreign field / That is for ever England'—Neville is wearing a Rupert Brooke mask to cover his shattered face—with 'That would be the bit with my nose under it; just fucking drive, will you?' (189).

Intertextuality

The inclusion of Virginia Woolf and, in a more offhand reference, Olive Schreiner invites an intertextual understanding of *Life Class*. John Brannigan links it to the obvious Woolf novel, *Mrs Dalloway*, which is partly about war damage, but continues that 'ultimately Barker's novel also reflects the fate of Lily Briscoe in *To the Lighthouse* [1927] in choosing art over marriage, in the implied incompatibility of a woman's artistic vision with the demands of marriage'.[11] No critic seems to have commented on the resonances of Elinor Brooke's surname, which may allude glancingly to Rupert but seems obviously, especially when she is called 'Miss Brooke', to invite comparison with Dorothea Brooke of *Middlemarch*, another woman determined never to marry. Avery links *Life Class* more broadly with 'key fin-de-siècle/early twentieth century texts such as Robert Louis Stevenson's *Dr. Jekyll and Mr. Hyde* (1886), Marie Corelli's [1855–1924] *The Sorrows of Satan* (1895) and Joseph Conrad's *The Secret Agent* (1907) [...]'.[12] More strikingly he also links Elinor's 'marginalised, unengaged view of the artist' to the secluded lady in Tennyson's poem 'The Lady of Shalott' (1833), a poetic figure who was also a frequent subject of *fin-de-siècle* paintings.[13] One critic, D. J. Taylor, in a mixed review, hailed Barker's ability to present trauma and the resulting psychological damage, but complained of her anachronistic use of language, which he identified as a mixture of times (contemporary, early twentieth century) and styles, a problem, he argued, that matters because elsewhere she has striven so hard for authenticity.[14]

Two intertextual elements apparently unnoticed—aside from the obvious Wyatt quotation—align the novels with James Joyce (1882–1941) and Dostoevsky. In *Toby's Room* Paul opens one of Toby's old books and reads 'Tobias Antony Brooke, Leybourne Farm, Netherton, Sussex, England, Great Britain, Europe, Northern Hemisphere, Earth, Solar System, Milky Way, the Universe' (103). This is very similar to the way Stephen Dedalus identifies himself in Joyce's *A Portrait of the Artist as a Young Man* (1916). And in the early pages of *Life Class* Paul, having bolted from the Slade in misery over his shortcomings as a painter, comes across a young woman, drunk, with her clothes dishevelled, being leered at by a portly middle-aged man who considers her easy pickings; Paul rescues the 'damsel in distress' (12), gives the older man a well-deserved and satisfying caning, and effects an ambiguous rescue. The whole scene echoes an incident involving Raskolnikov (another troubled, ambiguously placed student) in *Crime and Punishment* (1866).

One of a relatively small number of extended critical treatments of *Life Class* (in addition to Brannigan's and Avery's) appears in Fiona Tolan's essay 'Painting While Rome Burns' (2010), which links it with *On Beauty* (2005) by Zadie Smith (1975–), though without calling either a source for the other. She writes that both novels 'engage in a debate on the value and purpose of art and beauty'.[15] She relates it both to E. M. Forster (whose *Howards End* [1910] is the obvious intertext of *On Beauty*) and then to the philosophy of G. E. Moore (1873–1958), one of the intellectual forces of the Cambridge Apostles, a group that included Forster and many of the Virginia Woolf circle, including her husband Leonard Woolf (1880–1969) and Lytton Strachey (1880–1932), who were among the best known pacifists during the war; Barker's 'depiction of Elinor's association with Lady Ottoline Morrell and "that Bloomsbury crowd" (p. 200) brings the novelists [Barker and Smith] into contact with Moore's philosophical text' *Principia Ethica* (1903).[16] Tolan's conclusion seems to be that 'In *Life Class* [...] the central discussion of art's function remains a contested space: Elinor's withdrawal from history continues to be morally ambiguous, while Paul's witness of suffering produces powerful paintings tainted with fears of voyeurism and exploitation.'[17]

The scenes of Elinor as a part of the Bloomsbury group are conveyed in her diary, revealing some of her confusion and ambivalence (for instance, she is irritated that conscientious objectors assigned to farm work on Lady Ottoline Morrell's estate do not make the effort to do it well):

■ *Now I'm sitting in my bedroom listening to an owl hooting and wishing I could talk to Toby. Or Paul. Paul's in hospital in London, badly wounded, and I haven't even been to see him yet, so what does it mean when I say I want to talk to him? It's not even a conscious decision, not going to see him; I mean, I just can't seem to make myself do it. Ever since he volunteered to fight, we've been drifting further and further apart. Sometimes I wonder if there'll be anything left when we do, finally, meet. And then I feel terrible because while he was out there I virtually stopped writing to him altogether. [...] And now there he is in hospital with a lump of shrapnel in his leg— though I suppose they'll have got that out by now—and here I sit in a cosy little bedroom in a borrowed nightie, and... And none of it is my fault. And yet there's so much guilt [...]. (Toby's Room, 69)* □

Lara Tupper, reviewing *Life Class*, argued for art's function in making us face the reality of war (in part linking it to ongoing United States militarism) and declared, 'I think we need another war novel from Barker.'[18] And after a longer than usual pause, *Toby's Room* appeared, arguably another 'war novel'. Criticism of *Toby's Room* is so far limited to reviews. Some of them, struck by Barker's return, once again, to World War I just as *Downton Abbey*, the serial scripted by Julian Fellowes (1949–), and broadcast on ITV in England and PBS in the United States since 2010, became a sensation on television, devoted most of their attention to the continuing fascination of the war, nearly a hundred years after its beginning. The full headline on John Barber's review—'A portrait of the First World War that's anything but nice; Ground-breaking trilogy paints a picture of war very different from the quaint melodramatics of Downton Abbey'—exemplifies the linkage, while also surprisingly granting *Toby's Room* premature status as part of a trilogy.[19] John Vernon links the author herself to Paul Tarrant's obsession with working out how the war had changed people, including himself. Like other reviewers, he notes the mixture of fictional and real people, saying that their combination is seamless; and his discussion of the relationship with *Life Class* is astute: he suggests that *Toby's Room* is not so much a sequel—after all, it begins before *Life Class*, though carrying on after that book—as a development of it. Part One is set in 1912, but before the beginning of the plot of *Life Class*; Part Two is set in 1917, further along, and in fact deeper into the morass of war depicted in the Trilogy. Vernon points out that background information from each of the two novels can be found in the other, instancing why Elinor has short hair and why she is reluctant sexually.[20] Freya Johnston notes the repetitions that refer back not just to *Life Class* but to the whole *Regeneration* trilogy and links them to Elinor's own compulsion to keep doing the same thing over and over—in her case, a compulsion after Toby dies to paint landscapes each of which contains a spectral vision of him.[21]

Hermione Lee identifies the three interlocking subjects of the novel as the fate of Toby, which is of course most melodramatic and mentioned in the title; the proper relationship between a woman artist and the facts of war; and the questions around terribly disfigured surviving veterans—their treatment and the necessity of looking at them.[22] Lee also connects the novel, intertextually, to Virginia Woolf's novel *Jacob's Room* (1922), which Woolf wrote as a tribute to her own dead brother Thoby Stephen (1880–1906). Peter Kemp makes the same connection and also connects scenes at the Café Royal to D. H. Lawrence's *Women in Love* (1915).[23] Lucy Scholes celebrates Barker's fearlessness in using 'the shock factor'—by which she means both the initial act of incest and, later and more subtly, Elinor's uneasy aestheticizing of war wounds that should provoke her pity, her tendency to assimilate the shattered faces of the wounded men to the chipped sculptures they used to copy at the Slade. Scholes highlights Elinor's independence, alongside her demonstration of 'female confinement against male freedom', and elicits from Barker the statement that Elinor was both a sort of exemplar of feminine obstinacy and freedom and a not entirely likeable character.[24]

Richard Davenport-Hines's review makes an unusual point about Pat Barker's devotion to the war (which is registered as a strength in most reviews). While he calls it a 'meticulously crafted novel', and praises the use of the novelist's 'scrupulous gifts to depict the gruesome world of the Sidcup hospital and to honour its patients and staff', he concludes with a complaint against the drabness of the material, its sadness and hopelessness, which he construes as pointlessness.[25]

Bryan Appleyard returns to the ongoing question of Barker's postmodernism, strongly denying that she is a postmodernist, or even a modernist author, but one who writes with directness and clarity and avoids all experimentalism. He goes on to quote Barker as saying that she eschews experimental writing because of her insistence on being understood, as well as what seems a suspicion that experimental prose abandons the reader in the interest of the novelist's self-regard.[26] Appleyard concludes, on the basis of his conversation with her, with a suggestion found in other profiles: that if this is a trilogy, the third volume will not be about the war, but will follow the same characters in their later lives up to the Second World War. Lucy Scholes, in a slightly later conversation, elicited a more detailed forecast that, in her next novel, 'she turns her attention to another real-life historical figure, the Scottish medium Helen Duncan, who in 1944 was the last woman in Britain to be tried as a witch after revealing a supposed state secret during a wartime séance'.[27] This is a particularly rich suggestion: secrets, séances and spiritualism have run through Barker's fiction from nearly the beginning, and the book seems certain to return to the syndrome that war arms the population against all sorts of sinister and uncanny 'others'—like the homosexuals, the women with hypertrophied clitorises, the posthumous influence of Oscar Wilde and Walt Whitman, of *The Eye in the Door*.

Conclusion

Pat Barker has been, for the most part, fortunate in the intelligence and fairness of the critical response to her novels. When *Granta* magazine named her one of the twenty best British novelists under forty, in 1983, she was the author of only one published book, *Union Street*, with *Blow Your House Down* forthcoming (an extract was printed in *Granta*), but the judgement proved prescient—perhaps more so than for some of the other names listed there. Her reviews—and reviews are one form of criticism—have never been uniform raves, an experience she shares with every author; and they have not been uniformly insightful; but they have been generally positive and more often than not based on genuine understanding of what she is attempting in her fiction.

Reviews can be conservative, of course, and when she appears to change direction, reviewers may object. Hence at the onset of the *Regeneration* trilogy some of the periodical notices complained of what looked like a betrayal of the feminist project that seemed to animate at least her first three novels (*The Man Who Wasn't There* being slightly anomalous, both in itself and in the critical reactions it has generated); others lamented the loss of what they considered her grittily realistic, politically engaged, social-democratic analysis of Thatcher's Britain (there can be few novels that have been called 'gritty' as often as Pat Barker's). Then, when she turned away from the First World War to contemporary life in *Another World*, some of her critics were disappointed again (Eileen Battersby, for instance, who considered each book in the *Regeneration* trilogy one of the best novels of the twentieth century and the first two unjustly deprived of the Booker Prize, discovered that Barker was not a congenital novelist, once she turned her attention to other subject matter).

Literary criticism in the more traditional sense, published in books and critical journals, has provided many useful insights into Barker's work.

BOOKS

There have been four book-length, single-author studies of Barker's oeuvre. The first and in some ways still the standard (aside from its incompleteness due to its publication date) is Sharon Monteith's *Pat Barker*, published in 2001 in association with the British Council. Monteith is, as Pat Wheeler wrote, 'known worldwide for her work on Pat Barker', and the novelist herself has praised her critical insight.[1] Her book has a chapter on *Union Street* and *Blow Your House Down*, one on the *Regeneration* trilogy, and one each on the other novels, up through *Border Crossing*. In her introduction she provides an overview of what she considers the important subjects or themes of Barker's fiction, including gender, war, class, memory and history. In a balancing comment she places Barker in a 'materialist tradition'[2] but notes that the class-based approach does not undermine the aesthetic qualities of the fiction.

In Monteith's overview she disputes a tendency found in book reviewers to divide Barker's fictional output between the novels before the *Regeneration* trilogy and those after it; likewise she insists (quoting Barker in support) that turning towards male characters in the trilogy does nothing to undermine the author's feminism, which is not just about women. Alongside useful comments on the role of sex and sexuality, of class and capitalism, of masculinity and masculine violence, she touches on the critical discussion of Barker in connection with postmodernism and deconstructionism (the post-structuralist practice of semiotic analysis following Jacques Derrida), suggesting that in some ways the use of such labels limits understanding of the fiction, just as emphasis on the social realism of the early books, insofar as it emphasizes the sociological, tends to overlook their artistry. In her Postscript she adds some summary comments on ambiguity, the relations between Barker's novels and the other texts with which they have intertextual links, and her ongoing interest in boundaries and boundary-crossing.

Four years after Monteith's book, the second monograph on Barker's work appeared, John Brannigan's *Pat Barker*, published in 2005 by Manchester University Press in a series on Contemporary British Novelists. He could naturally go a bit further than Sharon Monteith, including *Double Vision* as the last text treated. Brannigan's introduction to the important themes and practices of Barker's work concurs with Monteith in mentioning gender and its creation, class and the question of class solidarity, memory and trauma. He adds several more details including what he calls the theme of dereliction; the incorporation of themes of fragility (Brannigan writes subtly about images of broken shells, windows, and other margins, particularly in the early novels); and (quoting from *Double Vision*, p. 27) 'figures of utter ruin'. Brannigan is also unusual among the critics of Barker's fiction in calling significant attention to religious themes and imagery.

His final chapter is a lucid critical overview, which traces the history of critical attention to Barker—locating its onset mostly after the trilogy—and touching on recurrent themes, including feminism and the alleged abandonment of it, history, psychology, memory, and gender. His comments on the questions of realism and postmodernism offer a useful explanation; he insists that realism is the best term for Barker's approach, while acknowledging that a case for her as a postmodernist can be made, though 'at a stretch'.[3] He cites her use of pastiche, her scepticism toward grand narratives, and her incorporation of disparate fictional forms in her work, but points out that Barker has consistently claimed that her novels represent the real and assist readers in understanding social conditions.

David Waterman's *Pat Barker and the Mediation of Social Reality* was published by Cambria Press in 2009. As the title suggests, it is more narrowly concerned with a particular theme than Monteith or Brannigan: that is, 'questions of representation: whether we examine how existing representations serve to maintain the status quo, or whether we are interested in how to represent the horrors of war or the "monstrosities" of civil life [...]'.[4] Among the themes to which Waterman draws careful attention are class and the possibilities of community; 'masculine' behaviour and its constraints, especially in a time of crisis (e.g. war); and—something he highlights more than many readers—Barker's use of the uncanny and the supernatural, her 'ghosts'. Waterman's summary statement reinforces his particular approach: Pat Barker 'asks us to make progress precisely by being skeptical toward the representations of normative social control';[5] both the emphasis on representation and the assumption that Barker has an activist political agenda at the heart of her fiction writing are characteristic. Waterman has joint chapters on the 'working-class' novels and the trilogy, and individual chapters on each of the other books, concluding with *Life Class*.

Mark Rawlinson's *Pat Barker* was published in the New British Fiction series in 2010. Like Waterman's, his discussion covers the oeuvre through to *Life Class*. There is an introduction on 'Why We Should Read Pat Barker'; a long section on the major works; and finally a section on criticism and contexts, which includes a discussion of her critical reception, particularly how that criticism came to include an 'academic apparatus of peer-reviewed, footnoted articles in learned journals, student essays marked for their conformity to academic models by university professors, and nowadays, what some regard as the gold standard of academic reputation, the single-author monograph'.[6] Rawlinson then essays to explain how Barker's work achieved this prominence, taking primarily an institutional approach. This chapter also criticizes the two film versions of Barker's fiction, *Stanley and Iris* and *Regeneration*.

In his introduction Rawlinson singles out as his main concern Barker's use of history, which he does not limit to books about the relatively remote past (that is, the First World War books), insisting that 'Contemporary fiction is historical because on one level there is no secure demarcation between factual and fictional stories. But on another level, history looms large because fictional stories are such a productive way of representing the contingency of the present, the dependence, that is, of our world and the entities which constitute it on earlier states of affairs.'[7] Among the features of Barker's use of history, Rawlinson highlights is repetition, in part because it is both a literary and a psychoanalytic concern. He also gives critical attention to memory and haunting.

Single-author monographs of narrower scope include one on the *Regeneration* trilogy and two books about the single novel *Regeneration*. Karen Patrick Knutsen's *Pat Barker's Regeneration Trilogy* was published in 2010; that its publisher is German and the author was supported by a grant from the Norwegian Research Council says much about Barker's European rather than just British importance. Knutsen announces at the outset that she has chosen to focus on 'trauma, class, gender and psychology' in her book. As a result she proceeds diachronically: as she explains, her discourses 'are not representative of one moment in history but involve changes and transformations in patterns of cultural experience through time. Within discourses, the past and the present are multiple and unstable.'[8] Accordingly her book, rather than being structured around the three books, is organized in five major chapters, 'Historical and Critical Contexts', 'Cultural Trauma', 'The Discourse of Class', 'The Discourse of Gender', and 'The Discourse of Psychology'. Knutsen's approach is more thoroughly informed by recent critical theory than some others; for instance, she does not just cite allusions and indebtedness but locates her understanding of intertextuality in Julia Kristeva's *Revolution in Poetic Language* (1974); and explains her use of 'discourse' as indebted to Michel Foucault, and 'dialogue' and 'dialogic' by reference to Bakhtin. Her book has a very thorough and useful bibliography.

Karin Westman's *Pat Barker's Regeneration: A Reader's Guide* was published in 2001. Short and direct, it contains chapters on the novelist (biography and career), the novel, its reception, its performance, and some suggestions for further reading and discussion questions. The 'Performance' chapter attends to the novel's sales, its impact on modern British thinking about the war, and some controversy, and devotes considerable attention to the film version, about which Westman has published a book chapter elsewhere. Westman's discussion of Barker's use of history brings some insight to the similarity and differences between *Regeneration* and some of the novels published in the same years, including Martin Amis's *Time's Arrow* (1991), Salman Rushdie's *The Satanic Verses* (1988), and *A History of the World in 10 ½ Chapters* (1989) by Julian Barnes (1946–), pointing out that unlike some of them

Barker's book does not 'signal' to the reader that it is playing with history, or incorporate techniques to remind the reader of its fictionality. 'While some authors prefer to emphasize the act of historical appropriation, Barker does not do so in *Regeneration*. [...] She does provide some historical information to tell us who is "real" and who must be, by contrast, "made up," but she offers this information in an "Author's Note" at the *end* of the novel, rather than at the beginning.'[9]

Published in 2009, *Regeneration* is a 'York Notes Advanced' book, clearly for the use of students, by Sarah Gamble. It includes historical background, on the Great War for instance; biography; a chapter on the text; and one on critical approaches, which illustrates how Barker's *Regeneration* might be accessed through gender theory, trauma theory, and Marxism. Chapters also include lessons for students on such matters as how to study a novel and how to read critically, and a glossary of literary terms, as well as summaries of the plot and character sketches of the major characters, in-text definitions of terms (like 'paradox') and marginal factoids (who Jesus was), provocative questions, and links to websites. It is announced as a guide to reading and not a replacement for reading or for studying secondary sources.

Beyond the single-author books on Barker, there are two important collections. The first is more comprehensive, differing from the second only in its extent. Edited by Sharon Monteith, Margaretta Jolly, Nahem Yousaf and Ronald Paul, *Critical Perspectives on Pat Barker* was published in 2005 by the University of South Carolina Press. There are eighteen chapters, by some of the foremost critics of Barker's work, among them Sharon Monteith and John Brannigan; Karin Westman (the chapter on the film of *Regeneration*); and Pat Wheeler, who would go on to edit the next Barker collection. The book is divided into five sections, thematically; within those it proceeds largely chronologically, in chapters that focus on one or two novels. The first chapter is Brannigan's, on *Union Street*; the last is by Monteith and Yousaf, on *Double Vision*. There is an important interview with Pat Barker, an article on teaching *Blow Your House Down*, and, somewhat unusually because it usually receives scantier critical attention, two chapters on *The Man Who Wasn't There*. The Introduction, by Nahem Yousaf and Sharon Monteith, gives a good account of what readers may expect, and will find, in the collection:

■ The essays in this collection represent scholarly interest worldwide. The collection is varied in approach and methodology, espousing no single way of 'reading Barker' over any other. [...] The size and breadth of the volume represents something of the critical interest devoted to Barker's work over the last two decades. Each novel has stimulated commentary and criticism from a variety of disciplines: theologians (Michael Bochenski), other writers and novelists (Michèle Roberts and Blake Morrison), playwrights and filmmakers (Sarah Daniels, Martin Ritt, and Gilles Mackinnon), as well as the preponderance of literary critics gathered here.[10] □

Another key feature of the Critical Perspectives volume is that its authors take both a critical and a pedagogical approach to Barker's works, a further testimony to the way in which her books had begun appearing in university curricula.

In 2011, Cambridge Scholars published *Re-Reading Pat Barker*, which was edited by Pat Wheeler. It is something of a companion to *Critical Perspectives on Pat Barker*: there is overlap in contributors (Sharon Monteith contributes the Foreword, John Brannigan a chapter, and Pat Wheeler, editor and contributor, had a chapter in the earlier compendium), and its nine chapters include discussions of the *Regeneration* trilogy and the earlier books (sometimes called the working-class novels); it supplements that compendium with two chapters each on *Border Crossing* and *Life Class* (published after *Critical Perspectives*) and two chapters on *Another World* alongside another that interestingly links *Another World* with *Union Street* and *Liza's England*. In short, it leans toward the later part of the Barker career, as perhaps makes sense after the extensive attention that the trilogy and earlier novels had received already. Sharon Monteith's Foreword links the two books, first listing some of Barker's concerns addressed in *Critical Perspectives*: 'a panoply of social and intellectual problems around ethics and morality, faith, crime, psychoanalysis and psychosis, memory and trauma, modernity and postmodernity and the politics of representation'; the new volume, she adds, 'returns to many of those ideas and extends them, particularly Barker's concern with art and vision, aesthetics and feeling, texturing her most recent fiction'.[11]

There has been an extensive secondary criticism of Barker in the form of periodical articles and portions of more miscellaneous books which attempt an overview, as the bibliography demonstrates. Among the latter might be the items by Childs (2005), Alexander (1989), Moseley (2003), Boyers (2005), Bradford (2007), Haywood (1997), Rennison (2005), Joannou (2004), Palmer (1989), Vickroy (2002), and Whitehead (2004). In addition there is much critical insight to be gained from the numerous interviews Barker has granted over the years. Sharon Monteith, who has interviewed her several times, comments on the 'self-consciousness of Barker's commentary on her writing practice' and its 'admixture of creative and critical commentary [...]'.[12]

Finally, there are many, many articles and essays on Barker's work, which cannot be summarized successfully. Perhaps a useful way to categorize them is by the subject matter to which they devote attention. Recurrent features of the criticism, and representative examples (some of which, of course, touch on more than one of these subjects), include

- *trauma*: Talbott (1997); Greif (2001); Vickroy (2004); Monteith and Yousaf (2005); Troy (2007)
- *memory*: Kirk (1999); Whitehead (2004); Knutsen (2005)
- *psychology and psychiatry*: Talbott (1997); Wyatt-Brown (1997); Nickerson and Shea (1997); Winter (2000); Shephard (2001); Mukherjee (2001); Bluestone (2003); Waterman (2003); Wessely (2006)
- *war and war writing*: Morrison (1996); Monteith (1997); Harris (1998); Slobodin (1998); Bergonzi (1999); Trumpener (2000); Winter (2000); Pellow (2001); Waterman (2003); Shapiro (2005); Shaddock (2006); Troy (2007); Mudge (2007); Korte (2007); Patten (2008); Waterman (2008); Meacham (2012)
- *gender*, including both women's issues and masculinity: Anderson (1990); Bauer (1990); Harris (1998); Malm (1998); Jolly (2000); Hitchcock (2002); Waterman (2003); Vickroy (2004); Shaddock (2006); Falcus (2007); Gamble (2007); Gallagher (2011)
- *class*: Dodd, K. and P. (1992); Smith (1995); Hitchcock (2000); Hitchcock (2002)

and

- *technical concerns*, among them the question, mentioned above, of
  - Barker's relationship to *realism*: Anderson (1990); Slobodin (1998); Löschnigg (1999); Bergonzi (1999); Brannigan (2003); Shapiro (2005); Wessely (2006); Bernard (2007)
  - and her enrichment of her fiction through *intertextuality*: Lanone (1999); Duckworth (2004); Joyes (2009)

Many critical articles address themselves to one or two of the novels and may be located in the bibliography.

DIRECTIONS FOR FUTURE CRITICISM

One promising project will be to devote more critical attention to Pat Barker and visual art and artists. As a writer, she has always used other literary texts, fictional and nonfictional, poetry and prose, to enrich the texture of her work, and critics have been alert to the ways in which her novels respond to—that is, answer back, or augment, or parody, or simply quote or allude to—other written texts. Incorporating well-known poets into the *Regeneration* trilogy provided an avenue to using quotations from or echoes of the verse of Sassoon and Owen. But since *Double Vision* (2003), there has been a growing interest in visual art. A main character in that book is a sculptor; her dead husband was a war photographer; there is considerable discussion of Goya's Disasters of War; and overall the question of how one represents, the ethics of representation, even (in the case of Kate Frobisher) the technique of how to represent in plastic material and the relationship of art (a statue of Jesus) to belief—all these issues are important. Critics have often suggested that Barker's novels foreground issues of representation by the way they are written. Starting in *Double Vision* these issues are foregrounded as part of the subject matter. The two novels since then, *Life Class* and *Toby's Room*, have painters as their main characters. What makes painting genuine? What can and cannot be painted? Is painting an escape from the nightmare of history (i.e. war) or is it necessarily implicated in history? How do painters bear witness to horrors? All these questions are raised in acute and subtle ways in these two novels. Critics have begun to think and write about them—see Avery (2011), Waterman (2008), Tolan (2010), and Brannigan (2011)—but there is scope for much more investigation of what Barker is doing in this turn from the literary to the visual.

An obvious direction for further criticism is on *Toby's Room*, which was published only in autumn of 2012. Among the questions critics might approach are the importance of the incest theme; the relationship to Virginia Woolf (through her inclusion as a character, the novel's reminder of her own book *Jacob's Room* and her brother Thoby Stephen); and, should this prove to be part of a second trilogy, the theory and practice of trilogy-ness.

It is impossible to claim that critics have ignored the question of realism in Pat Barker's work. But there remain at least two areas that deserve a clarifying treatment.

One is her use of the 'real' past. Some attempt to place her within the major tradition of historical fiction would be useful, in part because it would provide some answers to the objections by overly literal-minded critics, often professional historians, that she has deformed history by her use of it: that she has given her characters anachronistic slang; that her presentation of shellshock as hysteria is a postmodern understanding deriving from Elaine Showalter and pushed back onto unsuspecting World War I subalterns; that her characters 'would not have done' something she represents them as doing. Historical fiction is after all *fiction*, and a strong interpretation by someone who clearly understands that could unclutter discussion of her use of the war from picayune objections which seem to arise from a misunderstanding of the nature and freedoms of the novel.

And, though this may be difficult—in part because of the very slipperiness of the term 'postmodern'—a deep study of whether it makes most sense to call Barker's fiction postmodern, or realistic, would be invaluable. Too many critiques seem driven either by a negative view of realism (even a caricature of 'classic' 'nineteenth-century' realism, with some suggestion that it always includes omniscient narration or moralistic didacticism) or simply by a desire to give Barker the benefit of including her with the more daring of contemporary novelists, and thus use an elastic and capacious *ad hoc* definition of postmodernism. Does inclusion of Gothic elements, or the use, in a historical novel, of facts drawn from history books, or sly humour, really make her a postmodernist? Do her books accord with the definition of the genre provided in Linda Hutcheon's influential work on historiographic metafiction (which, after all, seems to require metafictional self-reflexivity and a *parodic* reuse of the historical past)? Perhaps they do, but to this point the identity has been asserted but not closely argued. Trying to adjudicate how the texts of her novels place her within, or outside, the world of metafiction or postmodernism would be an important step in criticism of Barker.

And finally, future criticism will need to be agile and alert to respond to future *fiction* by Pat Barker, which, if the past is any guide, will lead critics in new directions, perhaps confounding their current certainties and generalizations, as new and original fiction should.

Notes

INTRODUCTION

1. Flora Alexander, *Contemporary Women Novelists* (London: Edward Arnold, 1989), p. 244.
2. John Brannigan, *Pat Barker* (Manchester: Manchester University Press, 2005), p. 3.
3. Greg Harris, 'Compulsory Masculinity, Britain, and the Great War: The Literary-Historical Work of Pat Barker', *Critique: Contemporary Studies in Fiction* 39.4 (Summer 1998), pp. 290–304.
4. Margaretta Jolly, 'Toward a Masculine Maternal: Pat Barker's Bodily Fictions', in Sharon Monteith, Margaretta Jolly, Nahem Yousaf and Ronald Paul (eds), *Critical Perspectives on Pat Barker* (Columbia, SC: University of South Carolina Press, 2005), pp. 235–53.
5. Marie-Luise Kohlke, 'Pathologized Masculinity in Pat Barker's *Double Vision*: Stephen Sharkey's Monstrous Others', in Pat Wheeler (ed.), *Re-Reading Pat Barker* (Newcastle: Cambridge Scholars, 2011), p. 79.
6. Sarah C. E. Ross, 'Regeneration, Redemption, Resurrection: Pat Barker and the Problem of Evil', in James Acheson and Sarah C. E. Ross (eds), *The Contemporary British Novel Since 1980* (London: Palgrave Macmillan, 2005), p. 136.
7. Brannigan, *Pat Barker* (2005), p. 1.
8. Jolly (2005), p. 236.
9. Sharon Monteith, 'Warring Fictions: Reading Pat Barker', *Moderna Språk* 91 (1997), p. 127.
10. Mark Greif, 'Crime and Rehabilitation', *The American Prospect* (9 April 2001), p. 36.
11. Brannigan, *Pat Barker* (2005), p. 7.
12. John Brannigan, 'An Interview with Pat Barker', *Contemporary Literature* 46:3 (Autumn 2005), p. 369.
13. Mary Trabucco, 'Fire and Water in *Border Crossing*: Testimony as Contagion and Cure', Pat Wheeler (ed.), *Re-Reading Pat Barker* (Newcastle: Cambridge Scholars, 2011), p. 99.
14. Brannigan (2005), p. 10.
15. Sharon Monteith, *Pat Barker* (Tavistock, Devon: Northcote House in Association with the British Council, 2002), p. 108.
16. Monteith (2002), p. 110.
17. Brannigan, *Pat Barker* (2005), p. 4.
18. Brannigan, *Pat Barker* (2005), p. 127.
19. Brannigan, *Pat Barker* (2005), pp. 173 ff.
20. Ross (2005), pp. 132, 140.
21. Maria Holmgren Troy, 'Matrix, Metramorphosis, and the Readymade in *Union Street*, *Liza's England* and *Another World*', in Pat Wheeler (ed.), *Re-Reading Pat Barker* (Newcastle: Cambridge Scholars, 2011), p. 1.
22. Catherine Bernard, 'Pat Barker's Critical Work of Mourning: Realism with a Difference', *Études Anglaises* 60 (April–June 2007), pp. 174, 175.
23. Troy (2011), p. 9.
24. 'Best of Young British Novelists', *Granta* 7 (1983), p. 48.

25. Brannigan, 'An Interview' (2005), p. 368.
26. Brannigan, *Pat Barker* (2005), p. 3.
27. Jolly (2005), p. 236.

CHAPTER ONE

1. Michael Gorra, 'Laughter and Bloodshed', *The Hudson Review* 37.1 (Spring 1984), p. 154.
2. Gorra (1984), p. 155.
3. Elizabeth Ward, 'The Dark at the End of the Street', *Washington Post* (9 September 1984), Book World, p. 3.
4. Ivan Gold, 'North Country Women', *New York Times on the Web* (2 October 1983).
5. John Brannigan, 'The Small World of Kelly Brown: Home and Dereliction in *Union Street*', in Sharon Monteith, Margaretta Jolly, Nahem Yousaf and Ronald Paul (eds), *Critical Perspectives on Pat Barker* (Columbia, SC: University of South Carolina Press, 2005), p. 3.
6. John Brannigan, 'An Interview with Pat Barker', *Contemporary Literature* 46:3 (Autumn 2005), p. 372.
7. George Wotton, 'Writing from the Margins', in Ian A. Bell (ed.), *Peripheral Visions: Images of Nationhood in Contemporary British Fiction* (Cardiff: University of Wales Press, 1995), p. 206.
8. Brannigan, 'Small World' (2005), p. 4; David Waterman, *Pat Barker and the Mediation of Social Reality* (Amherst, NY: Cambria Press, 2009), p. 7; Mark Rawlinson, *Pat Barker* (London: Palgrave Macmillan, 2010), p. 20.
9. Monica Malm, '*Union Street*: Thoughts on Mothering', *Moderna Språk* 92 (January 1998), p. 143; Ian Haywood, *Working-class Fiction: From Chartism to* Trainspotting (London: Northcote House in association with the British Council, 1997), p. 145.
10. Sharon Monteith, *Pat Barker* (Tavistock, Devon: Northcote House in Association with the British Council, 2002), p. 17.
11. Penny Smith, 'Remembered Poverty: The North-East of England', in Ian A. Bell (ed.), *Peripheral Visions: Images of Nationhood in Contemporary British Fiction* (Cardiff: University of Wales Press, 1995), p. 114.
12. John Brannigan, *Pat Barker* (Manchester: Manchester University Press, 2005), p. 15.
13. Haywood (1997), p. 145; Blake Morrison, 'War Stories', *New Yorker* (22 January 1996), p. 79.
14. Fiona Tolan, 'Pat Barker', in Philip Tew, Fiona Tolan, and Leigh Wilson (eds), *Writers Talk: Conversations with Contemporary British Novelists* (London: Continuum, 2008), p. 19.
15. John Kirk, 'Recovered Perspectives: Gender, Class, and Memory in Pat Barker's Writing', *Contemporary Literature* XL.4 (1999), p. 609; Paulina Palmer, *Contemporary Women's Fiction: Narrative Practice and Feminist Theory* (Jackson: University Press of Mississippi, 1989), 42.
16. Brannigan, *Pat Barker* (2005), p. 28.
17. Kathryn Dodd and Philip Dodd, 'From the East End to *EastEnders*: Representations of the Working Class, 1890–1990', in Dominic Strinati and Stephen Wagg (eds), *Come on Down? Popular Media Culture in Post-War Britain* (London: Routledge, 1992), pp. 122, 124.
18. Palmer (1989), p. 123.
19. Sarah Brophy, 'Working-Class Women, Labor, and the Problem of Community in *Union Street* and *Liza's England*', in Sharon Monteith, Margaretta Jolly, Nahem Yousaf and Ronald Paul (eds), *Critical Perspectives on Pat Barker* (Columbia, SC: University of South Carolina Press, 2005), p. 25; Malm (1998), p. 143; David Waterman, *Pat Barker*

and the Mediation of Social Reality (Amherst, NY: Cambria Press, 2009), p. 35; Brophy (2005), p. 27.

20. Sarah Falcus, "'A Complex Mixture of Fascination and Distaste'": Relationships Between Women in Pat Barker's *Blow Your House Down*, *Liza's England* and *Union Street*', *Journal of Gender Studies* 16 (November 2007), p. 250.
21. Falcus (2007), p. 257.
22. Falcus (2007), p. 254.
23. Margaretta Jolly, 'After Feminism: Pat Barker, Penelope Lively and the Contemporary Novel', in Alistair Davies and Alan Sinfield (eds), *British Culture of the Postwar: An Introduction to Literature and Society 1945–1999* (London: Routledge, 2000), p. 62; Rawlinson (2010), p. 25.
24. Haywood (1997), p. 145.
25. Brannigan, 'Small World' (2005), p. 8; Kirk (1999), p. 605.
26. Falcus (2007), p. 250.
27. Rawlinson (2010), p. 25; Monteith (2002), p. 17.
28. Haywood (1997), 147.
29. Brophy (2005), p. 25.
30. Tolan (2008), p. 25.
31. James Procter, 'The Return of the Native: Pat Barker, David Peace and the Regional Novel After Empire', in Rachel Gilmour and Bill Schwarz (eds), *End of Empire and the English Novel Since 1945* (Manchester, Manchester University Press, 2011), pp. 204–5.
32. Flora Alexander, *Contemporary Women Novelists* (London: Edward Arnold, 1989), pp. 47–8.
33. Alexander (1989), p. 48.
34. Brannigan, *Pat Barker* (2005), p. 15.
35. Peter Hitchcock, *Dialogics of the Oppressed* (Minneapolis: University of Minnesota Press, 1993), p. 62.
36. Hitchcock (1993) 63.
37. Margaretta Jolly, 'Toward a Masculine Maternal: Pat Barker's Bodily Fictions', in Sharon Monteith, Margaretta Jolly, Nahem Yousaf and Ronald Paul (eds), *Critical Perspectives on Pat Barker* (Columbia, SC: University of South Carolina Press, 2005), pp. 241, 236.
38. Brannigan, *Pat Barker* (2005), p. 31; Rawlinson (2010), p. 22.
39. Sharon Monteith, 'Warring Fictions: Reading Pat Barker', *Moderna Språk* 91 (1997), p. 125.
40. Brophy (2005), p. 30.
41. Kirk (1999), p. 612.
42. Falcus (2007), p. 250.
43. Brannigan, *Pat Barker* (2005), p. 32.
44. Alexander (1989), pp. 49–50.
45. Maria Holmgren Troy, 'Matrix, Matremorphosis, and the Readymade in *Union Street*, *Liza's England* and *Another World*', in Pat Wheeler (ed.), *Re-Reading Pat Barker* (Newcastle: Cambridge Scholars, 2011), p. 3.
46. Troy (2011), p. 8.
47. Brannigan, 'Small World' (2005), p. 12.
48. Brophy (2005), p. 36.
49. Haywood (1997), p. 146.
50. Hitchcock (1993), p. 61.
51. Brannigan, *Pat Barker* (2005), p. 24; Brannigan, 'Small World' (2005), p. 10.
52. Alexander (1989), p. 49.
53. Ward (1984), p. 3.
54. Wotton (1995), p. 208.
55. Kirk (1999), p. 612.

56. Donna Perry, 'Going Home Again: An Interview with Pat Barker', *The Literary Review* 34.2 (Winter 1991), p. 236.
57. Vincent Canby, 'Middle-Aged and Not Quite Middle Class', *New York Times* (9 February 1990), section C, p. 12.
58. Peter Travers, 'Stanley and Iris', *Rolling Stone* (9 February 1990), p. 38.
59. Steve Grant, 'Stanley & Iris', in John Pym (ed.), *Time Out Film Guide* (London: Ebury Publishing, 2009), p. 1000.
60. Perry (1991), p. 236.
61. Nicci Gerrard, 'MSPrint: Review of Feminist Novels,' *The Guardian* (18 July 1984).
62. Katha Pollitt, 'Bait for a Killer', *New York Times* (21 October 1984), section 7, p. 7.
63. Pollitt (1984), col. 7, p. 7.
64. Ward (1984), p. 3.
65. Rob Nixon, 'An Interview with Pat Barker', *Contemporary Literature* 45.1 (Spring 2004), p. 15.
66. Kennedy Fraser, 'Ghost Writer: Pat Barker's Haunted Imagination', *New Yorker* (17 March 2008), p. 43.
67. Paul Simpson, 'Reclaiming the Invisible: *Union Street* and *Blow Your House Down*', *New Labor Forum* (1 September 2004), pp. 112, 113.
68. Alexander (1989), p. 50.
69. Katerina Andriotis, 'Pat Barker, *Blow Your House Down* and the Prostitution Debate', *Sexuality & Culture* 13 (2009), p. 54.
70. Monteith (2002), p. 21.
71. Maroula Joannou, 'Pat Barker and the Languages of Region and Class', in Emma Parker (ed.), *Contemporary British Women Writers* (Cambridge: D. S. Brewer, 2004), p. 48.
72. Ann Ardis, 'Political Attentiveness vs. Political Correctness: Teaching Pat Barker's "Blow Your House Down"', *College Literature* 18 (October 1991), pp. 47–8.
73. Dale M. Bauer, 'The Other "F" Word: The Feminist in the Classroom', *College English* 52 (April 1990), p. 393.
74. Michelle Hanson, 'Tuesday Women: Working Class Heroine', *The Guardian* (14 March 1989).
75. Rawlinson (2010), p. 32.
76. Rawlinson (2010), p. 33
77. Ardis (1991), p. 51.
78. Rawlinson (2010), p. 31.
79. Joannou (2004), p. 52; Brannigan, *Pat Barker* (2005), p. 37; Rawlinson (2010), p. 37.
80. Tolan (2008), p. 22.
81. Monteith (2002), p. 25.
82. Jolly (2000), p. 65.
83. Monteith (2002), p. 24
84. Ardis (1991), p. 49.
85. Haywood (1997), p. 147.
86. Rawlinson (2010), p. 35
87. Andrea Stevens, 'Violence Against Women', *New York Times* (21 October 1984), section 7, p. 9.
88. Palmer (1989), p. 88.
89. Palmer (1989), p. 89.
90. Peter Childs, 'Pat Barker: In the Shadow of Monstrosities', in *Contemporary Novelists: British Fiction Since 1970* (London: Palgrave Macmillan, 2005), p. 71.
91. Joannou (2004), p. 45.
92. Ardis (1991), p. 45.
93. Bauer (1990), p. 394.
94. Childs (2005), p. 68.
95. Palmer (1989), p. 89.

96. Brannigan, *Pat Barker* (2005), p. 44.
97. Childs (2005), p. 71.

CHAPTER TWO

1. Sarah Brophy, 'Working-Class Women, Labor, and the Problem of Community in *Union Street* and *Liza's England*', in Sharon Monteith, Margaretta Jolly, Nahem Yousaf and Ronald Paul (eds), *Critical Perspectives on Pat Barker* (Columbia, SC: University of South Carolina Press, 2005), p. 25; Margaretta Jolly, 'After Feminism: Pat Barker, Penelope Lively and the Contemporary Novel', in Alistair Davies and Alan Sinfield (eds), *British Culture of the Postwar: An Introduction to Literature and Society 1945–1999* (London: Routledge, 2000), p. 68.
2. John Kirk, 'Recovered Perspectives: Gender, Class, and Memory in Pat Barker's Writing', *Contemporary Literature* XL.4 (1999); Lyn Pykett, 'The Century's Daughters: Recent Women's Fiction and History', *Critical Quarterly* 29.3 (September 1987), p. 73.
3. Donna Perry, 'Going Home Again: An Interview with Pat Barker', *The Literary Review* 34.2 (Winter 1991), p. 237.
4. Kennedy Fraser, 'Ghost Writer: Pat Barker's Haunted Imagination', *New Yorker* (17 March 2008), p. 41.
5. Pauline Willis, 'Monday Women: Bulletin', *The Guardian* (15 September 1986); Norman Shrapnel, 'Books: A Last Stand for People', *The Guardian* (15 September 1986).
6. Phil Baker, et al., 'Paperbacks', *The Sunday Times* (31 March 1996).
7. Paul Driver, 'Liza Jarrett's Hard Life', *London Review of Books* 8:21 (4 December 1986), pp. 24–6.
8. Jonathan Yardley, 'Finding Hope Amid Hard Times', *Washington Post* (1 October 1986), D2.
9. Eden Ross Lipson, 'Liza Toughs It Out', *New York Times on the Web* (21 December 1986).
10. Brophy (2005), p. 26.
11. Sharon Monteith, *Pat Barker* (Tavistock, Devon: Northcote House in Association with the British Council, 2002), p. 33; and see Brophy (2005), pp. 27–31.
12. Ian Haywood, *Working-class Fiction: From Chartism to* Trainspotting (London: Northcote House in association with the British Council, 1997), p. 147; Kirk (1999), p. 622.
13. Pykett (1987), p. 73; Jolly (2000), p. 243.
14. Monteith (2002), p. 29.
15. Sarah Falcus, '"A Complex Mixture of Fascination and Distaste": Relationships Between Women in Pat Barker's *Blow Your House Down*, *Liza's England* and *Union Street*', *Journal of Gender Studies* 16 (November 2007), p. 258.
16. Sarah Falcus, 'Unsettling Ageing in Three Novels by Pat Barker', *Ageing & Society* 32 (2012), p. 1386.
17. Jolly (2000), p. 69; Peter Hitchcock, 'They Must Be Represented? Problems in Theories of Working-Class Representation', *PMLA* 115 (January 2000), p. 21.
18. Mark Rawlinson, *Pat Barker* (London: Palgrave Macmillan, 2010), p. 50; Flora Alexander, *Contemporary Women Novelists* (London: Edward Arnold, 1989), pp. 50–1.
19. Peter Hitchcock, *Dialogics of the Oppressed* (Minneapolis: University of Minnesota Press, 1993), p. 81.
20. Kirk (1999), pp. 611, 624.
21. Jenny Newman, 'Souls and Arseholes: The Double Vision of *Liza's England*', in Sharon Monteith, Margaretta Jolly, Nahem Yousaf and Ronald Paul (eds), *Critical Perspectives on Pat Barker* (Columbia, SC: University of South Carolina Press, 2005), p. 104.
22. Pykett (1987), p. 74; Linda Anderson, 'The Re-Imagining of History in Contemporary Women's Fiction', in Linda Anderson (ed.), *Plotting Change: Contemporary Women's Fiction* (London: Edward Arnold, 1990), p. 132.

23. Pykett (1987), p. 74; Anderson (1990), p. 134.
24. Newman (2005), p. 101.
25. Rawlinson (2010), p. 47.
26. Newman (2005), p. 101.
27. David Waterman, *Pat Barker and the Mediation of Social Reality* (Amherst, NY: Cambria Press, 2009), p. 24; Catherine Bernard, 'Pat Barker's Critical Work of Mourning: Realism with a Difference', *Études Anglaises* 60 (April–June 2007), p. 176.
28. Newman (2005), p. 109.
29. Sharon Monteith, 'Warring Fictions: Reading Pat Barker', *Moderna Språk* 91 (1997), p. 127.
30. Monteith (2002), pp. 50–1.
31. Rob Nixon, 'An Interview with Pat Barker', *Contemporary Literature* 45.1 (Spring 2004), p. 17.
32. Shena Mackay, 'Elvis and the Bogeyman', *The Sunday Times* (23 April 1989).
33. Norman Shrapnel, 'Books: A Last Stand for People', *The Guardian* (26 September 1986).
34. Herbert Mitgang, 'Books of the Times: A Story in the Imagination of a Boy', *New York Times* (8 December 1990), p. 18.
35. Penny Smith, 'Remembered Poverty: The North-East of England', in Ian A. Bell (ed.), *Peripheral Visions: Images of Nationhood in Contemporary British Fiction* (Cardiff: University of Wales Press, 1995), p. 115.
36. Monteith (1997), pp. 127, 125–6, 122.
37. John Brannigan, *Pat Barker* (Manchester: Manchester University Press, 2005), p. 77.
38. Rawlinson (2010), pp. 56–7.
39. Alan Lovell, '*The Uses of Literacy*: The Scholarship Boy', *Universities & Left Review* 1.2 (Summer 1957), p. 33.
40. Pat Wheeler, 'Transgressing Masculinities: *The Man Who Wasn't There*', in Sharon Monteith, Margaretta Jolly, Nahem Yousaf and Ronald Paul (eds), *Critical Perspectives on Pat Barker* (Columbia, SC: University of South Carolina Press, 2005), p. 132; Monteith (2002), p. 43.
41. Brannigan, *Pat Barker* (2005), p. 90.
42. Wheeler (2005), p. 130.
43. Waterman (2009), p. 44.
44. Sharon Monteith, 'Screening *The Man Who Wasn't There*: The Second World War and 1950s Cinema', in Sharon Monteith, Margaretta Jolly, Nahem Yousaf and Ronald Paul (eds), *Critical Perspectives on Pat Barker* (Columbia, SC: University of South Carolina Press, 2005), p. 115.
45. Monteith (2002), p. 42.
46. Rawlinson (2010), p. 58.
47. Monteith (2002), p. 47; Waterman (2009), pp. 43–4.
48. Wheeler (2005), p. 139.
49. Brannigan, *Pat Barker* (2005), p. 81.
50. Waterman (2009), p. 40; Brannigan, *Pat Barker* (2005), p. 84.
51. Monteith (2005), p. 117.
52. Monteith (2005), p. 120.
53. Rawlinson (2010), p. 57.
54. Monteith (2005), p. 118; Brannigan, *Pat Barker* (2005), p. 86.
55. Monteith (2002), p. 45; Brannigan, *Pat Barker* (2005), p. 79.
56. Monteith (2002), pp. 49–50.

CHAPTER THREE

1. Anne Whitehead, 'Open to Suggestion: Hypnosis and History in the *Regeneration* Trilogy', in Sharon Monteith, Margaretta Jolly, Nahem Yousaf and Ronald Paul (eds),

Critical Perspectives on Pat Barker (Columbia, SC: University of South Carolina Press, 2005), p. 215.

2. Richard Bradford, *The Novel Now: Contemporary British Fiction* (London: Blackwell, 2007), p. 84.

3. Paul Taylor, 'Hero at the Emotional Front', *The Independent* (2 June 1991), p. 32; Justine Picardie, 'The Poet Who Came Out of His Shell', *The Independent* (25 June 1991), p. 19.

4. Donna Perry, 'Interview with Pat Barker', in Donna Perry (ed.), *Backtalk: Women Writers Speak Out* (New Brunswick, NJ: Rutgers University Press, 1993), p. 51.

5. Perry (1993), p. 52.

6. Candice Rodd, 'A Stomach for War', *The Independent* (12 September 1993), p. 28.

7. Rob Nixon, 'An Interview with Pat Barker', *Contemporary Literature* 45.1 (Spring 2004), p. 6.

8. Sharon Monteith, 'Pat Barker' (interview), in Sharon Monteith, Jenny Newman and Pat Wheeler (eds), *Contemporary British and Irish Fiction: An Introduction Through Interviews* (London: Edward Arnold, 2004), p. 32.

9. John Brannigan, *Pat Barker* (Manchester: Manchester University Press, 2005), p. 167.

10. Karen Patrick Knutsen, 'Memory, War, and Trauma: Acting Out and Working Through in Pat Barker's *Regeneration Trilogy*', in Maria Holmgren Troy and Elisabeth Wennö (eds), *Memory, Haunting, Discourse* (Karlstad: Karlstad University Press, 2005), p. 162.

11. Bernard Bergonzi, *War Poets and Other Subjects* (Aldershot: Ashgate, 1999), p. 7.

12. Bergonzi (1999), pp. 6–9.

13. Ben Shephard, *A War of Nerves: Soldiers and Psychiatrists in the Twentieth Century* (Cambridge, MA: Harvard University Press, 2001), p. 109.

14. Bradford (2007), p. 86.

15. Mark Rawlinson, *Pat Barker* (London: Palgrave Macmillan, 2010), p. 68.

16. Bergonzi (1999), p. 13.

17. Bergonzi (1999), p. 14.

18. Brannigan, *Pat Barker* (2005), p. 94.

19. Martin Löschnigg, '"...the novelist's responsibility to the past": History, Myth, and the Narratives of Crisis in Pat Barker's *Regeneration* Trilogy (1991–1995)', *Zeitschrift für Anglistik und Amerikanistik* 47 (1999), pp. 220, 222.

20. Löschnigg (1999), pp. 223–4.

21. Löschnigg (1999), p. 227.

22. Katherine G. Nickerson and Steven Shea, 'W. H. R. Rivers: Portrait of a Great Physician in Pat Barker's *Regeneration* Trilogy', *The Lancet* 350 (19 July 1997), p. 205.

23. Anne M. Wyatt-Brown, 'Headhunters and Victims of War: W. H. R. Rivers and Pat Barker', *Proceedings of the 13th International Conference on Literature and Psychoanalysis* (Lisbon: Instituto Superior de Psicologia Aplicada, 1997), pp. 53–9.

24. Blake Morrison, 'War Stories', *New Yorker* (22 January 1996), pp. 82, 80.

25. Sharon Monteith, *Pat Barker* (Tavistock, Devon: Northcote House in Association with the British Council, 2002), p. 70; Lynda Prescott, 'Pat Barker's Vanishing Boundaries', in Nick Bentley (ed.), *British Fiction of the 1990s* (London: Routledge, 2005), p. 168; Karen Patrick Knutsen, *Reciprocal Haunting: Pat Barker's Regeneration Trilogy* (Münster: Waxmann, 2010), p. 41.

26. Bergonzi (1999), pp. 6, 8.

27. Pat Wheeler, '"Where Unknown, There Place Monsters": Reading Class Conflict and Sexual Anxiety in the *Regeneration* Trilogy', in Pat Wheeler (ed.), *Re-Reading Pat Barker* (Nottingham: Cambridge Scholars, 2011), p. 50.

28. Jay Winter, 'Shell-Shock and the Cultural History of the Great War', *Journal of Contemporary History* 35 (January 2000), p. 11.

29. Perry (1993), p. 52; Francis Spufford, 'Exploding Old Myths', *The Guardian* (9 November 1995), p. T2.

30. Lynda Prescott, 'Pat Barker, *The Ghost Road*', in David Johnson (ed.), *The Popular and the Canonical: Debating Twentieth-Century Literature 1940–2000* (London: Routledge, 2005), p. 170.
31. Ronald Paul, 'In Pastoral Fields: The Regeneration Trilogy and Classic First World War Fiction', in Sharon Monteith, Margaretta Jolly, Nahem Yousaf and Ronald Paul (eds), *Critical Perspectives on Pat Barker* (Columbia, SC: University of South Carolina Press, 2005), p. 149.
32. Paul (2005), pp. 154–5.
33. Paul (2005), p. 157.
34. Peter Hitchcock, 'What Is Prior? Working-Class Masculinity in Pat Barker's Trilogy', *Genders Online Journal* 35, www.genders.org/g35/g35_hitchcock.html (2002), p. 9.
35. Hitchcock (2002), p. 4.
36. Brannigan, *Pat Barker* (2005), p. 99.
37. Perry (1993), p. 51.
38. Mark Greif, 'Crime and Rehabilitation', *The American Prospect* (9 April 2001), p. 37.
39. Morrison (1996), p. 82; Löschnigg (1999), p. 222; and see Knutsen (2010), p. 19.
40. Wheeler (2011), p. 44.
41. Catherine Bernard, 'Pat Barker's Critical Work of Mourning: Realism with a Difference', *Études Anglaises* 60 (April–June 2007), pp. 178, 181.
42. Anne Whitehead, 'Pat Barker's *Regeneration* Trilogy', in Brian W. Shaffer (ed.), *A Companion to the British and Irish Novel 1945–2000* (London: Blackwell, 2005), p. 555.
43. David Waterman, 'Improper Heroes: Treating the Contagion of Hysteria, Homosexuality and Pacifisim in Pat Barker's World War I Trilogy', *Études Brittaniques contemporaines* 24 (2003), p. 5.
44. Waterman (2009), p. 70.
45. Dennis Brown, 'The *Regeneration* Trilogy: Total War, Masculinities, Anthropology, and the Talking Cure', in Sharon Monteith, Margaretta Jolly, Nahem Yousaf and Ronald Paul (eds), *Critical Perspectives on Pat Barker* (Columbia, SC: University of South Carolina Press, 2005), p. 192.
46. Margaretta Jolly, 'After Feminism: Pat Barker, Penelope Lively and the Contemporary Novel', in Alistair Davies and Alan Sinfield (eds), *British Culture of the Postwar: An Introduction to Literature and Society 1945–1999* (London: Routledge, 2000), p. 60.
47. Nixon (2004), p. 7.
48. Greif (2001), p. 36.
49. Robert Boyers, *The Dictator's Dictation: The Politics of Novels and Novelists* (New York: Columbia University Press, 2005), pp. 153, 156.
50. Patricia E. Johnson, 'Embodying Losses in Pat Barker's *Regeneration* Trilogy', *Critique* 46 (Summer 2005), p. 308.
51. Bergonzi (1999), p. 13.
52. Nick Hubble, 'Pat Barker's *Regeneration* Trilogy', in Philip Tew and Rod Mengham (eds), *British Fiction Today* (London: Continuum, 2006), p. 159.
53. Brannigan, *Pat Barker* (2005), p. 99.
54. Waterman (2009), p. 59.
55. Monteith (2002), p. 55.
56. Nickerson and Shea (1997), p. 207.
57. Morrison (1996), p. 78; Whitehead, 'Pat Barker's' (2005), p. 551; Johnson (2005), p. 308; Brannigan, *Pat Barker* (2005), p. 103; Monteith (2002), p. 69.
58. Brown (2005), p. 187; Margaretta Jolly, 'Toward a Masculine Maternal: Pat Barker's Bodily Fictions', in Sharon Monteith, Margaretta Jolly, Nahem Yousaf and Ronald Paul (eds), *Critical Perspectives on Pat Barker* (Columbia, SC: University of South Carolina Press, 2005), p. 246.
59. Knutsen (2010), p. 21.
60. Boyers (2005), p. 160.

61. Shephard (2001), p. 109.
62. Greif (2001), pp. 160–1.
63. John Brannigan, 'Pat Barker's *Regeneration* Trilogy: History and the Hauntological Imagination', in Richard J. Lane, Rod Mengham and Philip Tew (eds), *Contemporary British Fiction* (Cambridge: Polity, 2003), p. 14.
64. Laurie Vickroy, *Trauma and Survival in Contemporary Fiction* (Charlottesville: University of Virginia Press, 2002), p. 197.
65. Waterman (2009), p. 60.
66. Monteith (2002), p. 73.
67. Wheeler (2011), p. 57.
68. Spufford (1995), T2.
69. Boyers (2005), p. 159.
70. Winter (2000), p. 11.
71. Whitehead, 'Pat Barker's' (2005), p. 550.
72. Brannigan, *Pat Barker* (2005), p. 89.
73. Hitchcock (2002), p. 9.
74. Richard Slobodin, 'Who Would True Valour See', *History and Anthropology* 10 (1998), p. 309.
75. Gillian Glover, 'Barker Bites', *The Scotsman* (25 October 1995), p. 14.
76. Brown (2005), p. 187.
77. Brown (2005), p. 195.
78. Löschnigg (1999), p. 227.
79. Brannigan, *Pat Barker* (2005), pp. 112–13.
80. Knutsen (2010), p. 17.
81. Karen Patrick Knutsen, 'Memory, War, and Trauma: Acting Out and Working Through in Pat Barker's *Regeneration Trilogy*', in Maria Holmgren Troy and Elisabeth Wennö (eds), *Memory, Haunting, Discourse* (Karlstad: Karlstad University Press, 2005), p. 168.
82. Knutsen (2010), p. 17.
83. Vickroy (2002), p. 196.
84. Paul (2005), p. 148.
85. Brown (2005), p. 188.
86. Vickroy (2002), p. 192.
87. Knutsen (2010), p. 19.
88. Wheeler (2011), p. 45; Monteith (2002), p. 54; Whitehead, Open to Suggestion' (2005), p. 217.
89. Monteith (2002), p. 54.
90. Monteith (2002), p. 57.
91. Paul (2005), p. 152.
92. Monteith (2002), p. 58.
93. Whitehead, 'Pat Barker's' (2005), p. 552.
94. Whitehead, 'Open to Suggestion' (2005), pp. 209–10.
95. Knutsen (2010), p. 89.
96. Knutsen (2010), p. 79.

CHAPTER FOUR

1. Peter Kemp, 'Getting Under the Skin of a Nation at War', *The Sunday Times* (2 June 1991).
2. Justine Picardie, 'The Poet Who Came Out of His Shell Shock', *The Independent* (25 June 1991), p. 19.
3. Nick Rennison, *Contemporary British Novelists* (London: Routledge, 2005), pp. 26–7.
4. Herbert Mitgang, 'Healing a Mind and Spirit Badly Wounded in the Trenches', *New York Times* (15 April 1992), p. C21.

5. Ann-Louise Shapiro, 'The Fog of War: Writing the War Story Then and Now', *History and Theory* 44 (February 2005), p. 99.
6. Rudolf Weiss, 'Mise en abyme in Pat Barker's *Regeneration*', in Pavel Drábek and Jan Chovanec (eds), *Theory and Practice in English Studies* 2 (2004), p. 189.
7. Mark Rawlinson, *Pat Barker* (London: Palgrave Macmillan, 2010), p. 80.
8. Alistair Duckworth, 'Two Borrowings in Pat Barker's "Regeneration"', *Journal of Modern Literature* 27 (Winter 2004), p. 66.
9. Kaley Joyes, 'Regenerating Wilfred Owen: Pat Barker's Revisions', *Mosaic: a Journal for the Interdisciplinary Study of Literature* 42 (September 2009), p. 169.
10. Joyes (2009), pp. 178–9.
11. Joyes (2009), p. 185.
12. Joyes (2009), p. 175.
13. Weiss (2004), p. 192.
14. Kenneth O. Morgan, 'Britain and the Audit of War: The Prothero Lecture', *Transactions of the Royal Historical Society Sixth Series* 7 (1997), p. 133.
15. Karin Westman, *Pat Barker's Regeneration: A Reader's Guide* (New York and London: Continuum, 2001), p. 21.
16. Paul Taylor, 'Hero at the Emotional Front', *The Independent* (2 June 1991), p. 32; Mitgang (1992), p. C21.
17. Lavinia Greenlaw, 'All Noisy on the Western Front', *The New Republic* (21 April 1996), p. 40.
18. Duckworth (2004), p. 63.
19. Simon Wessely, 'Twentieth-Century Theories of Combat Motivation and Breakdown', *Journal of Contemporary History* 41 (April 2006), p. 282.
20. Eve Patten, '"Why Not War Writers?": Considering the Cultural Front', in Richard Pine and Eve Patten (eds), *Literatures of War* (Newcastle Upon Tyne: Cambridge Scholars Publishing, 2008), p. 18.
21. Greg Harris, 'Compulsory Masculinity, Britain, and the Great War: The Literary-Historical Work of Pat Barker', *Critique: Contemporary Studies in Fiction* 39 (Summer 1998), p. 302.
22. Westman (2001), p. 58.
23. Patten (2008), p. 23.
24. Ankhi Mukherjee, 'Stammering to Story: Neurosis and Narration in Pat Barker's *Regeneration*', *Critique* 43 (Fall 2001), p. 51.
25. Westman (2001), p. 26.
26. Westman (2001), p. 37.
27. Catherine Lanone, 'Scattering the Seed of Abraham: The Motif of Sacrifice in Pat Barker's *Regeneration* and *The Ghost Road*', *Literature & Theology* 13 (September 1999), p. 262.
28. Lanone (1999), p. 264.
29. Patricia E. Johnson, 'Embodying Losses in Pat Barker's *Regeneration* Trilogy', *Critique* 46 (Summer 2005), p. 314.
30. Lanone (1999), p. 261.
31. Westman (2001), p. 34.
32. Frances Stead Sellers, 'The Poet of the Trenches', *Washington Post* (3 April 1992), p. D1; Eddie Gibb, 'Minds Blown Apart by the Pity of War', *The Sunday Times* (24 November 1996).
33. C. Kenneth Pellow, 'Analogy in *Regeneration*', *War Literature and the Arts* 13 (2001), p. 131.
34. Pellow (2001), p. 135.
35. Pellow (2001), pp. 141–2.
36. Westman (2001), p. 33.
37. Laurie Vickroy 'A Legacy of Pacifism: Virginia Woolf and Pat Barker', *Women and Language* 27 (2004), p. 48.

38. Westman (2001), p. 49.
39. Karin Westman, 'Generation Not Regeneration: Screening Out Class, Gender, and Cultural Change in the Film of *Regeneration*', in Sharon Monteith, Margaretta Jolly, Nahem Yousaf and Ronald Paul (eds), *Critical Perspectives on Pat Barker* (Columbia, SC: University of South Carolina Press, 2005), p. 164.
40. Westman (2001), p. 14.
41. Vickroy (2004), p. 47.
42. Harris (1998), p. 295.
43. Vickroy (2004), p. 45.
44. Anne Barnes, 'Sassoon and the Glamour of War', *The Times* (15 August 1991).
45. Harris (1998), p. 292.
46. Westman (2001), p. 39.
47. Candice Rodd, 'A Stomach for War', *The Independent* (12 September 1993), p. 28.
48. Karen Patrick Knutsen, *Reciprocal Haunting: Pat Barker's Regeneration Trilogy* (Münster: Waxmann, 2010), pp. 59–60.
49. Knutsen (2010), p. 60.
50. Westman (2001), p. 53.
51. Westman (2001), p. 60.
52. Paul Taylor, 'Regeneration', in John Pym (ed.), *Time Out Film Guide* (London: Ebury Publishing, 2009), p. 877.
53. Sara Martin, 'Regenerating the War Movie: Pat Barker's *Regeneration* According to Gillies Macinnon', *Literature Film Quarterly* 30.2 (2002), p. 101.
54. Anne Whitehead, 'Pat Barker's *Regeneration* Trilogy', in Brian W. Shaffer (ed.), *A Companion to the British and Irish Novel 1945–2000* (London: Blackwell, 2005), p. 558.
55. Martin (2002), p. 98.
56. Westman, 'Generation' (2005), p. 162.
57. Westman, 'Generation' (2005), p. 168.
58. Westman (2005), p. 170.
59. Sharon Monteith, *Pat Barker* (Tavistock, Devon: Northcote House in Association with the British Council, 2002), p. 76.
60. Quoted in Westman (2001), p. 70.
61. Gibb (1996).

CHAPTER FIVE

1. Philip Hensher, 'Getting Better All the Time', *The Guardian* (26 November 1993), p. S4.
2. Carl Macdougall, 'Peep Holes into Weary World of War', *Herald of Scotland* (25 September 1993).
3. Eileen Battersby, 'A Roll Call of Causalities', *The Irish Times* (23 September 1993), p. 10.
4. Jessica Meacham, 'War, Policing and Surveillance: Pat Barker and the Secret State', in Adam Piette and Mark Rawlinson (eds), *The Edinburgh Companion to British and American War Literature* (Edinburgh: Edinburgh University Press, 2012), p. 285.
5. Richard Slobodin, 'Who Would True Valour See', *History and Anthropology* 10 (1998), p. 309.
6. Meacham (2012), p. 291.
7. John Brannigan, 'Pat Barker's *Regeneration* Trilogy: History and the Hauntological Imaginaion', in Richard J. Lane, Rod Mengham and Philip Tew (eds), *Contemporary British Fiction* (Cambridge: Polity, 2003), p. 19.
8. Macdougall (1993), p. 14.
9. Anna Grimshaw, 'The Eye in the Door: Anthropology, Film and the Exploration of Interior Space', in Marcus Banks and Howard Murphy (eds), *Rethinking Visual Anthropology* (New Haven, CT: Yale University Press, 1997), p. 39.

10. Sheryl Stevenson, 'The Uncanny Case of Dr Rivers and Mr Prior: Dynamics of Transference in *The Eye in the Door*', in Sharon Monteith, Margaretta Jolly, Nahem Yousaf and Ronald Paul (eds), *Critical Perspectives on Pat Barker* (Columbia, SC: University of South Carolina Press, 2005), p. 224.

11. Laurie Vickroy, *Trauma and Survival in Contemporary Fiction* (Charlottesville: University of Virginia Press, 2002), p. 29.

12. Eddie Gibb, 'Minds Blown Apart by the Pity of War', *The Sunday Times* (24 November 1996).

13. Lynda Prescott, 'Pat Barker, *The Ghost Road*', in David Johnson (ed.), *The Popular and the Canonical: Debating Twentieth-Century Literature 1940–2000* (London: Routledge, 2005), p. 353.

14. Stevenson (2005), p. 228.

15. Grimshaw (1997), p. 44.

16. Stevenson (2005), p. 221.

17. Monteith (2002), p. 61.

18. John Brannigan, *Pat Barker* (Manchester: Manchester University Press, 2005), p. 100.

19. Ben Shephard, *A War of Nerves: Soldiers and Psychiatrists in the Twentieth Century* (Cambridge, MA: Harvard University Press, 2001), pp. 7, 9.

20. Brannigan, *Pat Barker* (2005), p. 101.

21. Stevenson (2005), p. 222.

22. Stevenson (2005), p. 227.

23. Stevenson (2005), p. 225.

24. Stevenson (2005), p. 219.

25. Karen Patrick Knutsen, *Reciprocal Haunting: Pat Barker's Regeneration Trilogy* (Münster: Waxmann, 2010), p. 96.

26. Jim Shepard, 'Gentlemen in the Trenches', *New York Times on the Web* (15 May 1994).

27. Richard Bradford, *The Novel Now: Contemporary British Fiction* (London: Blackwell, 2007), p. 85.

28. Robert Boyers, *The Dictator's Dictation: The Politics of Novels and Novelists* (New York: Columbia University Press, 2005), pp. 162–3.

29. Eileen Battersby, 'Read, Remember and Celebrate', *The Irish Times* (9 November 1995), p. 15.

CHAPTER SIX

1. Lorna Sage, 'Both Sides', *London Review of Books* 17.10 (5 October 1995), p. 9.

2. Angela Lambert, 'In the Footsteps of Fallen Heroes', *The Independent* (9 November 1995), p. 2.

3. Eileen Battersby, 'Caught in the Harsh Glare of the Sun', *The Irish Times* (23 September 1995), p. 8; Eileen Battersby, 'Beyond Battles', *The Irish Times* (21 September 1995), p. 12.

4. Kate Kellaway, 'Billy, Don't Be a Hero', *The Observer* (27 August 1995), p. 16.

5. Francis Spufford, 'Violence Shocks, Love Hurts, Bullets Kill', *The Guardian* (22 September 1995), p. T12.

6. Lavinia Greenlaw, 'All Noisy on the Western Front', *The New Republic* (21 April 1996), p. 40.

7. Eileen Battersby, 'Win of Barker Novel Endorses Prize', *The Irish Times* (8 November 1995), p. 8.

8. Kenneth O. Morgan, 'Britain and the audit of War: The Prothero Lecture', *Transactions of the Royal Historical Society Sixth Series* 7 (1997), p. 131.

9. George Walden, 'Why We Picked Pat Barker—and Why It Matters', *Evening Standard* (8 November 1995), p. 9.

10. Boyd Tonkin, 'Fiction on the Ghost Road', *New Statesman and Society* 8.378 (10 November 1995), p. 41.

11. Daniel Johnson, 'Grandfather's Memories Inspired Booker Winner', *The Times* (8 November 1995).

12. Derwent May, 'War, Sex and a Heavy Cruiser', *The Times* (9 September 1995).

13. Jennifer Shaddock, 'Dreams of Melanesia: Masculinity and the Exorcism of War in Pat Barker's *The Ghost Road*', *Modern Fiction Studies* 52 (Fall 2006), p. 658.

14. Lynda Prescott, 'Pat Barker, *The Ghost Road*', in David Johnson (ed.), *The Popular and the Canonical: Debating Twentieth-Century Literature 1940–2000* (London: Routledge, 2005), p. 373.

15. Prescott (2005), p. 371.

16. Katherine G. Nickerson and Steven Shea, 'W. H. R. Rivers: Portrait of a Great Physician in Pat Barker's *Regeneration* Trilogy', *The Lancet* 350 (19 July 1997), p. 205.

17. Nickerson and Shea (1997), p. 207.

18. Patrick Rengger, 'The Bookers', *Globe and Mail* (4 November 1995).

19. Eileen Battersby, 'Read, Remember and Celebrate', *The Irish Times* (9 November 1995), p. 15.

20. Shaddock (2006), p. 660.

21. Karen Patrick Knutsen, *Reciprocal Haunting: Pat Barker's Regeneration Trilogy* (Münster: Waxmann, 2010), p. 113.

22. Claudia Roth Pierpont, 'Shell Shock', *New York Times Book Review* (31 December 1995), p. 5.

23. Francis Spufford, 'Exploding Old Myths', *The Guardian* (9 November 1995), p. T2.

24. Sharon Monteith, *Pat Barker* (Tavistock, Devon: Northcote House in Association with the British Council, 2002), p. 66.

25. Patricia E. Johnson, 'Embodying Losses in Pat Barker's *Regeneration* Trilogy', *Critique* 46 (Summer 2005), p. 311.

26. Nick Rennison, *Contemporary British Novelists* (London: Routledge, 2005), p. 29.

27. Sage (1995), p. 9.

28. Knutsen (2010), p. 71.

29. Shaddock (2006), p. 658.

30. Kellaway (1995), p. 16.

31. Spufford, 'Violence' (1995), p. T12.

32. Francis Spufford, 'Exploding Old Myths', *The Guardian* (9 November 1995), p. T2.

33. Prescott (2005), pp. 353, 379–80.

34. John Harvey, 'Fiction in the Present Tense', *Textual Practice* 20.1 (2006), p. 92.

35. Prescott (2005), pp. 379–80.

36. Knutsen (2010), p. 81.

37. Peter Kemp, 'War Has Been Her Greatest Obsession—and it Looms Large in her New Novel', *The Sunday Times* (1 July 2007), Culture section, p. 4.

CHAPTER SEVEN

1. Elizabeth Renzetti, 'A Sense of History Without the Cozy Veneer', *Globe and Mail* (23 December 1998), p. C1.

2. Eileen Battersby, 'The Pity of War and its Aftermath', *The Irish Times* (14 November 1998), p. 68.

3. Michael Arditti, 'Howls from Geordie's Ghost', *The Independent* (31 October 1998), p. 14; Natasha Walter, 'Geordie Goes to Hell', *The Guardian* (17 October 1998), p. 10.

4. Barry Unsworth, 'Haunted House', *New York Times* (16 May 1999), section 7, p. 6.

5. Anne Whitehead, 'The Past as Revenant: Trauma and Haunting in Pat Barker's *Another World*', *Critique* 45.2 (Winter 2004), pp. 129, 131.

6. John Brannigan, *Pat Barker* (Manchester: Manchester University Press, 2005), pp. 122–3.

7. Katie Trumpener, 'Memories Carved in Granite: Great War Memorials and Everyday Life', *PMLA* 115.2 (October 2000), p. 1100.

8. Sharon Monteith, *Pat Barker* (Tavistock, Devon: Northcote House in Association with the British Council, 2002), p. 87.

9. Nick Hubble, 'Pat Barker's *Regeneration* Trilogy', in Philip Tew and Rod Mengham (eds), *British Fiction Today* (London: Continuum, 2006), pp. 157, 158.

10. Heather Nunn and Anita Biressi, 'In the Shadow of Monstrosities: Memory, Violence, and Childhood in Another World', in Sharon Monteith, Margaretta Jolly, Nahem Yousaf and Ronald Paul (eds), *Critical Perspectives on Pat Barker* (Columbia, SC: University of South Carolina Press, 2005), pp. 254–5.

11. Suzie Mackenzie, 'Out of the Past', *The Guardian* (24 October 1998), p. 30.

12. Whitehead (2004), p. 139.

13. Brannigan, *Pat Barker* (2005), p. 132.

14. Brannigan, *Pat Barker* (2005), p. 129.

15. Arditti (1998), p. 14; Battersby (1998), p. 68.

16. Nunn and Biressi (2005), pp. 256–7.

17. Nunn and Biressi (2005), p. 260.

18. Whitehead (2004), p. 145.

19. Catherine Bernard, 'Pat Barker's Critical Work of Mourning: Realism with a Difference', *Études Anglaises* 60 (April–June 2007), p. 179. Quotation is from Anne Whitehead, 'Open to Suggestion: Hypnosis and History in the *Regeneration* Trilogy', in Sharon Monteith, Margaretta Jolly, Nahem Yousaf and Ronald Paul (eds), *Critical Perspectives on Pat Barker* (Columbia, SC: University of South Carolina Press, 2005), pp. 203–18.

20. Battersby (1998), p. 68; Unsworth (1999), section 7, p. 6; Monteith (2002), p. 80.

21. Julie Myerson, 'Still Shell-Shocked After All These Years', *Mail on Sunday* (25 October 1998), p. 36.

22. Sarah Gamble, 'North-East Gothic: Surveying Gender in Pat Barker's Fiction', *Gothic Studies* 9.2 (2007), p. 75.

23. Whitehead (2004), p. 131.

24. Maria Holmgren Troy, 'Memory and Literature: The Case of Pat Barker's *Another World*', in Andreas Kitzmann, Conny Mithander and John Sundhold (eds), *Memory Work: The Theory and Practice of Memory* (Frankfurt: Pater Lang, 2005), pp. 95–6.

25. Brannigan, *Pat Barker* (2005), p. 134; Whitehead (2004), p. 140; Judith Seaboyer, '"It Happened Once...It Can Happen Again. Take Care": Gothic Topographies in Pat Barker's *Another World*', in Pat Wheeler (ed.), *Re-Reading Pat Barker* (Newcastle: Cambridge Scholars, 2011), p. 70.

26. Brannigan, *Pat Barker* (2005), pp. 137–8.

27. Monteith (2002), p. 91.

28. Seaboyer (2011), p. 63.

29. Whitehead (2004), p. 140.

30. Gamble (2007), p. 72.

31. Monteith (2002), p. 91.

32. Gamble (2007), p. 73.

33. Margaretta Jolly, 'Toward a Masculine Maternal: Pat Barker's Bodily Fictions', in Sharon Monteith, Margaretta Jolly, Nahem Yousaf and Ronald Paul (eds), *Critical Perspectives on Pat Barker* (Columbia, SC: University of South Carolina Press, 2005), p. 250.

34. David Waterman, *Pat Barker and the Mediation of Social Reality* (Amherst, NY: Cambria Press, 2009), p. 106.

35. Monteith (2002), p. 92.

36. Anne Whitehead, *Trauma Fiction* (Edinburgh: Edinburgh University Press, 2004), p. 40; Nunn and Biressi (2005), pp. 258, 263.

37. Mike Hepworth, 'Generational Consciousness and Age Identity: Three Fictional Examples', in June Edmunds and Bryan S. Turner (eds), *Generational Consciousness, Narrative, and Politics* (Lanham, MD: Rowman and Littlefield, 2002), p. 131.

38. Maria Holmgren Troy, 'The Novelist as an Agent of Collective Remembrance: Pat Barker and the First World War', in Conny Mithander, John Sundholm and Maria

Holmgren Troy (eds), *Collective Traumas: Memories of War and Conflict in 20th-Century Europe* (Brussels: Peter Lang, 2007), p. 85.

39. Troy (2007), p. 93.
40. Troy (2007), p 75.
41. Brannigan, *Pat Barker* (2005), p. 123.
42. Nunn and Biressi (2005), p. 264.
43. Mark Greif, 'Crime and Rehabilitation', *The American Prospect* (9 April 2001), p. 37.
44. Monteith (2002), p. 96.
45. Harvey Bluestone, 'Border Crossing', *Psychiatric Services* 54 (December 2003), pp. 1655–6.
46. Robert McCrum, 'The Books Interview: Pat Barker', *The Observer* (1 April 2001), p. 17.
47. Mary Trabucco, 'Fire and Water in *Border Crossing*: Testimony as Contagion', in Pat Wheeler (ed.), *Re-Reading Pat Barker* (Newcastle: Cambridge Scholars, 2011), p. 105.
48. Julie Wheelwright, 'The Books Interview: Young Lives Between the Lines', *The Independent* (31 March 2001), p. 9.
49. Mary Morrissey, 'The Age of Innocence', *The Irish Times* (24 March 2001), p. 72.
50. Richard Eder, 'Shades of Gray', *New York Times* (18 March 2001), section 7, p. 1; Anna Burnside, 'Random Evil, Personality Disorders and Even the First World War', *Sunday Herald* (1 April 2001), p. 5.
51. Trabucco (2011), p. 110.
52. Monteith (2002), p. 95.
53. Michiko Kakutani, 'Books of the Times: Ominous Psychological Games that Unearth the Past', *New York Times* (16 March 2001), p. 42.
54. Monteith (2002), p. 98.
55. Trabucco (2011), p. 108.
56. Richard Restak, 'Reaching Out to an Adolescent Killer in a Tale that Mimics the News', *Washington Times* (15 April 2001), p. B8.
57. Trabucco (2011), p. 100.
58. Greif (2001), p. 38.
59. Waterman (2009), p. 122.
60. Greif (2001), p. 39.
61. Eder (2001), section 7, p. 1.
62. Eluned Summers-Bremner, 'Family at War: Memory, Sibling Rivalry, and the Nation in *Border Crossing* and *Another World*', in Sharon Monteith, Margaretta Jolly, Nahem Yousaf and Roland Paul (eds), *Critical Perspectives on Pat Barker* (Columbia, SC: University of South Carolina Press, 2005), p. 278.
63. Elizabeth Grice, 'Between Violence and Salvation', *Daily Telegraph* (31 March 2001), p. 7.
64. Maya Jaggi, 'Profile: Pat Barker, Dispatches from the Front', *The Guardian* (16 August 2003), p. 16; Ellen Warner, 'Fiction: As Committed as a Lover—and as Creepy as a Stalker', *Independent on Sunday* (24 August 2003), p. 16.
65. Neil Gordon, 'Something Not Quite Right', *New York Times* (14 December 2001), section 7, p. 12.
66. Jaggi (2003), p. 16; Rosemary Goring, 'Hope Floats in our War-Torn World', *The Herald* (9 August 2003), p. 12.
67. Sharon Monteith and Nahem Yousaf, '*Double Vision*: Regenerative or Traumatized Pastoral?' in Sharon Monteith, Margaretta Jolly, Nahem Yousaf and Roland Paul (eds), *Critical Perspectives on Pat Barker* (Columbia, SC: University of South Carolina Press, 2005), p. 283.
68. John Brannigan, '"To See and To Know": Ethics and Aesthetics in *Double Vision* and *Life Class*', in Pat Wheeler (ed.), *Re-Reading Pat Barker* (Newcastle: Cambridge Scholars, 2011), p. 15.

69. Barbara Korte, 'Touched by the Pain of Others: War Correspondents in Contemporary Fiction. Michael Ignatieff, *Charlie Johnson in the Flames* and Pat Barker, *Double Vision*', 88 (April 2007), p. 190.
70. Brannigan, *Pat Barker* (2005), p. 158.
71. Neil Gordon, 'Double Vision', *International Herald Tribune* (24 December 2003), p. 16.
72. Wendy Smith, 'Pat Barker: Of Death and Deadlines', *Publishers Weekly* (15 December 2003), p. 48.
73. Marie-Louise Kohlke, 'Pathologized Masculinity in Pat Barker's *Double Vision*: Stephen Sharkey's Monstrous Others', in Pat Wheeler (ed.), *Re-Reading Pat Barker* (Newcastle: Cambridge Scholars, 2011), p. 82.
74. Kohlke (2011), p. 86.
75. Kohlke (2011), p. 92.
76. Brannigan, *Pat Barker* (2005), p. 145.
77. Hubble, p. 154; Brannigan, *Pat Barker* (2005), p. 149.
78. Brannigan, *Pat Barker* (2005), p. 140.
79. Goring (2003), p. 12.
80. Monteith and Yousaf (2005), p. 284.
81. Mark Anthony Jarman, 'In and Out of the Frame', *Globe and Mail* (23 August 2003), p. D3.
82. Smith (2003), p. 48.
83. Monteith and Yousaf (2005), p. 296.

CHAPTER EIGHT

1. Anna Burnside, 'Random Evil, Personality Disorders and Even the First World War', *Sunday Herald* (1 April 2001), p. 5.
2. Susanna Rustin, 'A Life in Writing: Double Vision: Pat Barker Returns to the Setting of her Regeneration Trilogy for her 11th Novel', *The Guardian* (30 June 2007), p. 11.
3. Alan Cumyn, 'Pat Barker and the Crucible of Doom', *Globe and Mail* (28 July 2007), p. D4.
4. Alden Mudge, 'The Suffering of Others: Pat Barker's Vivid Portrait of the Face of War', Book Page (February 2007), http://bookpage.com/interviews/8441-pat-barker#.Uy WpMqtFA5s.
5. John Brannigan, '"To See and To Know": Ethics and Aesthetics in *Double Vision* and *Life Class*', in Pat Wheeler (ed.), *Re-Reading Pat Barker* (Newcastle: Cambridge Scholars, 2011), p. 18.
6. Peter Kemp, 'War Has Been her Greatest Obsession—and it Looms Large in her New Novel. But is this Pat Barker's Last Battle?' *The Sunday Times* (1 July 2007), Culture section, p. 4.
7. Michiko Kakutani, 'Exploring Small Stories of the Great War', *New York Times* (29 February 2008), p. E31.
8. Lee Randall, 'Back to the Western Front', *The Scotsman* (14 July 2007), p. 14.
9. Simon Avery, 'Forming a New Political Aesthetic: The Enabling Body in Pat Barker's *Life Class*', in Pat Wheeler (ed.), *Re-Reading Pat Barker* (Newcastle: Cambridge Scholars, 2011), p. 135.
10. Avery (2011), p. 146.
11. Brannigan (2011), p. 22.
12. Avery (2011), p. 140.
13. Avery (2011), p. 148.
14. D. J. Taylor, 'A Spattered Canvas: Pat Barker's New Novel Sutures Art and Battlefront Surgery in 1914', *The Guardian* (7 July 2007), p. 17.
15. Fiona Tolan, '"Painting While Rome Burns": Ethics and Aesthetics in Pat Barker's *Life Class* and Zadie Smith's *On Beauty*', *Tulsa Studies in Women's Literature* 29.2 (Fall 2010), p. 376.

16. Tolan (2010), p. 384.
17. Tolan (2010), p. 390.
18. Lara Tupper, 'A Review of *Life Class* by Pat Barker', *The Believer* (January 2008), online.
19. John Barber, 'A Portrait of the First World War that's Anything But Nice', *Globe and Mail* (10 November 2012), p. A11.
20. John Vernon, 'The Damage of War, Physical and Psychological', *International Herald Tribune* (9 October 2012), Leisure section, p. 11.
21. Freya Johnston, 'The Ghosts of War', *Daily Telegraph* (1 September 2012), p. 24.
22. Hermione Lee, 'Book of the Week: The Anatomy of War', *The Guardian* (11 August 2012), Review, p. 5.
23. Peter Kemp, 'Atrocity Exhibitions: Pat Barker Returns to the Trenches in a Chilling Look at Art, Disfigurement and the Horrors of War', *The Sunday Times* (2 September 2012), Features, p. 37.
24. Lucy Scholes, 'Pat Barker on "Toby's Room", Historical Fiction, and the Booker', *The Daily Beast* (online) (5 October 2012), np.
25. Richard Davenport-Hines, 'Brotherly Love', *The Spectator* (1 September 2012), p. 33.
26. Bryan Appleyard, 'Inspired by the Scars of a Generation', *The Sunday Times* (19 August 2012), Features, p. 15.
27. Scholes (2012).

CONCLUSION

1. Pat Wheeler, 'Introduction', in Pat Wheeler (ed.), *Re-Reading Pat Barker* (Newcastle: Cambridge Scholars, 2011), p. xiii; Merritt Moseley, Personal Interview with Pat Barker, June 2010.
2. Sharon Monteith, *Pat Barker* (Tavistock, Devon: Northcote House in Association with the British Council, 2001), p. 1.
3. John Brannigan, *Pat Barker* (Manchester: Manchester University Press, 2005).p. 173.
4. David Waterman, *Pat Barker and the Mediation of Social Reality* (Amherst, NY: Cambria Press, 2009), p. 3.
5. Waterman (2009), p. 170.
6. Mark Rawlinson, *Pat Barker* (London: Palgrave Macmillan, 2010),p. 157.
7. Rawlinson (2010), p. 15.
8. Karen Patrick Knutsen, *Reciprocal Haunting: Pat Barker's Regeneration Trilogy* (Münster: Waxmann, 2010), p. 18.
9. Karin Westman, *Pat Barker's Regeneration: A Reader's Guide* (New York and London: Continuum, 2001), p. 58.
10. Nahem Yousaf and Sharon Monteith, 'Introduction: Reading Pat Barker', in Sharon Monteith, Margaretta Jolly, Nahem Yousaf and Ronald Paul (eds), *Critical Perspectives on Pat Barker* (Columbia, SC: University of South Carolina Press, 2005), p. xiii.
11. Sharon Monteith, 'Foreword', in Pat Wheeler (ed.), *Re-Reading Pat Barker* (Newcastle: Cambridge Scholars, 2011), p. ix.
12. Monteith (2011), p. viii.

Select Bibliography

BOOKS BY PAT BARKER

(Details of first UK publication, with details of editions used for quotations in this guide, where different.)

Union Street (London: Virago, 1982).

Blow Your House Down (London: Virago, 1984).

Union Street and Blow Your House Down (London: Quality Paperbacks Direct, 1996).

Liza's England (Originally published as *The Century's Daughter*, retitled in 1996) (London: Virago, 1986). (New York: Picador, 1986), pagination is the same as for the UK Virago paperback.

The Man Who Wasn't There (London: Virago, 1989). (New York: Picador, 1989), pagination is the same as for the UK Virago paperback.

Regeneration (London: Viking, 1991). (New York: Plume, 1991), pagination is the same as for the UK Penguin paperback.

The Eye in the Door (London: Viking, 1993). (New York: Plume, 1993), pagination is the same as for the UK Penguin paperback.

The Ghost Road (London: Viking, 1995). (New York: Plume, 1995), pagination is the same as for the UK Penguin paperback.

The Regeneration Trilogy (London: Viking Penguin, 1996).

Another World (London: Viking, 1998). (New York: Farrar, Straus & Giroux, 1998), pagination is the same as for the UK Penguin paperback.

Border Crossing (London: Viking, 2001). (New York: Farrar, Straus & Giroux, 2001).

Double Vision (London: Hamish Hamilton, 2003). (New York: Picador, 2003).

Life Class (London: Hamish Hamilton, 2007). (New York: Anchor, 2007).

Toby's Room (London: Hamish Hamilton, 2012).

BOOKS ABOUT PAT BARKER

GENERAL

Brannigan, John. *Pat Barker* (Manchester: Manchester University Press, 2005). Through to *Double Vision*.

Monteith, Sharon. *Pat Barker* (Tavistock, Devon: Northcote House in Association with the British Council, 2002). Eighteen chapters on all the books through to *Border Crossing*; includes reflection on film versions and on the books in the classroom.

Monteith, Sharon, Margaretta Jolly, Nahem Yousaf and Ronald Paul (eds). *Critical Perspectives on Pat Barker* (Columbia, SC: University of South Carolina Press, 2005). Through to *Double Vision*.

Rawlinson, Mark. *Pat Barker* (London: Palgrave Macmillan, 2010). Through to *Life Class*.

Waterman, David. *Pat Barker and the Mediation of Social Reality* (Amherst, NY: Cambria Press, 2009). Through to *Life Class*.

Wheeler, Pat (ed.). *Re-Reading Pat Barker* (Newcastle: Cambridge Scholars, 2011). Nine chapters on various books; through to *Life Class*.

ON THE *REGENERATION* TRILOGY

Knutsen, Karen Patrick. *Reciprocal Haunting: Pat Barker's Regeneration Trilogy* (Münster: Waxmann, 2010).

ON *REGENERATION*

Gamble, Sarah. *Regeneration: York Notes Advanced* (London: York Press, 2009).
Westman, Karin. *Pat Barker's Regeneration: A Reader's Guide* (New York and London: Continuum, 2001).

BOOKS WITH SUBSTANTIAL DISCUSSION OF BARKER

GENERAL, OR COVERING MORE THAN ONE TITLE

Bradford, Richard. *The Novel Now: Contemporary British Fiction* (London: Blackwell, 2007).
Childs, Peter. *Contemporary Novelists: British Fiction Since 1970* (London: Palgrave Macmillan, 2005).
Rennison, Nick. *Contemporary British Novelists* (London: Routledge, 2005).

ABOUT *UNION STREET/BLOW YOUR HOUSE DOWN*

Alexander, Flora. *Contemporary Women Novelists* (London: Edward Arnold, 1989).
Haywood, Ian. *Working-class Fiction: From Chartism to* Trainspotting (London: Northcote House in association with the British Council, 1997).
Palmer, Paulina. *Contemporary Women's Fiction: Narrative Practice and Feminist Theory* (Jackson: University Press of Mississippi, 1989).

ABOUT *LIZA'S ENGLAND*

Hitchcock, Peter. *Dialogics of the Oppressed* (Minneapolis: University of Minnesota Press, 1993).

ABOUT THE *REGENERATION* TRILOGY

Bergonzi, Bernard. *War Poets and Other Subjects* (Aldershot: Ashgate, 1999).
Boyers, Robert. *The Dictator's Dictation: The Politics of Novels and Novelists* (New York: Columbia University Press, 2005).
Shephard, Ben. *A War of Nerves: Soldiers and Psychiatrists in the Twentieth Century* (Cambridge, MA: Harvard University Press, 2001).
Vickroy, Laurie. *Trauma and Survival in Contemporary Fiction* (Charlottesville: University of Virginia Press, 2002).
Whitehead, Anne. *Trauma Fiction* (Edinburgh: Edinburgh University Press, 2004).

BOOK CHAPTERS AND CRITICAL ARTICLES

GENERAL, OR COVERING MORE THAN ONE TITLE

Fraser, Kennedy. 'Ghost Writer: Pat Barker's Haunted Imagination', *The New Yorker* (17 March 17 2008), pp. 41–5.

Moseley, Merritt. 'Pat Barker (8 May 1943 –)', in *Dictionary of Literary Biography*, Volume 271, *British and Irish Novelists Since 1960* (Detroit, MI: Gale, 2003), pp. 39–48.

Prescott, Lynda. 'Pat Barker's Vanishing Boundaries', in Nick Bentley (ed.), *British Fiction of the 1990s* (London: Routledge, 2005), pp. 167–78.

Wheeler, Pat. 'Introduction', in Pat Wheeler (ed.), *Re-Reading Pat Barker* (Newcastle: Cambridge Scholars, 2011), pp. xii–xv.

Yousaf, Nahem and Sharon Monteith. 'Introduction: Reading Pat Barker', in Sharon Monteith, Margaretta Jolly, Nahem Yousaf and Ronald Paul (eds), *Critical Perspectives on Pat Barker* (Columbia, SC: University of South Carolina Press, 2005), pp. vii–xxii.

ABOUT *UNION STREET*

'Best of Young British Novelists', *Granta* 7 (1983).

Brannigan, John. 'The Small World of Kelly Brown: Home and Dereliction in *Union Street*', in Sharon Monteith, Margaretta Jolly, Nahem Yousaf and Ronald Paul (eds), *Critical Perspectives on Pat Barker* (Columbia, SC: University of South Carolina Press, 2005), pp. 3–13.

Brophy, Sarah. 'Working-Class Women, Labor, and the Problem of Community in *Union Street* and *Liza's England*', in Sharon Monteith, Margaretta Jolly, Nahem Yousaf and Ronald Paul (eds), *Critical Perspectives on Pat Barker* (Columbia, SC: University of South Carolina Press, 2005), pp. 24–39.

Dodd, Kathryn and Philip Dodd. 'From the East End to *EastEnders*: Representations of the Working Class, 1890–1990', in Dominic Strinati and Stephen Wagg (eds), *Come on Down? Popular Media Culture in Post-War Britain* (London: Routledge, 1992), pp. 116–32.

Falcus, Sarah. '"A Complex Mixture of Fascination and Distaste": Relationships Between Women in Pat Barker's *Blow Your House Down*, *Liza's England* and *Union Street*', *Journal of Gender Studies* 16 (November 2007), pp. 249–61.

Falcus, Sarah. 'Unsettling Ageing in Three Novels by Pat Barker', *Ageing & Society* 32 (2012), pp. 1382–98.

Gallagher, Lucy. '"He Had Always Believed That There Were Two Sorts of Women: The Decent Ones and the Rest": The Female Body, Dirt, and Domesticity in Pat Barker's *Union Street*', *Contemporary Women's Writing* 5.1 (January 2011), pp. 36–51.

Hitchcock, Peter. 'They Must Be Represented? Problems in Theories of Working-Class Representation', *PMLA* 115 (January 2000), pp. 20–32.

Jolly, Margaretta. 'After Feminism: Pat Barker, Penelope Lively and the Contemporary Novel', in Alistair Davies and Alan Sinfield (eds), *British Culture of the Postwar: An Introduction to Literature and Society 1945–1999* (London: Routledge, 2000), pp. 58–82.

Jolly, Margaretta. 'Toward a Masculine Maternal: Pat Barker's Bodily Fictions', in Sharon Monteith, Margaretta Jolly, Nahem Yousaf and Ronald Paul (eds), *Critical Perspectives on Pat Barker* (Columbia, SC: University of South Carolina Press, 2005), pp. 235–53.

Kirk, John. 'Recovered Perspectives: Gender, Class, and Memory in Pat Barker's Writing', *Contemporary Literature* XL.4 (1999), pp. 603–25.

Malm, Monica. '*Union Street*: Thoughts on Mothering', *Moderna Språk* 92 (January 1998), pp. 143–6.

Monteith, Sharon. 'Warring Fictions: Reading Pat Barker', *Moderna Språk* 91 (1997), pp. 124–9.

Smith, Penny. 'Remembered Poverty: The North-East of England', in Ian A. Bell (ed.), *Peripheral Visions: Images of Nationhood in Contemporary British Fiction* (Cardiff: University of Wales Press, 1995), pp. 103–21.

Troy, Maria Holmgren. 'Matrix, Metramorphosis, and the Readymade in *Union Street*, *Liza's England* and *Another World*', in Pat Wheeler (ed.), *Re-Reading Pat Barker* (Newcastle: Cambridge Scholars, 2011), pp. 1–12.

Wotton, George. 'Writing from the Margins', in Ian A. Bell (ed.), *Peripheral Visions: Images of Nationhood in Contemporary British Fiction* (Cardiff: University of Wales Press, 1995), pp. 194–215.

ABOUT *BLOW YOUR HOUSE DOWN*

Andriotis, Katerina. 'Pat Barker, *Blow Your House Down* and the Prostitution Debate', *Sexuality & Culture* 13 (2009), p. 54.

Ardis, Ann. 'Political Attentiveness vs. Political Correctness: Teaching Pat Barker's "Blow Your House Down"', *College Literature* 18 (October 1991), pp. 44–54.

Bartleet, Carina. 'Bringing the House Down: Pat Barker, Sarah Daniels, and the Dramatic Dialogue', in Sharon Monteith, Margaretta Jolly, Nahem Yousaf and Ronald Paul (eds), *Critical Perspectives on Pat Barker* (Columbia, SC: University of South Carolina Press, 2005), pp. 87–100.

Bauer, Dale M. 'The Other 'F' Word: The Feminist in the Classroom', *College English* 52 (April 1990), pp. 385–96.

Falcus, Sarah. '"A Complex Mixture of Fascination and Distaste": Relationships Between Women in Pat Barker's *Blow Your House Down*, *Liza's England* and *Union Street*', *Journal of Gender Studies* 16 (November 2007), pp. 249–61.

Joannou, Maroula. 'Pat Barker and the Languages of Region and Class', in Emma Parker (ed.), *Contemporary British Women Writers* (Cambridge: D. S. Brewer, 2004), pp. 41–54.

Smith, Penny. 'Remembered Poverty: The North-East of England', in Ian A. Bell (ed.), *Peripheral Visions: Images of Nationhood in Contemporary British Fiction* (Cardiff: University of Wales Press, 1995), pp. 103–21.

ABOUT *LIZA'S ENGLAND*

Anderson, Linda. 'The Re-Imagining of History in Contemporary Women's Fiction', in Linda Anderson (ed.), *Plotting Change: Contemporary Women's Fiction* (London: Edward Arnold, 1990), pp. 129–41.

Bernard, Catherine. 'Pat Barker's Critical Work of Mourning: Realism with a Difference', *Études Anglaises* 60 (April–June 2007), pp. 173–84.

Brophy, Sarah. 'Working-Class Women, Labor, and the Problem of Community in *Union Street* and *Liza's England*', in Sharon Monteith, Margaretta Jolly, Nahem Yousaf and Ronald Paul (eds), *Critical Perspectives on Pat Barker* (Columbia, SC: University of South Carolina Press, 2005), pp. 24–39.

Falcus, Sarah. '"A Complex Mixture of Fascination and Distaste": Relationships Between Women in Pat Barker's *Blow Your House Down*, *Liza's England* and *Union Street*', *Journal of Gender Studies* 16 (November 2007), pp. 249–61.

Falcus, Sarah. 'Unsettling Ageing in Three Novels by Pat Barker', *Ageing & Society* 32 (2012), pp. 1382–98.

Gildersleeve, Jessica. 'Her Story: *Liza's England* (*The Century's Daughter*)', in Pat Wheeler (ed.), *Re-Reading Pat Barker* (Newcastle: Cambridge Scholars, 2011), pp. 25–41.

Jolly, Magaretta. 'Toward a Masculine Maternal: Pat Barker's Bodily Fictions', in Sharon Monteith, Margaretta Jolly, Nahem Yousaf and Ronald Paul (eds), *Critical Perspectives on Pat Barker* (Columbia, SC: University of South Carolina Press, 2005), pp. 235–53.

Newman, Jenny. 'Souls and Arseholes: The Double Vision of *Liza's England*', in Sharon Monteith, Margaretta Jolly, Nahem Yousaf and Ronald Paul (eds), *Critical Perspectives on Pat Barker* (Columbia, SC: University of South Carolina Press, 2005), pp. 101–14.

Pykett, Lyn. 'The Century's Daughters: Recent Women's Fiction and History', *Critical Quarterly* 29.3 (September 1987), pp. 71–7.

Troy, Maria Holmgren, 'Matrix, Metramorphosis, and the Readymade in *Union Street*, *Liza's England* and *Another World*', in Pat Wheeler (ed.), *Re-Reading Pat Barker* (Newcastle: Cambridge Scholars, 2011), pp. 1–12.

alon,

ABOUT *THE MAN WHO WASN'T THERE*

Lovell, Alan. 'The *Uses of Literacy*: The Scholarship Boy', *Universities & Left Review* 1.2 (Summer 1957), pp. 33–4.

Monteith, Sharon. 'Screening *The Man Who Wasn't There*: The Second World War and 1950s Cinema', in Sharon Monteith, Margaretta Jolly, Nahem Yousaf and Ronald Paul (eds), *Critical Perspectives on Pat Barker* (Columbia, SC: University of South Carolina Press, 2005), p. 115.

Wheeler, Pat. 'Transgressing Masculinities: *The Man Who Wasn't There*', in Sharon Monteith, Margaretta Jolly, Nahem Yousaf and Ronald Paul (eds), *Critical Perspectives on Pat Barker* (Columbia, SC: University of South Carolina Press, 2005), pp. 128–46.

ABOUT THE *REGENERATION* TRILOGY

Brannigan, John. 'Pat Barker's *Regeneration* Trilogy: History and the Hauntological Imagination', in Richard J. Lane, Rod Mengham and Philip Tew (eds), *Contemporary British Fiction* (Cambridge: Polity, 2003), pp. 13–26.

Brown, Dennis. 'The *Regeneration* Trilogy: Total War, Masculinities, Anthropology, and the Talking Cure', in Sharon Monteith, Margaretta Jolly, Nahem Yousaf and Ronald Paul (eds), *Critical Perspectives on Pat Barker* (Columbia, SC: University of South Carolina Press, 2005), pp. 187–202.

Harris, Greg. 'Compulsory Masculinity, Britain, and the Great War: The Literary-Historical Work of Pat Barker', *Critique: Contemporary Studies in Fiction* 39 (Summer 1998), pp. 290–304.

Hitchcock, Peter. 'What Is Prior? Working-Class Masculinity in Pat Barker's Trilogy', *Genders Online Journal* 35, www.genders.org/g35/g35_hitchcock.html (2002), np.

Hubble, Nick. 'Pat Barker's *Regeneration* Trilogy', in Philip Tew and Rod Mengham (eds), *British Fiction Today* (London: Continuum, 2006), pp. 153–64.

Johnson, Patricia E. 'Embodying Losses in Pat Barker's *Regeneration* Trilogy', *Critique* 46 (Summer 2005), pp. 307–19.

Knutsen, Karen Patrick. 'Memory, War, Trauma: Acting Out and Working Through in Pat Barker's *Regeneration Trilogy*', in Maria Holmgren Troy and Elisabeth Wennö (eds), *Memory, Haunting, Discourse* (Karlstad: Karlstads University Press, 2005), pp. 161–71.

Löschnigg, Martin. '"…the novelist's responsibility to the past": History, Myth, and the Narratives of Crisis in Pat Barker's *Regeneration* Trilogy (1991–1995)', *Zeitschrift fur Anglistik und Amerikanistik* 47 (1999), pp. 214–28.

Morgan, Kenneth O. 'Britain and the Audit of War: The Prothero Lecture', *Transactions of the Royal Historical Society Sixth Series* 7 (1997), pp. 131–53.

Morrison, Blake. 'War Stories', *The New Yorker* (22 January 1996), pp. 78–82.

Mudge, Alden. 'The Suffering of Others: Pat Barker's Vivid Portrait of the Face of War', *Book Page* (February 2007), http://bookpage.com/interview/the-suffering-of-others.

Nickerson, Katherine G. and Steven Shea. 'W. H. R. Rivers: Portrait of a Great Physician in Pat Barker's *Regeneration* Trilogy', *The Lancet* 350 (19 July 1997), pp. 205–9.

Paul, Ronald. 'In Pastoral Fields: The *Regeneration* Trilogy and Classic First World War Fiction', in Sharon Monteith, Margaretta Jolly, Nahem Yousaf and Ronald Paul (eds), *Critical Perspectives on Pat Barker* (Columbia, SC: University of South Carolina Press, 2005), pp. 147–61.

Shapiro, Ann-Louise. 'The Fog of War: Writing the War Story Then and Now', *History and Theory* 44 (February 2005), pp. 91–101.

Slobodin, Richard. 'Who Would True Valour See', *History and Anthropology* 10 (1998), pp. 299–317.

Talbott, John E. 'Soldiers, Psychiatrists, and Combat Trauma', *Journal of Interdisciplinary History* 27 (Winter 1997), pp. 437–54.

Troy, Maria Holmgren. 'The Novelist as an Agent of Collective Remembrance: Pat Barker and the First World War', in Conny Mithander, John Sundholm and Maria Holmgren Troy (eds), *Collective Traumas: Memories of War and Conflict in 20th-Century Europe* (Brussels: Peter Lang, 2007), pp. 47–78.

Trumpener, Katie. 'Memories Carved in Granite: Great War Memorials and Everyday Life', *PMLA* 115.2 (October 2000), pp. 1096–103.

Vickroy, Laurie. 'A Legacy of Pacifism: Virginia Woolf and Pat Barker', *Women and Language*,27 (2004), pp. 45–50.

Waterman, David. 'Improper Heroes: Treating the Contagion of Hysteria, Homosexuality and Pacifism in Pat Barker's World War I Trilogy', *Études Brittaniques contemporaines* 24 (2003), pp. 5–18.

Wessely, Simon. 'Twentieth-Century Theories on Combat Motivation and Breakdown', *Journal of Contemporary History* 41.2 (April 2006), pp. 269–86.

Wheeler, Pat. '"Where Unknown, There Place Monsters": Reading Class Conflict and Sexual Anxiety in the *Regeneration* Trilogy', in Pat Wheeler (ed.), *Re-Reading Pat Barker* (Nottingham: Cambridge Scholars, 2011), pp. 43–61.

Whitehead, Anne. 'Open to Suggestion: Hypnosis and History in the *Regeneration* Trilogy', in Sharon Monteith, Margaretta Jolly, Nahem Yousaf and Ronald Paul (eds), *Critical Perspectives on Pat Barker* (Columbia, SC: University of South Carolina Press, 2005), pp. 203–18.

Whitehead, Anne. 'Pat Barker's *Regeneration* Trilogy', in Brian W. Shaffer (ed.), *A Companion to the British and Irish Novel 1945–2000* (London: Blackwell, 2005), pp. 550–60.

Winter, Jay. 'Shell-Shock and the Cultural History of the Great War', *Journal of Contemporary History* 35 (January 2000), pp. 7–11.

Wyatt-Brown, Anne M. 'Headhunters and Victims of War: W. H. R. Rivers and Pat Barker', *Proceedings of the 13th International Conference on Literature and Psychoanalysis* (Lisbon: Instituto Superior de Psicologia Aplicada, 1997), pp. 53–9.

ABOUT *REGENERATION*

Duckworth, Alistair. 'Two Borrowings in Pat Barker's "Regeneration"', *Journal of Modern Literature* 27 (Winter 2004), pp. 63–7.

Joyes, Kaley. 'Regenerating Wilfred Owen: Pat Barker's Revisions', *Mosaic: A Journal for the Interdisciplinary Study of Literature* 42.3 (September 2009), pp. 169–83.

Lanone, Catherine. 'Scattering the Seed of Abraham: The Motif of Sacrifice in Pat Barker's *Regeneration* and *The Ghost Road*', *Literature & Theology* 13 (September 1999), pp. 259–68.

Martin, Sara. 'Regenerating the War Movie: Pat Barker's *Regeneration* According to Gillies Mackinnon', *Literature Film Quarterly* 30.2 (2002), pp. 98–103.

Mukherjee, Ankhi. 'Stammering to Story: Neurosis and Narration in Pat Barker's "Regeneration"', *Critique* 43 (Fall 2001), pp. 49–62.

Patten, Eve. '"Why Not War Writers?": Considering the Cultural Front', in Richard Pine and Eve Patten (eds), *Literatures of War* (Newcastle Upon Tyne: Cambridge Scholars Publishing, 2008), pp. 17–29.

Pellow, C. Kenneth. 'Analogy in *Regeneration*', *War Literature and the Arts* 13 (2001), pp. 130–46.

Ross, Sarah C. E. 'Regeneration, Redemption, Resurrection: Pat Barker and the Problem of Evil', in James Acheson and Sarah C. E. Ross (eds), *The Contemporary British Novel Since 1980* (London: Palgrave Macmillan, 2005), pp. 131–41.

Weiss, Rudolf. 'Mise en abyme in Pat Barker's *Regeneration*', in Pavel Drábek and Jan Chovanec (eds), *Theory and Practice in English Studies* 2 (2004), pp. 189–94.

Westman, Karin. 'Generation Not Regeneration: Screening Out Class, Gender, and Cultural Change in the Film of *Regeneration*', in Sharon Monteith, Margaretta Jolly, Nahem Yousaf and Ronald Paul (eds), *Critical Perspectives on Pat Barker* (Columbia, SC: University of South Carolina Press, 2005), pp. 162–74.

ABOUT *THE EYE IN THE DOOR*

Grimshaw, Anna. 'The Eye in the Door: Anthropology, Film and the Exploration of Interior Space', in Marcus Banks and Howard Murphy (eds), *Rethinking Visual Anthropology* (New Haven, CT: Yale University Press, 1997), pp. 36–52.

Meacham, Jessica. 'War, Policing and Surveillance: Pat Barker and the Secret State', in Adam Piette and Mark Rawlinson (eds), *The Edinburgh Companion to British and American War Literature* (Edinburgh: Edinburgh University Press, 2012), pp. 285–93.

Stevenson, Sheryl. 'The Uncanny Case of Dr Rivers and Mr Prior: Dynamics of Transference in *The Eye in the Door*', in Sharon Monteith, Margaretta Jolly, Nahem Yousaf and Ronald Paul (eds), *Critical Perspectives on Pat Barker* (Columbia, SC: University of South Carolina Press, 2005), pp. 219–32.

ABOUT *THE GHOST ROAD*

Harvey, John. 'Fiction in the Present Tense', *Textual Practice* 20.1 (2006), pp. 71–98.

Lanone, Catherine. 'Scattering the Seed of Abraham: The Motif of Sacrifice in Pat Barker's *Regeneration* and *The Ghost Road*', *Literature & Theology* 13 (September 1999), pp. 259–68.

McCloskey, Mark. 'The Ghost Road', *Magill's Literary Annual* (1996), pp. 1–3.

Prescott, Lynda, 'Pat Barker, *The Ghost Road*', in David Johnson (ed.), *The Popular and the Canonical: Debating Twentieth-Century Literature 1940–2000* (London: Routledge, 2005), pp. 344–99.

Shaddock, Jennifer. 'Dreams of Melanesia: Masculinity and the Exorcism of War in Pat Barker's *The Ghost Road*', *Modern Fiction Studies* 52 (Fall 2006), pp. 656–74.

Walden, George. 'Why We Picked Pat Barker—and Why It Matters', *Evening Standard* (8 November 1995), p. 9.

ABOUT *ANOTHER WORLD*

Falcus, Sarah. 'Unsettling Ageing in Three Novels by Pat Barker', *Ageing & Society* 32 (2012), pp. 1382–98.

Gamble, Sarah. 'North-East Gothic: Surveying Gender in Pat Barker's Fiction', *Gothic Studies* 9.2 (2007), pp. 71–82.

Hepworth, Mike. 'Generational Consciousness and Age Identity: Three Fictional Examples', in June Edmunds and Bryan S. Turner (eds), *Generational Consciousness, Narrative, and Politics* (Lanham, MD: Rowman and Littlefield, 2002), pp. 131–44.

Nunn, Heather and Anita Biressi. 'In the Shadow of Monstrosities: Memory, Violence, and Childhood in *Another World*', in Sharon Monteith, Margaretta Jolly, Nahem Yousaf and Ronald Paul (eds), *Critical Perspectives on Pat Barker* (Columbia, SC: University of South Carolina Press, 2005), pp. 254–65.

Seaboyer, Judith. '"It Happened Once...It Can Happen Again. Take Care": Gothic Topographies in Pat Barker's *Another World*', in Pat Wheeler (ed.), *Re-Reading Pat Barker* (Newcastle: Cambridge Scholars, 2011), pp. 63–78.

Summers-Bremner, Eluned. 'Family at War: Memory, Sibling Rivalry, and the Nation in *Border Crossing* and *Another World*', in Sharon Monteith, Margaretta Jolly, Nahem Yousaf and Ronald Paul (eds), *Critical Perspectives on Pat Barker* (Columbia, SC: University of South Carolina Press, 2005), pp. 266–82.

Troy, Maria Holmgren. 'Matrix, Metramorphosis, and the Readymade in *Union Street*, *Liza's England* and *Another World*', in Pat Wheeler (ed.), *Re-Reading Pat Barker* (Newcastle: Cambridge Scholars, 2011), pp. 1–12.

Troy, Maria Holmgren. 'Memory and Literature: The Case of Pat Barker's *Another World*', in Andreas Kitzmann, Conny Mithander and John Sundhold (eds), *Memory Work: The Theory and Practice of Memory* (Frankfurt: Pater Lang, 2005), pp. 85–103.

Whitehead, Anne. 'The Past as Revenant: Trauma and Haunting in Pat Barker's *Another World*', *Critique* 45.2 (Winter 2004), pp. 129–46.

ABOUT *BORDER CROSSING*

Bluestone, Harvey. 'Border Crossing', *Psychiatric Services* 54 (December 2003), pp. 1655–6.

Greif, Mark. 'Crime and Rehabilitation', *The American Prospect* (9 April 2001), pp. 36–9.

Summers-Bremner, Eluned. 'Family at War: Memory, Sibling Rivalry, and the Nation in *Border Crossing* and *Another World*', in Sharon Monteith, Margaretta Jolly, Nahem Yousaf and Ronald Paul (eds), *Critical Perspectives on Pat Barker* (Columbia, SC: University of South Carolina Press, 2005), pp. 266–82.

Trabucco, Mary. 'Fire and Water in *Border Crossing*: Testimony as Contagion', in Pat Wheeler (ed.), *Re-Reading Pat Barker* (Newcastle: Cambridge Scholars, 2011), pp. 99–112.

ABOUT *DOUBLE VISION*

Brannigan, John. '"To See and To Know": Ethics and Aesthetics in *Double Vision* and *Life Class*', in Pat Wheeler (ed.), *Re-Reading Pat Barker* (Newcastle: Cambridge Scholars, 2011), pp. 13–24.

Kohlke, Marie-Louise. 'Pathologized Masculinity in Pat Barker's *Double Vision*: Stephen Sharkey's Monstrous Others', in Pat Wheeler (ed.), *Re-Reading Pat Barker* (Newcastle: Cambridge Scholars, 2011), pp. 79–98.

Korte, Barbara. 'Touched by the Pain of Others: War Correspondents in Contemporary Fiction. Michael Ignatieff, *Charlie Johnson in the Flames* and Pat Barker, *Double Vision*', *English Studies: A Journal of English Language and Literature* 88 (April 2007), pp. 183–94.

Monteith, Sharon and Nahem Yousaf. '*Double Vision*: Regenerative or Traumatized Pastoral?' in Sharon Monteith, Margaretta Jolly, Nahem Yousaf and Ronald Paul (eds), *Critical Perspectives on Pat Barker* (Columbia, SC: University of South Carolina Press, 2005), pp. 283–300.

ABOUT *LIFE CLASS*

Avery, Simon. 'Forming a New Political Aesthetic: The Enabling Body in Pat Barker's *Life Class*', in Pat Wheeler (ed.), *Re-Reading Pat Barker* (Newcastle: Cambridge Scholars, 2011), pp. 131–50.

Brannigan, John. '"To See and To Know": Ethics and Aesthetics in *Double Vision* and *Life Class*', in Pat Wheeler (ed.), *Re-Reading Pat Barker* (Newcastle: Cambridge Scholars, 2011), pp. 13–24.

Tolan, Fiona. '"Painting While Rome Burns": Ethics and Aesthetics in Pat Barker's *Life Class* and Zadie Smith's *On Beauty*', *Tulsa Studies in Women's Literature* 29.2 (Fall 2010), pp. 375–93.

Waterman, David. 'The "Fear of Being Irrelevant" in a Time of War: Representing Self and Other in Pat Barker's *Life Class*', *Krieg und Literatur / War and Literature* 14 (2008), pp. 49–60.

INTERVIEWS AND PROFILES

Brannigan, John. 'An Interview with Pat Barker', *Contemporary Literature* 46:3 (Autumn 2005), pp. 367–92.

Jaggi, Maya. 'Profile: Pat Barker, Dispatches from the Front', *The Guardian* (16 August 2003), p. 16.

Johnson, Daniel. 'Grandfather's Memories Inspired Booker Winner', *The Times* (8 November 1995).

McCrum, Robert. 'The Books Interview: Pat Barker', *Observer* (1 April 2001), p. 17.

Monteith, Sharon. 'Pat Barker' (interview), in Sharon Monteith, Jenny Newman and Pat Wheeler (eds), *Contemporary British and Irish Fiction: An Introduction Through Interviews* (London: Edward Arnold, 2004), pp. 19–35.

Nixon, Rob. 'An Interview with Pat Barker', *Contemporary Literature* 45.1 (Spring 2004), pp. 1–21.

Perry, Donna. 'Interview with Pat Barker', in Donna Perry (ed.), *Backtalk: Women Writers Speak Out* (New Brunswick, NJ: Rutgers University Press, 1993), pp. 43–62.

Scholes, Lucy. 'Pat Barker on "Toby's Room", Historical Fiction, and the Booker', *The Daily Beast* (online), 5 October 2012.

Smith, Wendy. 'Pat Barker: Of Death and Deadlines', *Publishers Weekly* (15 December 2003), pp. 48–9.

Wheelwright, Julie. 'The Books Interview: Young Lives Between the Lines', *The Independent* (31 March 2001), p. 9.

REVIEWS

UNION STREET

Ward, Elizabeth. 'On the Seamy Side of the Street', *The Washington Post Book World* (18 September 1983), p. 3.

STANLEY AND IRIS

Grant, Steve. 'Stanley & Iris', in John Pym (ed.), *Time Out Film Guide* (London: Ebury Publishing, 2009), p. 1000.

BLOW YOUR HOUSE DOWN

Gerrard, Nicci. 'Guardian Women: MSPrint/Reviews of Feminist Novels', *The Guardian* (18 July 1984).

Pollitt, Katha. 'Bait for a Killer', *New York Times* (21 October 1984), section 7, p. 7.

Stevens, Andrea. 'Violence Against Women', *New York Times* (21 October 1984), section 7, p. 9.

Ward, Elizabeth. 'The Dark at the End of the Street', *The Washington Post Book World* (9 September 1984), p. 3.

LIZA'S ENGLAND

Driver, Paul. 'Liza Jarrett's Hard Life', *London Review of Books* 8:21 (4 December 1986), pp. 24–6.

Lipson, Eden Ross. 'Liza Toughs It Out', *New York Times* (21 December 1986), section 7, p. 6.

Shrapnel, Norman. 'Books: A Last Stand for People', *The Guardian* (26 September 1986).

Willis, Pauline. 'Monday Women: Bulletin', *The Guardian* (15 September 1986).

THE MAN WHO WASN'T THERE

Mackay, Shena. 'Elvis and the Bogeyman', *The Sunday Times* (23 April 1989).

Mitgang, Herbert. 'Books of the Times: A Story in the Imagination of a Boy', *New York Times* (8 December 1990), p. 18.

REGENERATION

Barnes, Anne. 'Sassoon and the Glamour of War', *The Times* (15 August 1991).
Kemp, Pater. 'Getting Under the Skin of a Nation at War', *The Sunday Times* (2 June 1991).
Mitgang, Herbert. 'Healing a Mind and Spirit Badly Wounded in the Trenches', *New York Times* (15 April 1992), p. C21.
Picardie, Justine. 'The Poet Who Came Out of His Shell Shock', *The Independent* (25 June 1991), p. 19.
Sellers, Frances Stead. 'The Poet of the Trenches', *Washington Post* (3 April 1992), p. D1.
Taylor, Paul. 'Hero at the Emotional Front', *The Independent* (2 June 1991), p. 32.

REGENERATION/BEHIND THE LINES (FILM)

Taylor, Paul. 'Regeneration', in John Pym (ed.), *Time Out Film Guide* (London: Ebury Publishing, 2009), p. 877.

THE EYE IN THE DOOR

Battersby, Eileen. 'A Roll Call of Casualties', *The Irish Times* (23 September 1993), p. 10.
Hensher, Philip. 'Getting Better All the Time', *The Guardian* (26 November 1993), p. S4.
Macdougall, Carl. 'Peep Holes into Weary World of War', *Herald of Scotland* (25 September 1993).
Rodd, Candice. 'A Stomach for War', *The Independent* (12 September 1993), p. 28.
Shepard, Jim. 'Gentlemen in the Trenches', *New York Times on the Web* (15 May 1994).

THE GHOST ROAD

Baker, Phil et al. 'Paperbacks', *The Sunday Times* (31 March 1996).
Battersby, Eileen. 'Beyond Battles', *The Irish Times* (21 September 1995), p. 12.
Battersby, Eileen. 'Caught in the Harsh Glare of the Sun', *The Irish Times* (23 September 1995), p. 8.
Battersby, Eileen. 'Read, Remember and Celebrate', *The Irish Times* (9 November 1995), p. 15.
Battersby, Eileen. 'Win of Barker Novel Endorses Prize', *The Irish Times* (8 November 1995), p. 8.
Gibb, Eddie. 'Minds Blown Apart by the Pity of War', *The Sunday Times* (24 November 1996).
Glover, Gillian, 'Barker Bites', *The Scotsman* (25 October 1995), p. 14.
Greenlaw, Lavinia. 'All Noisy on the Western Front', *The New Republic* (21 April 1996), pp. 38–41.
Kellaway, Kate. 'Billy, Don't Be a Hero', *The Observer* (27 August 1995), p. 16.
Lambert, Angela. 'In the Footsteps of Fallen Heroes', *The Independent* (9 November 1995), p. 2.
May, Derwent. 'War, Sex and a Heavy Cruiser', *The Times* (9 September 1995).
Pierpont, Claudia Roth. 'Shell Shock', *New York Times Book Review* (31 December 1995), p. 5.
Rengger, Patrick. 'The Bookers', *Globe and Mail* (4 November 1995).
Sage, Lorna. 'Both Sides', *London Review of Books* 17.10 (5 October 1995), p. 9.
Spufford, Francis. 'Exploding Old Myths', *The Guardian* (9 November 1995), p. T2.
Spufford, Francis. 'Violence Shocks, Love Hurts, Bullets Kill', *The Guardian* (22 September 1995), p. T12.

Thorpe, Michael. 'The Walking Wounded', *World and I* 14.10 (October 1999), p. 258 (an omnibus review of the trilogy).

Tonkin, Boyd. 'Fiction on the Ghost Road', *New Statesman and Society* 8.378 (10 November 1995), p. 41.

ANOTHER WORLD

Arditti, Michael. 'Howls from Geordie's Ghost', *The Independent* (31 October 1998), p. 14.

Battersby, Eileen. 'The Pity of War and its Aftermath', *The Irish Times* (14 November 1998), p. 68.

Mackenzie, Suzie. 'Out of the Past', *The Guardian* (24 October 1998), p. 30.

Myerson, Julie. 'Still Shell-Shocked After All These Years', *Mail on Sunday* (25 October 1998), p. 36.

Renzetti, Elizabeth. 'A Sense of History Without the Cozy Veneer', *Globe and Mail* (23 December 1998), p. C1.

Unsworth, Barry. 'Haunted House', *New York Times* (16 May 1999), section 7, p. 6.

Walter, Natasha. 'Geordie Goes to Hell', *The Guardian* (17 October 1998), p. 10.

BORDER CROSSING

Burnside, Anna. 'Random Evil, Personality Disorders and Even the First World War', *Sunday Herald* (1 April 2001), p. 5.

Eder, Richard. 'Shades of Gray', *New York Times* (18 March 2001), section 7, p. 1.

Gordon, Neil. 'Something Not Quite Right', *New York Times* (14 December 2001), section 7, p. 12.

Grice, Elizabeth. 'Between Violence and Salvation', *Daily Telegraph* (31 March 2001), p. 7.

Kakutani, Michiko. 'Books of the Times: Ominous Psychological Games that Unearth the Past', *New York Times* (16 March 2001), p. 42.

Restak, Richard. 'Reaching Out to an Adolescent Killer in a Tale that Mimics the News', *Washington Times* (15 April 2001), p. B8.

DOUBLE VISION

Gordon, Neil. 'Double Vision', *International Herald Tribune* (24 December 2003), p. 16.

Goring, Rosemary. 'Hope Floats in our War-Torn World', *Herald* (9 August 2003), p. 12.

Jarman, Mark Anthony. 'In and Out of the Frame', *Globe and Mail* (23 August 2003), p. D3.

Morrissey, Mary. 'The Age of Innocence', *The Irish Times* (24 March 2001), p. 72.

Warner, Ellen. 'Fiction: As Committed as a Lover—and as Creepy as a Stalker', *Independent on Sunday* (24 August 2003), p. 16.

LIFE CLASS

Cumyn, Alan. 'Pat Barker and the Crucible of Doom', *Globe and Mail* (28 July 2007), p. D4.

Kakutani, Michiko. 'Books of the Times: Exploring Small Stories of the Great War', *New York Times* (29 February 2008), p. E31.

Kemp, Peter. 'War Has Been her Greatest Obsession—and it Looms Large in her New Novel. But is this Pat Barker's Last Battle?' *The Sunday Times* (1 July 2007), Culture section, p. 4.

Randall, Lee. 'Back to the Western Front', *The Scotsman* (14 July 2007), p. 14.

Rustin, Susanna, 'A Life in Writing: Double Vision: Pat Barker Returns to the Setting of her Regeneration Trilogy for her 11th Novel', *The Guardian* (30 June 2007), p. 11.

Taylor, D. J. 'A Spattered Canvas: Pat Barker's New Novel Sutures Art and Battlefront Surgery in 1914', *The Guardian* (7 July 2007), p. 17.

Tupper, Lara. 'A Review of *Life Class* by Pat Barker', *The Believer* (January 2008), www.believermag.com/issues/200801/?read=review_barker.

TOBY'S ROOM

Appleyard, Bryan. 'Inspired by the Scars of a Generation', *The Sunday Times* (19 August 2012), Features, pp. 14, 15.

Barber, John. 'A Portrait of the First World War That's Anything But Nice', *Globe and Mail* (10 November 2012), p. A11.

Davenport-Hines, Richard. 'Brotherly Love', *The Spectator* (1 September 2012), p. 33.

Kemp, Peter. 'Atrocity Exhibitions: Pat Barker Returns to the Trenches in a Chilling Look at Art, Disfigurement and the Horrors of War', *The Sunday Times* (2 September 2012), Features, pp. 36, 37.

Johnston, Freya. 'The Ghosts of War', *Daily Telegraph* (1 September 2012), pp. 24, 25.

Lee, Hermione. 'Book of the Week: The Anatomy of War', *The Guardian* (11 August 2012), Review, p. 5.

Vernon, John. 'The Damage of War, Physical and Psychological', *International Herald Tribune* (9 October 2012), Leisure section, p. 11.

Index